SHOCKWAVES

SHOCKWAVES:
THE GLOBAL IMPACT
OF SEXUAL HARASSMENT

Susan L. Webb

MasterMedia Limited • New York

Published 1994 by MasterMedia Limited

MASTERMEDIA and colophon are registered trademarks
of MasterMedia Limited

Library of Congress Cataloging-in-Publication Data
Webb, Susan L.
    Shockwaves : the global impact of sexual harassment / Susan L. Webb
        p.   cm.
    Includes bibliographical references.
    ISBN 0-942361-91-1 (hard) : $19.95 — ISBN 0-942361-90-3 (pbk.) : $9.95
    1. Sexual harassment of women. 2. Sex discrimination in employment.
    I. Title. II. Title: Shockwaves
HD6060.3.W428 1994
331.4'133—dc20   94-1724
                                                         CIP

Cover Concept by Gordon Doucette
Book Design by Alan L. Marks
Production Services by Lynn & Turek Associates
Manufactured in the United States of America
10 9 8 7 6 5 4 3 2 1

To my mother and father,
Kathryn and Bob Webb

CONTENTS

Introduction   *ix*

PART ONE: FROM CALM TO CHAOS

1 Initial Impact: The Click Heard
  'Round the World   *3*
2 Revisiting Sexual Harassment:
  What Is It?   *12*

PART TWO: FROM AROUND THE WORLD

3 First Shockwaves: The State
  of Sexual Harassment Worldwide   *49*
4 Second Shockwaves: International
  Understanding and Action   *68*
5 Global Reverberations:
  Country by Country   *93*

PART THREE: FROM THE UNITED STATES

6 Pushing Limits in the United States   *181*
7 Sexual Harassment In U.S. Industries   *224*
8 Young People, Schools, and Education   *294*

PART FOUR: LOOKING AHEAD

9 What Can Be Done?   *317*
10 Final Thoughts: Is the End In Sight?   *338*

About the Author   *358*
Resources   *360*
References   *421*
Additional Resources from the Author   *429*

Introduction

I'm sure you'll understand if I tell you that being in the sexual harassment business for the past fourteen long years has required that I maintain a certain balance, perspective, and to some extent, even a sense of humor.

Through the years, I've heard stories that are strange, weird, crazy, and sometimes hilarious—though they often turn out to have less than funny endings. I've also heard stories that are truly tragic and damaging for everyone—even those only remotely involved. The things people do to each other, especially at work, have been a constant source of amazement. Now, I'm more often disappointed than surprised that the same kinds of things keep happening over and over.

The Clarence Thomas–Anita Hill hearings were a discouraging time for everyone I know who watched or kept track of the goings-on. Regardless of which side you were on—his, hers, didn't know, or didn't care—you have to admit, watching the questions and testimony unfold between a Supreme Court Justice nominee and a prominent law professor—both African-American—was depressing. The nasty allegations, and the very process of nationally televised Senate hearings, came together to make an already ugly situation even uglier.

For me, there was another element that proved discouraging. I was continually asked during and after the hearings if I felt hopeful, as others did, that the hearings and the publicity they generated, would make a positive impact on the problem of sexual harassment. In other words, didn't I think people would be more knowledgeable? My answer was what depressed me the most: No.

Despite the fact that sexual harassment has been getting a great deal of attention as a concept and as an identified problem since at least 1980, we seemed to have made very little progress at the time of the Thomas–Hill hearings. Again and again, day after day, I heard people express the same misinformed and uneducated opinions about sexual harassment that they had held and expressed before the hearings. The only difference was they were expressing those same opinions more loudly. In short, most people before, during, and after the Thomas–Hill mess, had very little, if any, genuine or in-depth understanding of what sexual harassment actually is.

It was during the hearings that I agreed to write my book *Step Forward*, not as in "step forward and complain," but as in "isn't it about time we all took a step forward on understanding this problem (as opposed to two steps back)?" It was written as a simple, straightforward handbook to provide people with a basic understanding of the problem and its impact.

So all went reasonably well, at least as far as I was concerned. The book was published in December 1991, just seven weeks after the Thomas–Hill hearings. Sales were great, and I was finished and could rest for a while. But now, somehow, here we are again, barely two years later.

This book—*Shockwaves*—actually started the summer after the Thomas–Hill controversy. I was on summer vacation, sitting by the pool with my mother in Oklahoma, telling her that I was bored, bored, bored with the same old sexual harassment work, and that I had to think of something new and interesting for me about the issue, since I wasn't ready to leave it behind.

I told her that the only truly new and exciting thing for me after fourteen years of dealing with the subject was the idea of studying sexual harassment around the world, on a global scale. This was especially interesting since I had continued to receive hundreds of letters and clippings from people in scores of countries—all about sexual harassment. So I began this book.

When I actually started writing *Shockwaves*, I began with what has always been my basic belief—that workplace sexual harassment falls on the same continuum as other gender-based biases, offenses, and crimes, such as sexual assault, wife abuse, and rape. Sometimes the behaviors may be less severe—at what I call the lighter-gray end of the continuum. These behaviors are usually verbal, and include jokes, comments, and supposedly cute, sexist remarks. Other times the behaviors are more severe, or at the darker-gray end of the continuum—rape and physical violence against women, for example. But whether light gray or dark gray, the point is that all these behaviors are essentially on the same continuum. Regardless of their severity, these behaviors are about dominance, power, and victimization.

As I continued to research and write, my thoughts about sexual harassment moved in two somewhat opposite directions. On the one hand, I began to find less and less humor or amusement in even the least severe cases of sexual harassment. There were just too many instances of it at all levels, pouring in from all over the world, to find very much of it funny anymore. All acts of sexual harassment seemed serious.

At the same time, with reports of atrocities against women coming in daily from around the globe, workplace sexual harassment somehow seemed a less severe and less important issue to deal with. These atrocities include the multiple rapes of girls as young as age 8, and the purposeful impregnation of those girls by members of military forces; the murder of female infants and the abortion of female fetuses because of cultural preferences for boys; and the continual cultural practice of female genital mutilation (removal of the clitoris).

But then I came back, full circle, to my basic belief in the continuum. Certainly the rape and murder of young girls is of more immediate concern than a hostile work environment—but it all is still on the same continuum. It all is still about power, dominance, and victimization, lack of respect, and disregard for half of humanity.

Coming back to where I started, I realized that this book had to take the broadest scope possible. The "global impact of sexual harassment" could not be limited to a geographical overview, as I had originally intended. Global had to mean *everywhere* and *in every aspect of our lives*—in all countries, in all types and sizes of businesses and industries, and in all facets of society. That meant also looking at our families, schools, workplaces, and religious institutions, at our health professions and relationships with healers—even in public places, such as bars, restaurants, streets, parks, and walkways.

A friend, upon hearing this idea, laughed and said I'd have to change the name of *Shockwaves* from the "Global Impact," to the "Intergalactic Perspective," the implication being I'd taken on a bit much. Perhaps. Nevertheless, I had to expand the theme, and I hope you benefit from the broader scope.

Sexual harassment is simply one among the many offenses in this world directed primarily at one group. It is aimed at, and has the most direct impact on, women. But we must take stock, now, and realize that sexual harassment is just a few shades of gray away from the worst sex-based crimes in the world, and that it affects everyone. It is a problem of humanity—women, men, children—in every nook and cranny of the world.

Seattle, Washington
January 1994

SHOCKWAVES

PART ONE:
FROM CALM TO CHAOS

1

INITIAL IMPACT: THE CLICK HEARD 'ROUND THE WORLD

The name Anita Hill now conveys so much more than the woman herself that it can be used as a verb. The phrase suggests taking action and standing up for women's rights, as in 'Let's Anita Hill this issue of child care.'

Anna Quindlen
Columnist
The New York Times

More than thirty years have passed since Betty Friedan wrote her groundbreaking book *The Feminine Mystique,* in which she talked of the "clicks" that women hear ... sharp and distinct, like the sound of a light switch being flipped on. A click, Friedan said, is a woman's sudden and overwhelming awareness of something negative, demeaning, or discriminatory happening to her.

Most women remember hearing their first click. I certainly remember mine. It happened in 1971, when I was one of the few women graduate students in economics at the University of Oklahoma. During a class on Soviet economics, the professor asked a fairly difficult question. When I raised my hand, he called on me, and I gave the correct answer.

The professor said nothing. He looked instead at a male student sitting behind me and asked the same question. The student gave exactly the same answer I had just given. This time the professor smiled broadly and commended him for being correct. Click. I remember wondering at the time if words had actually come out of my mouth, or if I had just imagined giving the answer.

For most of the last twenty years or so, the clicks haven't seemed as loud or distinct as they were in the beginning. Maybe women became so used to the clicks that they just didn't sound as loud, or maybe there were so many clicks that they merged into a sort of a humming sound, or maybe women were so busy doing—having careers, husbands and kids all at the same time—that they simply didn't have time to listen. Whatever happened, the clicks seemed to have faded for a while.

In recent years, though, new and louder clicks have occurred. The first was in 1990 and involved sportswriter Lisa Olsen, who said she was sexually harassed by players of the New England Patriots football team, who allegedly displayed parts of their bodies in close proximity to her face. Lots of people heard this click—men as well as women—since, after all, the story took place in a football locker room and was often reported in the sports section of newspapers.

Then, in 1991, one of the nation's premiere neurosurgeons, Dr. Frances Conley, resigned her post at Stanford because of what she described as ongoing verbal and physical harassment by her fellow surgeons. This time the click had a louder and different sound. After all, Conley was a distinguished surgeon who charged she was being harassed by her peers in the operating room—not jocks in a locker room.

In the fall of that same year, we experienced what I call the "click heard 'round the world"—Clarence Thomas and Anita Hill. Things have not been the same since Senate confirmation hearings for Supreme Court Justice Thomas riveted the nation (and much of the world) following Hill's allegations of sexual harassment. Nor will they ever be the same again. This "click," or better yet—explosion—was the public airing of very private issues, witnessed by the world. Not only did the hearings push the issue of sexual harassment to the front burner in the United States, but everywhere, throughout the world, we also began hearing stories of sexual harassment, sexual abuse, and discrimination.

In the days and weeks following the Thomas hearings, it was especially interesting to watch reactions from different parts of the world and to see those reactions change, at least somewhat, over time. Journalist Lark Borden with the Rochester, N.Y., *Democrat & Chronicle* wrote about this phenomenon in an article titled "So, How Did the Hearings Play in Paris?"

Britain was "clearly horrified," Borden wrote, citing a *London Times* story headlined, "Voyeurs Tune in to a Modern Martyrdom." The story reported that the hearings had "high comedy, moments such as the one when Senator Edward Kennedy, of all people, intoned solemnly, 'I hope we can clear this room of the dirt and innuendo.'"

London's *Sunday Times* said, "Extreme feminism is now a state of religion in America."

The rest of Europe responded similarly. A Denmark newspaper, *Extrabladet*, enacted a 100-day moratorium on all political coverage of the United States, citing disgust with all the squabbling going on. Italy's *Corriere Della Sera* reported, "It would be unthinkable for [Italian] men in high places to resign over a visit to a prostitute."

Liberation, a left-wing Parisian newspaper wrote, "Odious America is laid bare, revealing the naked brutality between the races and the sexes, on a background of purity and ruthless power struggles." *Le Figaro*, also published in Paris, said Anita Hill "was a foot soldier in a political machination destined to torpedo the confirmation of Judge Thomas."

An international business lawyer from New York who was working in Brussels was quoted: "These hearings, according to my European colleagues, may have been America's best exports to Europe since 'Dallas,' 'Dynasty,' and 'Married ... With Children.' Too bad those shows aren't more representative of real life."

However, as French sociologists pointed out, much of the action taking place in France, and most believe the rest of the world as well, is a consequence of actions taken by the United States and Canada with regard to sexual harassment. Watching the difficulties in the United States during the Thomas-Hill controversy must have proved particularly interesting to those in other countries.

Despite initial reactions ranging from discounting the problem and trivializing the issue of sexual harassment to outright ridicule and laughter, responses changed again with the passage of a time. Soon the problem of sexual harassment was being more seriously discussed, publicized, and acted upon in scores of countries.

As the issue gained momentum, we began hearing more and more stories of sexual harassment from around the world, truly as if shockwaves were reverberating over and over again. Here are a few examples culled from hundreds of reports:

- In Cambodia, United Nations peacekeepers were accused by women of sexual harassment. The women said, in a letter to the head of the U.N. Transitional Authority in Cambodia, "We ... feel a sense of outrage at the unacceptable behavior of some male UNTAC personnel ... Sexual harassment occurs regularly in public restaurants, hotels and bars, banks, markets and shops to the point where many women feel highly intimidated." The peacekeeping group included 175 people, mostly Western or Cambodian women working for aid organizations.
- In Canada, one survey showed that 4 out of 10 women reported being sexually harassed at work and 8 percent reported sexual harassment or abuse by their doctors. In response, the Canadian government established a commission to inquire into violence against women, set up a gender sensitivity program for judges to attend, and

began to revamp laws to define obscenity as that which subordinates, degrades, or dehumanizes women.

- In Japan, an August 1991 survey showed that 70 percent of the women who responded experienced "seku-hara" at work and said their primary complaint was the "failure to be recognized as full human beings." Ninety percent said they were sexually harassed on the way to and from work.

- In France, a man was recently sentenced under a new criminal code to a year in jail for physically sexually harassing his female subordinate. When a recent survey indicated 21 percent of the women who responded said they had been sexually harassed, women challenged the report. Sexual harassment is seen as normal behavior in France, the women said, thus 21 percent was far too low. Still, other women said they would not consider it sexual harassment if they were asked to take their clothes off during a job interview.

- In Ireland, a speaker at a women's conference in Dublin called Leinster House, where the Irish political leaders work, a "groper's paradise" where sexual harassment is severe and condoned. Most women do not complain because they are desperate to keep their jobs in a time of high unemployment, she said.

- In Korea, the Korean National Railroad designated two of every ten coaches on Seoul-area commuter trains for "women only" in response to complaints of sexual harassment by men on the trains. The coaches have been reported to be about 97 percent full of women passengers—"afraid of pawing male passengers"—said *IHT* newspaper.

- In Morocco, the government banned a march planned by nineteen women's groups to protest sexual harassment. Government officials gave no reason for the ban.

According to a recent survey of twenty-three countries by the

International Labour Organisation (ILO), sexual harassment is a major problem for women of the world. In a three-hundred page report, the ILO said labor laws offer the best remedy for stopping sexual harassment in the workplace. Yet, only seven of the countries surveyed—Australia, Canada, France, New Zealand, Spain, Sweden, and the United States—have laws mentioning sexual harassment. Six countries—Australia, Canada, Ireland, Switzerland, the United Kingdom, and the United States—define sexual harassment by judicial decision.

The ILO said awareness of sexual harassment has come a long way in a relatively short period of time, with the United States in the legal and judicial forefront. But the report also shows there is still much to be done:

- In Austria, a 1986 survey showed almost 31 percent of women reported serious harassment incidents.
- In Czechoslovakia, a survey showed almost 18 percent of women had been sexually harassed physically and almost 36 percent verbally, but no courts have dealt with the issue.
- In Denmark, a survey showed 11 percent of women said in 1991 that they had been sexually harassed and 8 percent had lost jobs because of it.
- In Germany, 6 percent of women who responded to a 1990 survey had resigned from at least one job because of sexual harassment.
- In the United States, 40 to 60 percent of working women consistently say they have experienced sexual harassment at work, resulting in a staggeringly high cost to them and the companies they work for. According to *Treasury Magazine,* corporate America may have to spend $1 billion during the next five years to settle sexual harassment lawsuits as more companies are sued for sex-related offenses—and lose those suits—because of the current social climate, new legislation, and expanded judicial interpretations of sexual harassment laws.

Women in the United States are not alone. Around the world, in Estonia, Finland, Sweden, Israel, Germany, the former Soviet Union, Australia, England, the Dominican Republic ... study after study reveals the same thing—40 to 60 percent of working women experience sexual harassment.

Sexual Harassment of Girls (and Boys)

One of the most discouraging statistics comes from the United States—the very country that is supposed to be leading in the fight against sexual harassment of women. These depressing numbers have to do with girls, and in some cases boys, who from elementary school through college are being sexually harassed on a daily basis.

In 1993, Lou Harris and Associates surveyed 1,632 students in grades eight to eleven. Results showed sexual harassment has reached "epidemic proportions" in U.S. schools, with 81 percent of girls, and almost as many boys, saying they had been sexually harassed. Types of harassment reported by the students included jokes, sexual comments, and looks, and being grabbed or touched, intentionally brushed up against in a sexual way, and mooned or flashed.

Titled "Hostile Hallways," the survey documented what many have known to be a problem for years. Indeed, many people feel that the harassment our children face at school is merely a reflection of our media culture. Anne Bryant from the American Association of University Women said, "The kind of violence we see on television, in newspapers, in movies sends signals that behavior which is hurtful to others is not wrong."

With our daughters regularly facing sexual harassment at school, it's no wonder that, according to NBC Nightly News reporter Mary Alice Williams, " ... research shows that when girls enter their teenage years they begin to lose esteem, censure their opinions, ratchet back their expectations ... "

WHAT'S TO BE DONE?

The obvious question at this point is what can people, societies, and countries do about this incredible, seemingly growing, never-ending problem? The answer is fairly simple—not easy—but simple. For the most basic and first steps, we should use the same approach—direct, comprehensive, and ongoing—used in companies and other organizations that want to stop and prevent harassment. The parallels are clear:

1. *Top management support = top leader support.*
   We must elect, appoint, and support political leaders—those in "top management" of countries—who believe that sexual harassment is a serious problem, that it's against our laws and standards, and that it's bad for business, which in this sense means the business of society: to provide a safe, healthy, and productive living and working environment for its citizens and their children.
2. *Written, posted policy statements = law and policy.*
   Just as a company must have policies, governments must have them in the form of rules, regulations, and state and federal laws. While some of the world's countries have laws that specifically address sexual harassment, only a handful have effective legislation. We must ensure that all countries have legislation that speaks to the problem of sexual harassment, and that these laws are fairly applied to and interpreted for our daily lives.
3. *Procedures for getting and handling complaints = establishment or designation of agencies or commissions for processing complaints.*
   In only a very few countries do official procedures exist, either through the courts, civil rights agencies, or human rights commissions. Official channels must be established to encourage victims of sexual harassment to come forward, stand up for their rights, and demand that instances of sexual harassment be remedied.

4. *Training for all employees = education and awareness
   for citizens.*
   I am repeatedly asked by employees in my workshops—
   employees who also are concerned parents—to tell
   them what the schools are doing regarding sexual
   harassment training and awareness. So far my answer is
   "not much," though this is beginning to change in several countries. We must ensure that men and women,
   boys and girls, know the impact that sexual harassment
   and other forms of sexual inequity and sexual violence
   have on us all.
5. *Follow-up and follow-through = continuing attention
   through regulatory control and monitoring.*
   Now that the problem of sexual harassment has been
   placed on the "front burner," we must keep it there. We
   must continue to address this issue long after it is no
   longer deemed newsworthy. It simply will not go away
   by itself; it requires that we all work together to bring
   about its end.

A recent article reported that the French believe their country's new attention to the sexual harassment problem is
because of the efforts of women in the United States. For
some people, having other countries look to the United States
for support or guidance feels like another burden or responsibility to bear. It seems that we've really not accomplished very
much, yet even so, other people, especially women, in other
countries continue to watch the United States closely for help
in solving problems of harassment and discrimination.

In her book *Revolution From Within,* Gloria Steinem is
somewhat encouraging on this point. Steinem said we are
only in the first twenty-five years of a hundred-year-long wom-
en's movement, that we have more time, that we weren't supposed to be finished by now and that we are actually making
some progress. It does help to think of the effort with a long-
term perspective. But there is still so much more to be done.

2

REVISITING SEXUAL HARASSMENT: WHAT IS IT?

> *What is a feminist? Really? I am reminded of Rebecca West's response: 'I myself have never been able to find out precisely what feminism is. I only know that people call me a feminist whenever I express sentiments that differentiate me from a doormat.' She said that in 1913. Some things have not changed.*
>
> Clarence Page
> *December 1991*
> *Tribune Media*
> *Services, Inc.*

Two incidents reported by the *Los Angeles Times*, in an article cleverly titled "Harassment Watch: Dinosaurs on Parade," vividly show that despite our progress, old-time sexual harassment in its most overt form is alive and well.

In the first incident, the *Los Angeles Times* reported that the Ventura County district attorney asked the State Bar to investigate lawyer Douglas Palaschak for allegedly running newspaper ads for secretarial help as a way of finding young women for sexual or romantic relationships. Palaschak also faced felony drug charges. When women answered the ads, Palaschak allegedly asked them to sign a contract stating that they and he "mutually consent to all words, acts, sexual innuendo, sexual acts, touching, lewd behavior, etc." The contract also specified non-work duties he wanted his secretaries to perform: "Sex and romance would be nice."

Only one of the fifty women Palaschak hired in the previous year signed the contract, the *Times* reported. That woman worked one day and quit.

The second and less amusing incident involved William L'Heureux, the Mariposa County Welfare Director, who was charged with telephoning female welfare recipients for lewd and lascivious purposes. L'Heureux faced two misdemeanor counts of using public records to obtain the phone numbers and a third count of using a false name for lewd and lascivious purposes.

The *Times'* closing quote is to the point: "We were beginning to hope that allegations of such blatant sexual harassment were becoming relics. Evidently, not so."

Dinosaurs aren't confined to California. Jon Margolis of the *Chicago Tribune* reported on a counter-suit filed in Wyoming in response to a sexual harassment action filed by three women who had been employed as police dispatchers. The male counter-suers alleged it was the women who did the harassing, and that one of the women actually bit a former deputy sergeant on the buttocks. The sergeant claimed that the biting caused him to suffer loss of self-esteem.

Margolis commented, "One does not know what to make of this. It is heartening that the Washakie County law enforcement establishment does not include buttocks-biting inside the scope of a dispatcher's duties. But it's dismaying that a Wyoming cop can suffer loss of self-esteem merely from having a lady (well, a woman) bite him in the behind."

Crazy indeed.

My work also has brought me face to face with dinosaurs. Once during a live radio interview, the commentator decided to lecture me about my behavior toward him. Remember, this was live radio, not a taped delay. He had asked me a question about a "girl in the newsroom who wore inappropriate clothing to work" and whether or not she was bringing the problem of sexual harassment on herself. (If only I had a nickel for every time I've heard that question ...)

In an effort to be fair to everyone involved in the situation, part of my explanation was that while clothing that is overly sexual is not appropriate for the office, sometimes young people who are new to the work force, such as this girl, did not know how to dress professionally and needed a little guidance. He then told me that this girl was 35 years old.

I responded that when he used the word "girl" I thought he meant a very young and inexperienced female. That's when the lecture, or should I say diatribe, began. He told me on the air that he was sick and tired of people telling him how to talk, that this "thing" about the word girl was ridiculous, and I should stick to the point at hand—sexual harassment.

He was so angry and agitated that I never did get the chance to explain to him and his listeners that he had just demonstrated very clearly what sexual harassment is about— power, lack of power, disrespect, and disregard of women. I am not suggesting I was being harassed—rather, I was simply experiencing a perfect example of the underlying causes of harassment, both for me as the guest on his program, and for the "girl" he was discussing.

Another memorable moment occurred during a flight back to Seattle from New York. I had told the flight attendant that I was not a particularly good flyer and asked her to please check with me once in a while to see how I was doing. She said "fine" and came by every so often to chat.

About halfway through the flight, the captain came out of the cockpit and we met—I was standing near the galley, ahead of the first-class section. He laughed and said he'd heard I didn't fly too well, and that dancing might take my mind off it (though at this point I was doing fine). He then proceeded to take me loosely in his arms and dance me around the small open area directly behind the cockpit, but in front of passengers. He asked me what I did for a living that required I travel so much, and I told him I was a sexual harassment consultant. He then decided to tell me and two female flight attendants standing with us several off-color jokes.

The three of us smiled politely, admittedly in shock, and the captain went back into the cockpit. None of us could believe what had just happened—we said as much to each other, shook our heads in wonder, and I returned to my seat. Here certainly was a man who "didn't get it."

Obviously, the definition of sexual harassment and appropriate and inappropriate behavior is still quite misunderstood. I honestly think that this man had no malicious intent, but what on earth was he thinking (if he was thinking at all)?

DEFINING SEXUAL HARASSMENT

Whatever it is and isn't, the definition of sexual harassment has become as muddled and confused—and sometimes as muddied—as the definition of a feminist. Such confusion is not new. Some people believe this kind of confusion is purposeful, for if you muddy the definition of a term, then what it stands for also becomes less clear.

The problem with defining sexual harassment is not, as many people believe, that it is a subjective definition varying from one person to the next. The difficulty stems from the fact that there are at least three definitions, all with a slightly different perspective. If people understand each definition, and agree upon which one they are using, disagreement of what is and what is not harassment in a particular situation will occur less often.

The Behavioral Definition

The most common behavioral definition of sexual harassment is "deliberate and/or repeated sexual or sex-based behavior that is not welcome, not asked for, and not returned." There are three major elements and two qualifiers to this definition:

1) The behavior in question has to be sexual in nature or sex-based. In other words, it's a behavior with some sort of

sexual connotation to it, or one that occurs because of the sex of the person, male or female, that it is being directed to.

The range of behaviors with sexual connotations is wide, and the behaviors don't necessarily mean that the two people intend to have sex. Behaviors can range from the light-gray end of the continuum—including joking, innuendoes, flirting, and asking someone out for a date—to the dark-gray end—forced fondling, attempted or actual rape, and sexual assault.

Sex-based behaviors—those that occur on account of a person's sex—also can be broadly based. The point is they are negative behaviors that are primarily directed to, or have an impact on, only one sex or gender. These kinds of negative gender-related behaviors include derogatory remarks made by men or women—in other words, a serious battle of the sexes at work.

> The darker gray, or more severe, the sexual behavior is, the fewer times it needs to be repeated before reasonable people define it as harassment. The lighter gray, or less severe, the behavior is, the more times it needs to be repeated. This is one of the two "qualifiers" to the behavioral definition—the severity of the behavior must be considered in conjunction with its frequency.

2) The behavior must be deliberate and/or repeated. Some forms of sexual behavior are so graphic and offensive that the first time they occur they are considered deliberate, inappropriate, and sometimes even illegal actions. Other behaviors must be repeated over and over again before they become harassment.

If we were to use a continuum and put the light-gray sexual behaviors at one end—the joking, flirting, and slightly off-color remarks—and the dark-gray sexual behaviors at the other end—forced fondling, attempted rape, and serious sexual slurs—most of us would agree that the dark-gray behaviors are definitely not permissible. Where we have difficulty and disagreement is at the light-gray end. What one person sees as joking, another finds offensive and degrading.

Even comments made in a joking manner may not be bothersome the first few times. But day after day, joke after joke, such comments cease to be funny or amusing to the person who's receiving them. While the behavior may not be considered illegal sexual harassment, it still has a negative and damaging impact on the employee receiving it.

3) The final major element in the behavioral definition of sexual harassment is that the behavior is not welcome, asked for, or returned. We are not talking about mutual behaviors that people engage in together or enjoy. What two people do that is mutual is simply that, mutual, and is usually permissible as long as it doesn't interfere with their work or create a hostile or offensive work environment for others. (I say usually because there are some mutual behaviors that may not be defined as harassment because they are mutual, but nevertheless are still not permissible in the work environment—mutual buttocks grabbing, mutual graphic sexual jokes, etc.)

When considering the welcomeness of the behaviors, some people try to place the sole responsibility on the victim or receiver for setting limits. They claim "it's not sexual harassment unless she or he says so." That's not quite right.

> The lighter gray the behavior is, the more responsibility the receiver has to speak up, (because some people like this kind of behavior, and unless something is said, no one will know it's offensive). The darker gray the behavior is, the less responsibility the receiver has to speak up. The initiator should be sensitive enough to know that these behaviors are inappropriate in the first place.

The three elements—*sexual or sex-based behavior* that is *deliberate and/or repeated*, and *not welcome, asked for, or returned*—along with the two qualifiers of *varying frequency of repetition* and *varying responsibilities of the sender and receiver*—comprise a complete behavioral definition of sexual harassment.

This definition covers more than what a purely legal one might. However, studies have shown light-gray harassment tends to get worse when it is not addressed and stopped. By including light, moderate, and severe types of behavior in a definition of harassment, situations are more likely to be resolved before legal action is necessary.

Sexual harassment may be verbal, non-verbal, or physical. Verbal jokes, cracks, comments, and remarks are probably the most common form of harassment—what you're likely to see most often in complaints and investigations. Non-verbal harassment can be just as serious—certain kinds of looks, gestures, leering, ogling, pictures or cartoons. Physical harassment, such as touching, pinching, rubbing, or supposedly accidentally brushing against someone's breasts or buttocks, can be the most severe form of harassment and can involve criminal charges.

Remember, sexual harassment is really about power. The harasser either thinks or knows, consciously or unconsciously, that he or she has more power than the harassee. If not, there would be no harassment—the harassee could turn to the harasser and demand it stop and there would be no issue.

When asked why they file lawsuits or formal complaints outside their organizations—why they did not solve the problem in-house—victims of harassment give two reasons: 1) "I didn't think anyone would take me seriously." This says that they felt powerless. They thought or knew that others would laugh or tell them they were being too sensitive. 2) "I couldn't get it stopped any other way." Again, this indicates a feeling of powerlessness to stop unwanted behaviors.

Identifying Harassment Using the Behavioral Definition

To identify sexual harassment using the behavioral definition, ask the following questions for each behavior that occurred:

1) *Was the behavior sexual (about sex) or sex-based (directed to or having an impact on only one sex or gender)?* I actually plot each behavior on a light-gray/dark-gray continuum to get some picture of its severity first:

- At the lightest end of the continuum are behaviors that have the potential of being sexual harassment, particularly if they are repeated enough times, but also are socially acceptable in certain situations. These behaviors are more likely to be called inappropriate or out of line, but not truly harassment, especially if just one instance has occurred.

- Subtle (or light gray) sexual behaviors are sometimes socially acceptable, but some reasonable men and women would see them as offensive and want them stopped. The receivers usually don't want anything done to the sender at this point, other than for him or her to stop. The behavior is bothersome and worth mentioning, but would not warrant a formal complaint if this were the only behavior that occurred.

- Moderate (or medium gray) sexual behaviors are not socially acceptable, and reasonable men and women would see them as offensive and want them stopped. The behavior is serious enough that some action must be taken against the sender (such as warning letters or reprimands) in addition to having him or her stop the behavior. The behavior is offensive and could warrant a complaint even if it were the only one that occurred.

- Severe (or dark gray) sexual behaviors are never socially acceptable and are so graphic or severe that one instance can call for serious disciplinary action such as probation, suspension, or termination of the offending person. Included in this category are physical behaviors such as attempted and actual rape or sexual assault, and verbal behaviors such as serious sexual slurs.

2) *Was each behavior deliberate and/or repeated?* If not deliberate, and truly accidental, then most likely it cannot be labeled as harassment. If not accidental, then how often was each behavior repeated? Remember the qualifier—the lighter gray, or less severe, the behavior is, the more repetitions required to label it harassment; the darker gray, or more severe, the fewer repetitions needed to call it harassment. Keep in mind that repeated instances of similar behaviors can

---

Continuum of Behaviors

To determine whether a particular behavior constitutes sexual harassment, begin by plotting the behavior on this continuum:

LIGHT *   SOCIALLY ACCEPTABLE IN CERTAIN SITUATIONS, BUT CAN POTENTIALLY BE SEXUAL HARASSMENT IF IT IS REPEATED ENOUGH TIMES

SUBTLE   SOMETIMES SOCIALLY ACCEPTABLE, BUT SOME REASONABLE MEN AND WOMEN WOULD BE OFFENDED AND WANT THE BEHAVIOR STOPPED

MODERATE   NOT SOCIALLY ACCEPTABLE; REASONABLE MEN AND WOMEN WOULD BE OFFENDED AND WANT THE BEHAVIOR STOPPED

SEVERE **   NEVER SOCIALLY ACCEPTABLE, AND ARE SO GRAPHIC AND SEVERE THAT ONE INSTANCE DEMANDS ACTION

* Light behaviors are more likely to be called inappropriate or out of line, but not truly harassment, especially if only one instance has occurred.

** Severe behaviors include physical abuse such as attempted and actual rape or sexual assault, and verbal abuse such as serious sexual slurs.

constitute repetitions—three different verbal sexual remarks, for example, could be treated the same as three repetitions of the same comment.

3) *Was each behavior welcome, or asked for, or returned?* Again, remember the qualifier—the lighter gray the behavior, the more responsibility the receiver has to speak up; the darker gray the behavior, the less responsibility the receiver has to speak up and the more responsibility the sender has to monitor his or her own behavior. Did the receiver tell or indicate to the sender that the behavior was unwelcome? Was such notice necessary, or should the sender have known better in the first place?

4) *If the behaviors were reciprocated in any way, was there a balance between the seriousness of the sender's behavior and the receiver's returned behavior?* One of the arguments often presented is that the complainant or receiving employee liked the behavior, engaged in it, asked for it, encouraged it, etc. If this is the case, then both (or all of) the parties should be talked to so that these types of behavior are stopped (though not labeled sexual harassment since they were welcomed.)

However, in some cases when a person tells an off-color joke in response to someone who has just told an off-color joke, it appears that the jokes were welcomed and there was a "balance" in terms of the severity of the conduct. But when the original sender of the joke interprets the receiver's response as an invitation to go to a higher or more severe level—such as physical grabbing of buttocks or breasts, then the balance has shifted and the behavior is no longer justified.

An Assessment Checklist

Another argument you'll hear is that sexual harassment is "subjective" and "depends on the victim's perceptions." Of course, to some extent this is true, for what is harassing to one person may not be to another; there are no lists of right and wrong behaviors.

However, there are factors that can be considered. Below are factors based on the premise that the identification of sexual harassment should be made as a result of an objective assessment. The question to be asked is, "How would a reasonable person in the same or similar circumstances perceive the conduct?" with the perception of the victim and the intent of the harasser taken into consideration.

We've already covered some of these factors, but some are new. All are worth reviewing:

- Severity of the conduct: generally behaviors can be placed along a continuum ranging from mild to severe. While no hard lines can be drawn, general groupings can be made.
- Number and frequency of encounters: the number of incidents and the time span between each is important. What seems less severe when happening only once may become more serious when repeated often and with persistence.
- Apparent intent of the harasser: the question to be asked is what reasonable people would have meant had they acted in a similar manner. Also important is whether the behavior was directed at the victim or simply overheard or seen.
- Relationship of the two employees: studies reveal that people generally expect higher levels of conduct from supervisors. What may be permissible from a coworker is inappropriate from supervisory personnel and may be more serious and more threatening because of the power relationship. Also to be considered is the nature of their interpersonal relationship—do they generally get along well, have they had an ongoing feud for some time, or were they involved romantically?
- Victim's provocation: the behavior of the victim should be considered but not over-weighted. Blaming the vic-

tim is a common pattern that should be avoided. However, if the receiving employee does provoke or illicit such behavior, then it loses its "unwelcome" connotation.

• Response of the victim: it is generally assumed that the victim has some responsibility for communicating that a particular behavior is unwelcome. This responsibility makes more sense when considered in light of the severity of the conduct directed toward him or her. The more severe the conduct, such as forced fondling or attempted rape, the less responsibility the victim has to express objection. The milder the conduct, such as jokes or teasing, the more responsibility the victim has to speak up. This factor should be weighted since many victims are afraid to respond honestly, especially when the offending employee is a supervisor or a well-liked coworker.

• Effect on the victim: an assessment should be made of the consequences of the offensive behavior on the employee and the seriousness of the "injury." Was the employee, for example, humiliated, physically injured, demoted, or denied a promotion?

• Work environment: reasonable people usually expect different behaviors depending on the nature of the work environment. What is appropriate in a blue-collar factory may not be appreciated or appropriate in a white-collar office.

• Public or private situations: different types of harassing behaviors could be more or less serious depending on whether they happened publicly or privately.

• Men–women ratio: studies have shown that the higher the ratio of men to women in the work environment, the more likely sexual harassment is to occur.

Each of these factors must be considered in their relationship to each other. Various factors should be given different weights depending on the particular situation. In some situations, such as physical sexual abuse, only one factor may be relevant. In this instance, the behavior is so severe, that the other factors are of little relevance. However, with situations such as verbal harassment, all factors may be required to make an objective assessment.

Finally, after considering the above factors, look at the overall picture to assess the serious of the harassment claim and assign it one of the following levels of severity:

- **Level 0:** An insignificant complaint from an oversensitive employee; refer back to the employee for resolution and possible counseling. Or, a false, malicious, or capricious complaint that needs to be referred back to the complaining employee and calls for action against this employee.
- **Level 1:** Behavior is not harassment but was inappropriate and creates potential for trouble; the behavior should be watched and at least mentioned to the offending employee.
- **Level 2:** Light-gray harassment; good that it was brought out in the open to be dealt with now; the behavior can and must be stopped and remedied quickly and easily.
- **Level 3:** Moderate harassment; a serious infraction that requires some disciplinary action.
- **Level 4:** Severe harassment; calls for more serious disciplinary action, and the potential exists for legal action; the remedy is complicated and lengthy.

EEOC Definition of Sexual Harassment

In 1980, the U.S. Equal Employment Opportunity Commission (EEOC) issued guidelines on sexual harassment to reaffirm its position that sexual harassment is a form of illegal sex discrimination. The EEOC explicitly stated that the guidelines on sexual harassment also applied to harassment based on race, color, religion, national origin, or sex. The commission has since said that other protected categories, such as age, also are included in its anti-harassment policies. The guidelines clearly state what the EEOC believes constitutes sexual harassment, as well as what it perceives the employer's responsibility to be in dealing with sexual harassment. Many countries have used the guidelines as models for their own policies.

EEOC Guidelines: Section A

Unwelcome sexual advances, requests for sexual favors, and other verbal or physical conduct of a sexual nature constitute harassment under any of four conditions:

1) When such behavior is either explicitly or implicitly part of a manager's or supervisor's decision to hire or fire someone. When submitting to sexual conduct is a term or condition of employment, it is illegal whether the request or demand was made outright or simply implied. Showing that such a request was implied might involve looking at employment records before and after the request was rejected. Actions that amount to the same thing as an explicit request are illegal.

2) When such behavior is used to make other employment decisions such as pay, promotion, or job assignment. Employment decisions are illegal any time they are based on whether an employee submitted or refused to submit to some form of sexual conduct. The employment decision does not have to actually cost the employee his or her job, nor does the sexual conduct have to be an actual request for sex. The supervisor who plays favorites with workers who go along with his habit of telling dirty jokes or making sexual comments, and who bends the rules in their favor is making employment decisions based on willingness to submit to sexual conduct.

The preceding two conditions have been labeled by the U.S. courts as "quid pro quo" harassment, which means "this for that." It occurs when someone with the power to do so, usually a supervisor or manager, offers some kind of tangible job benefit for submission to sexual harassment. In these cases, U.S. courts have held the employer strictly liable—responsible even if the employer did not know the harassment was occurring and even if the employer has a policy forbidding such behavior.

3) When such behavior has the purpose or effect of unreasonably interfering with the employee's work.

4) When such behavior creates an intimidating, hostile, or offensive work environment.

U.S. courts have labeled the preceding two conditions as "hostile work environment" harassment ("poisoned environment" in some other countries), where the damage caused by sexual behaviors does not have to be a tangible economic consequence (such as losing a promotion), but includes the atmosphere of the work environment. When that atmosphere becomes so negative it affects the employee's ability to do his or her job, the sexual behavior causing it is illegal harassment.

EEOC included the words "purpose or effect" to indicate that intent to harm is not a necessary element of sexual harassment. If an employee's unwanted sexual behaviors create a hostile work environment and interfere with another employee's work performance, the intent of the first employee may be irrelevant.

To fit EEOC's definition, sexual harassment must have two characteristics: it is unwelcome and unwanted, and it has an impact on the employee's job or work environment. Other countries have followed suit with these two characteristics, (though some have included only tangible aspects—*quid pro quo* harassment—and have declined to address *hostile work environment* harassment). Nevertheless, the intent of a person's behavior, whether the behavior is face-to-face or behind another employee's back, during breaks or in locker rooms, may be irrelevant if it affects the work environment.

Section B

Each claim of sexual harassment should be examined separately. Consideration should be given to the context in which the behavior took place, the nature of the behavior, and the record as a whole. Other countries have used the case-by-case basis in their formal policies, statements and court decisions.

Sections C and D

These sections define the liability of the employer. Section C says the employer may be held "strictly liable" for harassment by supervisors—even when the employer is not aware of the harassment and even when there is a policy forbidding such behavior. Section D says the employer is liable for coworker harassment when the employer knows of the harassment and fails to take immediate and appropriate action.

Several U.S. courts ruled in 1983 that "strict liability," where the victim can file a charge without notifying management of the harassment, applies only in *quid pro quo* harassment cases where a tangible job benefit was affected. If it is *hostile work environment* harassment, the victim must allow the employer the opportunity to take appropriate action before the victim can file a complaint. While this issue is still being addressed by the courts, most U.S. courts have ruled that in the case of *quid pro quo* harassment or harassment by a supervisor, the employer is automatically liable.

Section E

The employer may be held responsible for sexual harassment

of its employees by people who are non-employees—such as customers or the general public—when the employer knows of the harassment and does not take appropriate action. In these cases the extent of the employer's control over the situation is examined closely and if, in any way, the employer can stop the harassment, it is responsible for doing so. In the United States, this has become known as "third-party harassment" and has been receiving considerable attention recently. Other countries have enacted similar policies.

Section F

Employers should take all necessary steps to prevent sexual harassment from occurring. This includes policy statements, training for employees, and grievance procedures. Other countries make similar suggestions or requirements.

Section G

If an employee submits to sexual requests and gains benefits from that, then other qualified employees may sue on the basis of sex discrimination for not being allowed those same benefits or opportunities. If a supervisor gives the best assignments to a subordinate because of their sexual activities, other employees, both male and female, could claim sex discrimination because they were not allowed the same job assignments. This section was upheld by a federal court in Delaware but has been challenged in at least one other court as action based on the personal proclivities of the supervisor rather than sex discrimination.

U. S. Courts Define Sexual Harassment

In 1982 and 1983, two U.S. Circuit Courts of Appeal adopted their own classification scheme for sexual harassment cases, identifying (*Henson v. City of Dundee* and *Katz v. Dole*) two basic varieties: 1) Harassment in which a supervisor demands sexual consideration in exchange for job benefits (*quid pro quo)*; and 2) Harassment that creates an offensive environment (*condition of work* or *hostile work environment* harassment).

Quid pro quo sexual harassment, as defined by the courts, encompasses all situations in which submission to sexually harassing conduct is made a term or condition of employment, or in which submission to or rejection of sexually harassing conduct is used as the basis for employment decisions affecting the individual who is the target of such conduct. In the *Henson* case, the court stated four elements that a plaintiff must prove to establish a case of *quid pro quo* sexual harassment:

1) that he or she belongs to a protected group (is male or female);
2) that he or she was subject to unwelcome sexual harassment;
3) that the harassment complained of was based on sex; and
4) that the employee's reaction to harassment complained of affected tangible aspects of the employee's compensation, terms, conditions, or privileges of employment.

Condition of work or *hostile work environment* sexual harassment, as defined by the courts, is roughly equivalent to definitions found in the EEOC's guidelines; that is, unwelcome and demeaning sexually related behavior that creates an intimidating, hostile and offensive work environment.

In the *Henson* case, the circuit court reversed the lower court's holding that the plaintiff must show some tangible job detriment in addition to the hostile work environment created by sexual harassment. The court said that although not every instance or condition of work environment harassment gives rise to a sex discrimination claim, a plaintiff who can prove a number of elements can establish a claim.

These five elements are similar to those for *quid pro quo* harassment (also outlined in the *Henson* case):

1) the employee belongs to a protected group under Title VII of the 1964 Civil Rights Act;
2) the employee was subject to unwelcome sexual harassment;
3) the harassment complained of was based on sex;
4) the harassment complained of affected a term, condition or privilege of employment; and
5) the employer knew, or should have known, of the harassment in question and failed to take prompt remedial action.

The First U.S. Supreme Court Decision on Sexual Harassment

On June 19, 1986, the U.S. Supreme Court ruled that sexual harassment on the job is illegal discrimination even if the victim suffers no economic loss. The Court held that "the language of Title VII is not limited to 'economic' or 'tangible' discrimination," and the law's phrase "terms, conditions or privileges" of employment indicates congressional intent to "strike at the entire spectrum of disparate treatment of men and women," including harassment which creates a hostile work environment.

The Court quoted the *Henson* ruling saying, "Sexual harassment which creates a hostile or offensive environment for members of one sex is every bit the arbitrary barrier to sexual equality at the workplace that racial harassment is to racial equality. Surely, a requirement that a man or woman run a gauntlet of sexual abuse in return for the privilege of being allowed to work and make a living can be as demeaning and disconcerting as the harshest of racial epithets."

The Court reiterated that not all workplace behavior that may be defined as harassment can be said to affect terms or conditions of employment. To be actionable it must be sufficiently severe or pervasive to "alter the conditions of the victim's employment and create an abusive working environment." The court's key holdings were:

1. Sexual harassment is a form of sex discrimination illegal under Title VII of the 1964 Civil Rights Act.
2. Sexual harassment is illegal even if the victim suffered only a *hostile work environment* and not loss of economic or tangible job benefits.
3. Employers are not automatically liable for sexual harassment by their supervisors.
4. Lack of knowledge of the harassment does not automatically relieve the employer of liability for supervisors' harassment.
5. The complainant's consent to the behavior does not relieve the employer of liability. The question is not the "voluntariness" of the complainant's participation, but whether or not her conduct indicated that the behavior was unwelcome.
6. The complainant's behavior, such as provocative speech and dress, may be considered in determining whether the complainant found particular sexual advances unwelcome.

Since the 1986 Supreme Court ruling, other U.S. courts have continued to define and refine what constitutes sexual harassment. The courts' decisions have, for the most part, become somewhat predictable and followed a pattern parallel to that of racial harassment. While some people believed (or hoped) that the courts would narrow the scope of what they consider discriminatory sexual harassment, this has not been the case. Actually the opposite has occurred—initial rulings limited the scope of what was defined as harassment, and subsequent rulings broadened the definition.

Pinups and Sexual Harassment: Robinson v. Jacksonville Shipyards

In January 1991, the Sixth U.S. Circuit Court of Appeals in Florida ruled that nude pinups in the workplace can constitute sexual harassment (*Robinson v. Jacksonville Shipyards*). In this case, a female shipyard welder accused her employer of sexual harassment and won, with the court ruling that posting pictures of nude and partly nude women is a form of sexual harassment.

In other cases, courts have found that pornographic pictures may contribute to an atmosphere of sexual harassment. But the new decision is thought to be the first finding that such pictures are sexual harassment, in and of themselves.

The federal district court judge in Jacksonville, Florida, Howell Melton, said that the employer, Jacksonville Shipyards, Inc., and two of its employees, were directly liable for the harassment and rejected what he called their "ostrich defense." The company claimed that it was unaware of many of the woman's complaints.

The judge said that the shipyard maintained a boys' club atmosphere with a constant "visual assault on the sensibilities of female workers." Pictures included pinup calendars and close-ups of female genitals posted on the walls. The judge went on to say that the sexualized atmosphere of the workplace had the effect of keeping women out of the shipyard.

The opinion also said, "A pre-existing atmosphere that deters women from entering or continuing in a profession or job is no less destructive to and offensive to workplace equality than a sign declaring "men only." The shipyard was ordered to institute a sexual harassment policy written by the National Organization for Women's (NOW) Legal Defense and Education Fund. The New York-based women's advocacy group brought the case to trial.

The decision found both verbal and visual sexual harassment, and described thirty pornographic pictures displayed at the shipyard. One picture showed a woman's pubic area with a spatula pressed against it. Some of the pictures came from calendars provided by tool companies and included a nude woman bending over with her buttocks and genitals exposed. Another showed a frontal view of a female torso with the words "U.S.D.A. Choice" written on it. The verbal harassment included explicit sexual remarks.

The decision said that when the plaintiff told coworkers that their behavior was sexual harassment, they took her complaint as a new subject of ridicule and denied they were harassing her. Two other female employees testified that they also were subjected to sexual harassment in the form of remarks, pinches and sexual teasing.

According to the testimony, the female welder complained repeatedly to her supervisors about the pictures. A supervisor told her at one meeting where she complained that the company had no policy against the pictures and that the men had "constitutional rights" to post them, so he would not order the pictures removed. According to the ruling, the shipyard had no system to record sexual harassment complaints and supervisors had no instructions to document complaints.

The judge ordered the shipyard to pay legal fees but did not order them to provide back pay for time lost from work. The woman said she had missed work days because of the strain of the harassment, but the judge said her estimates of missed days were too vague. Under Title VII, no other damages were available at the time.

Lawyers involved cited *Robinson v. Jacksonville Shipyards* as another case in which expert witness testimony of sexual stereotyping was used. Based on the testimony, the judge said the women were subject to "sex role spillover," where the women are evaluated by coworkers and supervisors based on the women's sexuality and sexual worth rather than their value as workers.

Alison Wetherfield of the NOW Legal Defense and Education Fund said, "Judge Melton understands how damaging and illegal it is for women workers to be given the message that they are welcome at work only so long as they accept the stereotypical role of sex object … [and] recognizes the impossible position many harassed women are in, in a very sensitive and unusual way." According to the decision, women are still rare in this shipyard's skilled jobs, with only six women (compared with eight hundred forty-six men) employed as skilled craft workers in 1986. The company has never employed a woman in a supervisory position such as foreman, leadman, or quarterman.

A year after the suit was filed the company instituted a new sexual harassment policy forbidding employees from making any kind of sexual conduct a condition of employment or from creating an intimidating, hostile or offensive work environment (as per the EEOC Guidelines). The policy was posted on bulletin boards but the employees received no training. The court ruled that the policy had little or no effect on what it said was a sexually hostile work environment and that the company did not adequately communicate the new policy to employees. The latest policy, ordered by the court, calls for the offensive pictures to be removed and for workers to be educated about sexual harassment. It provides for penalties, including warnings, suspensions, and firings for those who violate the policy.

Affirmative Action Chief Ousted Over Shipyard Case

In May 1992, the new affirmative action chief of the City of Jacksonville, Florida, was terminated after it was revealed that he had been found liable for failure to prevent sexual harassment in the landmark *Jacksonville Shipyard* case. John A. Stewart resigned at the mayor's request, one day after beginning his $42,500-a-year position as director of the city's efforts to recruit, hire, and promote women and minorities.

Stewart's resignation came after *The Florida Times-Union* noted in an article that he was found liable last year in the shipyard case. He was personnel officer at the shipyard when the suit was filed in 1986. In the court ruling, Judge Melton said, "Stewart is liable for the hostile work environment to which Robinson [the plaintiff] was subjected."

The Reasonable Woman Decision: Ellison v. Brady

On January 23, 1991, a second and even more important land-mark ruling was made by the Ninth U.S. Circuit Court of Appeals in San Francisco. This case, *Ellison v. Brady*, has serious implications with regard to investigating and resolving complaints. In its ruling, the Ninth Circuit Court—which covers several Western states—established a new legal standard called the "reasonable woman" standard. This case is especially important to employers, not only because of the expanded definition of sexual harassment, but also because the court indicated that it expects swift and decisive actions in response to harassment in the workplace.

In the *Ellison* case, the employer's response to the harassment was to repeatedly counsel the harasser, instructing him to leave the woman alone, and to transfer him to a different facility for four months—a response many employers would deem appropriate. In fact, before the *Ellison* case went to the federal court, the EEOC had held that the employer, the Internal Revenue Service, was not liable because it had taken sufficient steps to remedy the situation.

The Ninth Circuit disagreed. The court found fault with the employer's not having consulted the victim about the harasser's return to the office; for not reprimanding the man with probation, suspension or some other type of discipline; and finally, for transferring the woman to avoid further conflict, even though she had requested the transfer. The court also said that in some cases, the mere presence of an employee who has harassed a coworker may create a hostile work environment, so that the only reasonable recourse is to discharge the alleged harasser. The *Ellison* decision suggests that managers take the following preventative steps to protect themselves, their organizations, and their employees:

- develop a clear sexual harassment policy statement and grievance procedures, spelling this out in the employee manual;
- tell employees that harassment is taken from the victim's perspective so employees should be sensitive to the feelings and viewpoints of their coworkers;
- treat sexual harassment as a serious employee infraction, taking prompt and remedial action to correct the situation; if harassment continues, the harasser should be disciplined with suspension, demotion, or some other form of concrete discipline;
- include the victim in determining the appropriate action, at least when consideration is being given to allowing the harasser to work alongside the victim;
- do not alter the terms or conditions of the victim's employment when responding to the incidents of harassment;
- consider whether the harasser must be terminated because his or her mere presence creates a hostile work environment for the victim; and
- show that the severity of conduct varies inversely with the frequency of the conduct.

The Court also said that:

- an understanding of the victim's perspective requires an analysis of the different perspectives of men and women;
- a female employee may state a *prima facie* case of hostile environment sexual harassment by alleging conduct that a reasonable woman would consider sufficiently severe; however, the employer does not have to accom-

modate the idiosyncrasies of the rare hypersensitive employee;

• the reasonable woman standard is not static but will change over time as the views of reasonable women change; and

• there can be unlawful sexual harassment even when harassers do not realize that their conduct creates a hostile working environment.

In this case, the plaintiff, Ms. Kerry Ellison, was an agent for the IRS office in San Mateo, California. Her coworker, Mr. Sterling Gray, who worked about twenty feet from her, asked her out for lunch one day in June 1986 and they went out to eat. A few months later, Gray asked her out again, for drinks and lunch, and Ellison refused and made it clear that she was not interested. Gray then started to write her love letters.

In an October 1986 note scribbled on a message pad, he wrote "I cried over you last night and I'm totally drained today." She continued to refuse his further advances which he made in person and in writing and finally asked a coworker to tell Gray to leave her alone, all to no avail. A few days later he wrote in a three-page, single-spaced letter saying "I know that you are worth knowing with or without sex ... "

Ellison said she was frightened by his attention and "frantic" about what he might do next. She filed a complaint with her employer alleging sexual harassment. The alleged harasser was counseled, instructed to leave Ellison alone, and eventually transferred to another location. Three months later he was allowed to return to Ellison's office under two conditions: 1) that he complete additional training for a month at another location; and 2) that he leave Ellison alone when he returned.

The victim was not consulted about Gray's transfer or the conditions of his return. When Ellison learned that Gray was returning to her workplace, she requested and received a transfer. Then she filed suit.

The trial court federal judge dismissed the case ruling that

Gray's actions were "isolated and genuinely trivial" applying the "reasonable person" test to the circumstances. The court ruled that the average adult, regardless of sex, would not have found Ellison's workplace hostile. But in January 1991, the appeals court, the Ninth Circuit court, reversed the lower court decision and threw out the reasonable person rule. The court ruled that a hostile work environment must be judged from the perspective of the victim, in this case, the "reasonable woman."

This means that the victim's feelings must play a crucial role in identifying a series of actions as sexual harassment and that many employers will have to adopt a broader perspective in addressing sexual harassment complaints. Supervisors, especially male supervisors, should no longer disregard complaints because they do not find the behaviors offensive; it is the victim's perception that must be taken into account.

According to attorney Steven Winterbauer, " ... *Ellison* marks a significant departure from the prevailing standard governing claims of sexual harassment. The Ninth Circuit has joined a growing minority of courts taking an increasingly aggressive stance against workplace harassment. This trend appears to be a good indication of the future development of employment law."

"The case has helped reverse a 154-year old legal convention of determining sexual harassment based on what is known as the "reasonable man" (more recently the "reasonable person") standard. This [the old standard] says that determination of harassment is based on what the court believes a reasonable man would think."

ONE MORE TIME, WHAT EXACTLY IS SEXUAL HARASSMENT?

That question still has no definitive answer, particularly on a global scale with all the world's countries and their varying values, cultures, and norms. Nevertheless, there are some points of agreement, country to country, so for now, a good basic answer is to think in these terms: *For behavior to be considered sexual harassment it must meet these criteria: 1) it occurs because of the persons sex—it is related to or about sex; 2) it is unwelcome, not returned, not mutual; and 3) it affects the terms or conditions of employment, in some cases including the work environment itself.*

Definitions of Harassment Expand: Street Harassment

Northwestern University law professor Cynthia Grant Bowman published a sixty-page article in the March 1993 issue of *Harvard Law Review* on "street harassment" of women. Bowman says that "wolf-whistles, sucking noises and catcalls" directed at women in public places, as well as comments that "range from 'Hello, baby' to vulgar suggestions and outright threats" are part of a "spectrum of means by which men objectify women and assert coercive power over them." Bowman suggests making such harassment illegal, or at least to make the harassers subject to civil suits.

In her article, Bowman said "any incident of harassment, no matter how harmless, reinforces fear of rape by demonstrating that any man may choose to invade a woman's personal space, physically or psychologically ... ."

While Bowman argues that cultural change is the only real solution, Mickey Kaus, writing in *The New Republic,* offers three possible solutions. First, he cites Amitai Etzioni, in his

book *The Spirit of Community*, who does not want to
"notch" the first amendment by forbidding what some see as
offensive speech, but who suggests re-education of harassers.
Why not require them to attend "classes that will teach them
civility?" Kaus suggests that this rings too much of state-spon-
sored re-education of its citizens.

A second alternative would be to give the targets of street
harassment the right to sue for civil damages, but Kaus says,
this might be a "recipe for gross litigiousness. Do we really
want every woman who feels 'dissed' to be able to require a
judge to assess the 'reasonableness' of the dissing?"

The third alternative, which Kaus believes to be the most
satisfactory, is to delegate the required judgments to the
police by making "street harassment" a misdemeanor, just as
are other public disturbances. Pennsylvania currently has a
state law penalizing anyone who intentionally "engages in a
course of conduct or repeatedly commits acts which alarm or
seriously annoy" another person. While Kaus believes that
police would only arrest the most egregious violators, this
approach would at least provide a basis for telling offenders
to "move along." Further Kaus says, the law might stimulate
the cultural change that is ultimately the true, long-term
answer to the problem of "street harassment."

ACLU Changes Policy on Defining Sexual Harassment

The American Civil Liberties Union (ACLU), at its April 1993
meeting in New York, adopted a new stance on sexual harassment. In doing so, the organization rejected complaints that it
was ignoring the free speech rights of male workers and
agreed that courts should make it easier for women to bring
sexual harassment complaints.

While the ACLU was initially founded to defend free
speech, it has had to defend itself in recent years against criticisms that it bends its policies to competing interests, such as

freedom of speech versus racial justice or the elimination of sexual harassment in the workplace. The positions that the ACLU takes have no power in and of themselves, but the organization is an extremely active participant in court cases throughout the United States. It files more briefs with the U.S. Supreme Court that any group except the Justice Department.

The recent change in policy was linked to a case heard by the Supreme Court later in 1993. As reported in the April 1993 *Webb Report*, the court agreed to decide a case, *Harris v. Forklift Systems Inc.*, in which a lower court ruled that a woman must suffer psychological harm and interference with her job performance in order to support a claim of sexual harassment. Nadine Strossem, president of the ACLU, said the organization must focus its own views on such an issue if it wants to file a brief in this case.

Thus the board voted to change the current policy that sexual harassment only occurred if there is a pattern of behavior directed at an employee that "demonstrably hinders or completely prevents" her from doing her job. The board voted to make it easier to bring charges by loosening the definition and saying that the offensive behavior need not be aimed directly at the individual bringing the complaint.

"Many women are still second-class citizens," said Mary Ellen Gale of the ACLU's Southern California chapter. "It's important for the ACLU to recognize that sexual harassment is widespread and devastating and a fundamental violation of women's equal rights that does real harm to real women in the real world."

Benson Wolman, a board member representing Ohio who opposed the policy change, was concerned about subordinating the free speech rights of the men who might make sexual remarks to the rights of women to not be subjected to such comments. "I'm disturbed we would adjust a policy that would result in slighting the free speech rights of other employees ... We wouldn't tolerate these circumstances in other areas of the law."

Brand New: Sexual Harassment Insurance Against Lawsuits

In response to the recent upsurge in sexual harassment complaints and suits, several national insurers have begun offering what they call employment practice liability coverage. The policies are to protect companies against race, age, and sex discrimination suits filed by their employees.

Discrimination and wrongful termination lawsuits have increased significantly. Experts believe this is a result of the 1991 Civil Rights Act and the Americans with Disabilities Act—and because of increased awareness of sexual harassment following the Hill–Thomas controversy. Victims of discrimination or harassment who were once reluctant to come forward are now more willing to bring suits.

While most corporations carry some form of general liability insurance covering employee accidents or injuries, such insurance does not usually apply to discrimination—often seen by insurers as a willful, intentional act. Chubb Insurance Co. has written policies for approximately twelve companies since it introduced the coverage. The policies cover the company, its board, officers, and employees.

Lexington Insurance sold twenty-five policies in a recent six-month period, representing approximately $50 million in coverage. Defense for discrimination suits can be expensive, costing up to $700,000 if the case goes to trial.

Critics believe such insurance is unnecessary and expensive. Experts say the best way for a company to protect itself is by spending money instead on preventative programs, including policies, procedures, and employee training.

Continuing Twists and Turns

Sexual harassment is continuing to take both the old predictable road and new roads at the same time. Some fairly standard methods for identifying harassment are being recognized worldwide, while at the same time, new and unusual types of sexual harassment are being labeled. Sexual harassment now includes harassment by women, by men, by boys, and by girls—at work, at school, at play, and even in the strangest ways.

One recent story, reported in several U.S. newspapers, is of high-tech sexual harassment by computer. Women report that as personal computer use and on-line services increase in popularity, sexual harassment through computers is more and more of a problem. There are more than forty-five thousand bulletin board services available, so that a computer and a computer modem allows for entry into a worldwide network of people discussing art, music, politics, technology, and even the meaning of life.

The anonymity of e-mail allows hostilities to surface as well. One University of Illinois speech professor said she was shocked to see a pair of breasts—constructed from hundreds of punctuation marks—appear on her computer screen. "I was surprised ... but I was not surprised, given the problems in our culture, that when you get a new form of communication there's a gender hierarchy set up," she said.

Another woman, a freelance writer on the West Coast, received harassing e-mail messages, including rape threats laced with profanity. Supposedly the remarks were meant as retaliation for anti-sexist comments she had made to a computer discussion group. When she asked others on her network if they had been sexually harassed, more than 75 percent said yes.

Wendy Reid Crisp, national director of the National Association of Female Executives, says fear of high-tech harassment can impede women's ability to advance in the workplace. She said obscene techno-talk is "serious psychological harassment ... it's tied to your ability to earn a living."

Most incidents of computer sexual harassment have been at U.S. universities where there is easy access to Internet, the massive, loosely organized computer network that carries messages for an estimated fifteen million users every day. Cheris Kramarae, co-editor of the publication *Women, Information, Technology, Scholarship,* says that computer harassment discourages women from studying in areas where they are already under-represented, such as computer sciences, mathematics, and physics.

According to *USA Today,* Internet users can assess vast amounts of information on nearly any subject. One new group called "alt.binaries.pictures.erotica:" contains subjects such as nude Asian women, sadomasochism, bestiality, and pictures of naked children. All such material can be sent anonymously to other Internet users.

Because there is no commission or governing body in the United States to oversee transmissions of Internet, the regulation of content must be done by the individual institutions using the systems. Currently the Federal Communications Commission has authority to pursue harassment cases since most computer transmissions are done over the telephone. Although FCC officials said they are not yet aware of any such cases being pursued, it would be handled in the same manner as someone making obscene telephone calls and complaints would be forwarded to the U.S. Department of Justice for investigation and prosecution.

Robert Charles, a Washington lawyer who followed the issue of free speech and computer networks, says there is little legal precedent about improper comments over computers and that high-tech sexual harassment is a new issue that the courts will soon have to contend with.

No one is aware of any actual litigation involving sexual harassment by computer, but Charles and other experts say it's just a matter of time. He said "Since computer bulletin boards and electronic messaging are used in the working environment by tens of millions of people daily, there is certainly potential for a sexual harassment complaint based upon continuous, intimidating or offensive communications."

Interesting to note also, is that the University of New

South Wales in Australia launched an investigation into the implications of electronic mail after a series of claims of sexual, racial, and defamatory abuse during the first six months of 1993.

No doubt, sexual harassment will continue to show up in new and unusual ways for many years to come.

PART TWO:
FROM AROUND THE WORLD

3

FIRST SHOCKWAVES: THE STATE OF SEXUAL HARASSMENT WORLDWIDE

Sexual harassment is inextricably linked with power and takes place in societies which often treat women as sex objects and second-class citizens. Most likely harassed are women who are divorced, separated, widowed, single parents, lesbian, from ethnic minorities, who work in non-traditional jobs, are new to the work force, younger, or with temporary jobs or on contracts.

U.N. International Labour Organisation 1992

Not long ago when I was being interviewed by a Japanese journalist about sexual harassment in the United States and Japan, she asked how I would explain to Japanese men in a meeting that I would not serve them tea. At the time, I didn't quite understand the question, so I asked who the men were in this hypothetical meeting. They are "presidents of companies, just as you, Susan," the journalist replied. I told her I would explain to these men that I, too, was a company president, and that perhaps we should ask someone other than a president to serve tea to us all. (I dared not mention the possibility that we could each take a turn serving tea to each other). She acted almost as if she did not hear my answer, but of course she did. She was simply responding as the men in the meeting would. "But you are the woman in the room," she said. "Why will you not serve tea?"

Despite my continued and repeated explanations of power, authority, respect, stature, etc., she repeated the same question over and over: but why will you not serve tea? Finally she laughed and teasingly said, "but still, Susan, you are the woman," and that was that. End of discussion. It seems in meetings such as the one she described, we were not likely to get past the one, overriding aspect of my being female—nothing else would matter. It certainly is cause for thought about the true state of sexual harassment and equality in the world today.

Sometimes it just takes time for emotions to cool and thought to be given for things to change, seemingly on their own. Reports in 1993 from the United States indicated that public opinion had indeed changed over time when it came to whether people believed Clarence Thomas's or Anita Hill's accounts of alleged sexual harassment. The surveys showed that with the passage of time (and perhaps after giving the situation more thought), more people believed Professor Hill's claims later than had believed her at the time she made the complaints to the Senate sub-committee.

There also was immediate positive reaction at the time of the hearings from many women in the United States. According to the February 1992 issue of *Glamour* magazine, about 15 percent of the people who wrote Professor Hill after the confirmation hearings for Judge Thomas revealed personal accounts of sexual harassment. Many of the women who wrote Hill were "older women who had experienced harassment during the Depression or when their husbands were serving in World War II," said *Glamour* editor Susan Sedman. "They wrote of feeling they had to put up with almost anything from their bosses to keep their family going." Younger women cited similar situations "when they found themselves newly divorced."

From the time of the Thomas–Hill controversy until today, more and more women in the United States have come forward with stories of sexual harassment and discrimination, showing increasing anger and impatience at the conditions they face.

According to Lynn Povich, editor-in-chief of *Working Woman* magazine, there are three primary reasons why working women are so fed up with the government:

1. Economically, working women suffer most when the economy goes sour. This is because women are paid less than their male counterparts to begin with, are likely to be lower in the hierarchy at work, and in many cases are single mothers who bear the financial burden of raising their children, Povich said.
2. The controversy surrounding the Thomas–Hill hearings showed how badly women are actually treated and the degree to which Congress does not take women seriously. The vetoing of the Family Leave Bill during the Bush administration and the continual under-funding of women's health research show the same conclusions, Povich said. [The Family Leave Bill was resurrected with the change of administrations and signed into law in early 1993 by President Clinton.]
3. The entire "family values" issue, which some say made women's lives a political football, further served to politicize women, particularly during the last presidential election, Povich said.

Women mustn't be ignored or patronized, Povich said. "Women have the political power and the economic clout to make a difference. We are 51 percent of the population and 45 percent of the work force."

THE GLOBAL NUMBERS

Worldwide, research indicates that sexual harassment is indeed a global problem with global implications. Recent surveys in Austria, Belgium, Canada, Czechoslovakia, Denmark, Estonia, Finland, France, Germany, the Netherlands, Portugal, the former Soviet Union, Spain, Sweden, the United Kingdom, and the United States show sexual harassment to be widespread. The studies also validate, over and over, basically the same results, trends, and conclusions of earlier studies.

The results of studies vary somewhat depending on the size of the sample group, those surveyed and their level of awareness, and the way questions are posed. For example, asking women if they have been subjected to certain types of sexual behavior may result in higher percentages saying "yes" than if they are asked if they have been sexually harassed—since many may not be aware of what that phrase means. On the other hand, it has been suggested in U.S. research that asking women if they have been sexually harassed will result in higher percentages saying "yes" because American women are especially sensitive to the issue.

Because of these different research methods, as well as cultural differences, survey results within a country may vary from study to study. Furthermore, it is difficult to compare countries and determine which have a "worse" problem than others. The point is, regardless of research difficulties, all the studies and surveys to date reveal the same thing—that sexual harassment is a serious problem in the world's workplaces, with serious implications for its victims, its perpetrators, companies and organizations, and countries as a whole.

In terms of actual numbers, the earliest studies, conducted in the United States in the mid-1970s, show that from 40 to 60 percent of working women and approximately 15 percent of working men have personally experienced sexual harassment. International studies show there are no typical victims of sexual harassment, but that those most likely to be harassed are people perceived as vulnerable and financially dependent. The myth that physical attractiveness is related to being a victim of harassment is just that—a myth.

Blame the harasser, not yourself!

A sixty-five year old woman who worked as a secretary for a government agency told me she believed the myth that it was her fault—something in the way she behaved or because of her attractiveness—that caused a younger man to make vulgar, sexually suggestive remarks to her. To change the situation, she changed herself. She began pulling her hair back in a bun, she never wore sweaters or V-neck blouses, and most of the time she tried to keep her jacket on to hide her full-breasted figure. She said she changed her mind about it being her fault when one day the young man came up with white lotion in his hand, acting as if it were semen, and said, "See what you made me do!" and laughed loudly. She realized then that nothing in her behavior was causing him to treat her so disrespectfully. Sexual harassment is about the harasser being at fault, not the victim.

Since people perceived as vulnerable and financially dependent are those most likely to be harassed, it follows that subordinates are most likely victims of harassment. "Subordinate" may mean the location of a person in an organizational hierarchy, or it may simply mean the status of being a woman—so incidents of female supervisors being harassed by their peers and even their own subordinates can occur.

Specifically, those most likely to be sexually harassed throughout the world are divorced, separated and widowed women (since they have no man to protect them), single parents, lesbians, women from ethnic minorities, women who work in traditionally male jobs, new work force entrants, younger women, and women with temporary employment assignments or contracts. According to the International Labour Organisation's (ILO) 1992 study on harassment,

"Sexual harassment is inextricably linked with power and takes place in societies which often treat women as sex objects and second-class citizens."

The ILO study goes on to state that international research indicates that while women are more likely than men to be harassed, men who are subjected to harassment have the same kind of vulnerabilities: young men new to the work force, men working in traditionally female jobs, men from ethnic and racial minorities, and gay men. Harassment of men is more likely to take the form of joking and teasing as opposed to actual sexual overtures. Because of cultural pressures to be sexually active, available, and willing at all times (or to at least act as if they are), the number of instances where men are harassed may be under-reported.

A thirty-five year old man who worked in management at a large electrical utility told me that at his previous job, at another company, his female boss told him directly that she was sexually interested in him. When he told her that he was newly married and not interested in his boss, she informed him that if he didn't go along "my name would be mud in the company, and it was—for two years." After two years of putting up with slights and mistreatment from her, he quit, never complaining to anyone.

On a different occasion at a sexual harassment workshop, a man who worked in city government told me privately that a male department head would occasionally come up behind him in the hallway and swat him on the butt, as might happen on the football field among players. He didn't know if it was a sexual approach or not, but he was very embarrassed and ashamed by it. When asked if he had told anyone, he replied, "Just my wife." The behavior had gone on for years.

A Serious Problem Around the World

The similar, and often identical, results from sexual harassment surveys around the world are not surprising, but they are revealing of what harassment is truly about—a serious problem related to gender. Whether those harassing or harassed are office workers, police officers, attorneys, waiters or waitresses, whether they are European, North or South American, Asian, African—the results show the same patterns worldwide when it comes to sexual harassment. The numbers of victims, the percentages of people reporting they have been sexually harassed, the impact of harassment on them, their responses, and the types of harassment they have experienced all tend to look the same from country to country.

Taiwan

The Modern Women's Foundation (MWF) was organized in 1987 to help and protect women in the Taipei area from being sexually victimized. In 1991, the foundation surveyed 972 women of different occupational backgrounds in Taipei. Of those who responded, nearly 37 percent said they had personally experienced sexual harassment at work at least once, and 70 percent knew that their friends had suffered similar experiences. Respondents said that most harassment occurs at work.

Helene H. Lin, a marriage counselor and an associate professor of psychology at Soochow University in Taipei, said: "Sexual harassment is part of everyday life ... it has a long tradition in Chinese society."

France

In 1991 a study commissioned by the Secretary of State for Women's and Consumer's Rights, found that 21 percent of the 1,300 women surveyed said they had personally experienced sexual harassment. Of these women, 12 percent said the sexual advances were a type of coercion or blackmail; 63 percent said they were subjected to propositions and gestures; 60 percent reported continual unwanted sexual advances despite refusing previous advances; and 48 percent reported a hostile or offensive work environment.

The victims said their harasser was their employer in 29 percent of the cases; was their supervisor in 26 percent of the incidents; was a coworker 22 percent of the time; and was a client 27 percent of the time. Commerce and handicrafts sectors reported the highest number of female victims—18 percent; the industrial sector reported 17 percent; the medical and hospital sector reported 14 percent; and the leisure industry—bars, restaurants, and hotel industries reported 10 percent. Of the women who were harassed, 24 percent said they experienced negative consequences and 14 percent said they were forced to resign or were fired. In 19 percent of the cases, the women said the harassment also was detrimental to the harasser.

Japan

The Tokyo Metropolitan Government conducted a survey in 1991 which found that 81 percent of the respondents—both men and women—think that touching the hand or body of a person should be considered sexual harassment. Seventy-one percent of the men and 52 percent of the women said they think jokes or comments about a person's body is a form of sexual harassment; 25 percent of both men and women think staring at a person without a reason is sexual harassment; and 61 percent of both men and women think that having to serve alcohol at work parties or being subjected to sexual advances of drunken coworkers is also sexual harassment.

When asked why they believe sexual harassment occurs, 50 percent said it is because men and women are not seen as equal partners at work; 21 percent cited a lack of equal education between men and women; and 19 percent said it is because women are seen as sex objects. Fifty-one percent said they have heard about sexual harassment at work; 46 percent said it hinders equal relationships in the workplace; 26 percent said it is a personal problem at work; 23 percent said it is a social problem, not a workplace problem; and 2 percent said it is not a problem at all.

The Netherlands

To date, only one study has been conducted on sexual harassment in the Netherlands. It was commissioned by the government and conducted at the University of Groningen in 1986. Three case studies were used as the basis of the survey: a small business, a large city government, and an industrial company. The results indicated that 58 percent of the women responding said they had personally experienced sexual harassment, with 25 percent of them feeling their work environment was negatively affected—some to such an extent that they quit or were transferred to other areas. The women reported sexual harassment that was ongoing rather than a one-time incident (as most harassment studies show), and in some instances occurred on a daily basis between the men and women at work. Verbal harassment was the most common, with physical harassment to a lesser degree.

This study also validated earlier conclusions that sexual harassment is most likely to occur in workplaces in which exists a disproportionate ratio of men to women, or vice versa. Where there are nearly equal numbers of men and women, particularly in the same or very similar job categories, sexual harassment is less likely to occur. Another way of looking at this phenomenon is to note that in those organizations where men and women are in more traditional positions—the majority of employees are men or the majority of power positions are held by men—sexual harassment is likely to take place with an expected frequency. According to the

ILO study, "Sexual harassment occurs most often when the traditional roles of men and women are challenged by women taking up employment in a traditionally male-dominated sector, or when women are employed in high level positions."

Norway

In a 1988 study by a research group called Trak 88, 41 percent of the women responding said they had been subjected to unwanted sexual touching many times; 40 percent said sometimes; 9 percent said they had been touched once; and 9 percent said they had never been touched. The research group indicated that the sample group was small and not considered representative. However, it was still disturbing that even in a small sample group, 21 percent of the women said they had been raped or subject to attempted rape at the workplace. Also, 38 percent said they had been pressured to have sex (9 percent said they had been pressured many times, and 18 percent said they had been pressured one time).

Spain

The Women's Section of the General Union of Workers commissioned a study in 1986 to examine sex discrimination and sexual harassment in Spain. The study included women from six different economic sectors in Madrid.

The respondents said that 84 percent of them had experienced sexual comments, jokes, and remarks; 55 percent had been subjected to sexual looks or gestures; 27 percent had experienced pressure for dates or sexual advances; and 4 percent had been subjected to attempted sexual intercourse. The study also showed that women age 26 to 30 were more likely to be harassed because they were younger and supposedly sexually experienced. While results showed that women who were divorced, separated, or widowed were not more likely to experience sexual harassment, they were more likely to experience severe harassment when harassment did occur. Airline attendants and journalists reported the most frequent sexual harassment. Harassers were reported just as likely to be coworkers as supervisors. Effects on the victims, as in other studies, were shown to be anxiety, stress, depression, loss of self-esteem, absenteeism, and loss of productivity. The women who responded to the survey were not well-informed on their rights and legal avenues with regard to sexual harassment in the workplace.

Sweden

In 1987, Sweden's first study on sexual harassment was commissioned by the Equal Opportunities Ombudsman and the results were submitted to the Ministry of Labour. The survey included women from nine trade unions from both public and private sectors. Results showed that 17 percent of the women who responded said they had experienced some type of sexual harassment in the workplace, with the most frequent type being unwelcome verbal comments and touching (70 percent reported experiencing both). Nearly 33 percent of those who said they had been harassed also said they had received unwelcome requests for sex or sexual favors; half reported being harassed by supervisors or coworkers.

Of the women who said they were harassed, approximately one-third said the only solution was to leave their job, either by quitting, taking sick leave, or a leave of absence. While the study showed that women of all ages, salary ranges, positions, etc., can be victims of harassment, young women and women in male-dominated occupations appeared most likely to be sexually harassed.

United Kingdom

Michael Rubenstein, a well-known and respected expert on sexual harassment who is based in the United Kingdom, reported to the ILO on a number of smaller studies that have been conducted in the country. The government's Labour Research Department found in a 1987 study that 73 percent of the respondents reported some form of sexual harassment, with the most common types being suggestive remarks or verbal comments (reported by 48 percent); sexist or patronizing behavior (reported by 45 percent); and unnecessary touching and unwanted physical contact (reported by 34 percent).

Rubenstein also reported on a 1991 study of the clients of the Alfred Marks Bureau, an employment agency. This study found that 47 percent of the women and 14 percent of the men said they had been sexually harassed (those figures are nearly identical to major U.S. studies in 1980 and 1988 indicating 40-42 percent of women and 14-15 percent of men had been sexually harassed). Forty-three percent said they had experienced touching, pinching, or grabbing; 41 percent experienced suggestive comments and innuendoes; 32 percent experienced direct sexual propositions; 10 percent had been ogled, leered at, or subjected to suggestive looks; and 6 percent experienced comments about their bodies.

The United States

According to the American Management Association, 52 percent of their member companies have dealt with allegations of sexual harassment in the past five years, and nearly 60 percent of the cases resulted in disciplinary action against the offender. The survey was of 524 firms.

The survey also showed that 17 percent of the sexual harassment claims were dismissed without action, and 14 percent led to dismissal of the offender. Besides termination, other disciplinary action included formal reprimands (27 percent), probation or suspension (14 percent), or a transfer of the offender to another position (6 percent). The rest of the cases were settled with counseling or by mediation between the two parties.

Only 50 percent of the cases were brought to the companies' attention through formal complaints. Usually cases were developed through informal reports, third-party observations, or anonymous communications from workers to management. Nearly 75 percent of the companies responding said that they have formal policies and procedures in place and 40 percent offer training on the subject of sexual harassment.

Sixty percent of companies on the West coast reported claims; 41 percent in North Atlantic states; and 36 percent in New England. Small companies were more likely to dismiss allegations of harassment, while the larger firms were more likely to take disciplinary action.

Two surveys on sexual harassment that were published by *Working Woman* magazine in June 1992 should prove valuable to those concerned about the problem. One survey, published in the magazine's February 1992 issue, elicited more than 9,000 responses from readers. The other survey followed up on *Working Woman's* ground-breaking 1988 survey by looking again at the same Fortune 500 companies featured in that previous study.

Women know what sexual harassment is, the surveys showed. Only 15 percent were not sure about the line between harassment and harmless behavior. Human resource executives were even stricter than women about defining what constitutes sexual harassment.

More than 60 percent of the women said they personally had been sexually harassed, and more than 33 percent knew someone who had been harassed. Most women still don't complain, though—only 25 percent actually reported incidents. Companies reported receiving fewer than five complaints a month.

Most of the human resource executives surveyed, and 75 percent of the women, said provocative dress, behavior or hypersensitivity on the part of women is not the cause of harassment. Half of the human resources executives reported that the "love affair gone sour" is not the cause either.

Women and human resources executives differed on how they saw their companies responding to complaints. Only 20 percent of the women thought complaints were given justice by their companies, while more than 70 percent of the human resources managers thought justice was served in the way their companies handled problems.

"The old prey on the young, and the powerful on the less powerful," said *Working Woman*. The most common incident involves the female subordinate under 34 being harassed by a male over 35, according to both the women and the human resources executives who responded. Nearly 30 percent of cases involve women age 18–24; in 83 percent of cases, the harasser is a more powerful person than the victim.

More likely to be sexually harassed are women in managerial positions who earn more than $50,000 annually and women in male-dominated industries, the study showed. Other studies of female chemical engineers, lawyers, and executives have found that approximately 60 percent experience harassment.

Incidents of sexual harassment which are reported to human resources are usually severe. The problem appears in the 1992 *Working Woman* study as even more serious than the 1988 study. Human resource executives in 1992 report that 50 percent of the cases involve pressure for dates or sexual favors, as compared with only 29 percent in 1988. Touching or cornering is involved in 34 percent of the cases according to 1992 responses, with only 26 percent of this nature in 1988. According to the human resources executives, most of the cases reported are valid—68 percent as compared with 64 percent in 1988.

More than 50 percent of women responding said the desire to bully and humiliate is the reason for most sexual harassment. Nearly half the women said they had been harassed by known "chronic harassers." This supports past data that showed harassers tend to harass or bother multiple people, multiple times, with regard to multiple issues—racial, sexual, generally negative, unfair behavior. In other words, a few men cause most of the problems.

While 79 percent of the women said they would tell a friend who's being harassed to stand up to the harasser, only 40 percent who were harassed themselves told the harasser to stop, and only 26 percent reported the harassment. Trying to ignore the harassment was still the most commonly used tactic (46 percent of the cases). When women told the harasser to stop, one out of three times it worked—the harasser quit. Only one of four times was successful when the women tried to ignore or avoid the harasser.

Women who were harassed reported such negative effects as being fired or forced to quit, undermined self-confidence, impaired health, and long-term career damage. Health problems given were headaches, fatigue, nausea, sleep and appetite disturbances, and more frequent colds and urinary tract infections—similar to those that come from other stressful situations.

Of women who responded, 21 percent said complaints are dealt with justly. But more than 60 percent said charges are completely ignored or offenders are given only token reprimands, and 55 percent who tried reporting harassment said nothing happened to the harasser.

Of human resource executives who responded, 80 percent said most offenders in their companies are handled fairly, but in the 1988 survey 90 percent said the same. According to Freada Klein, who analyzed the *Working Woman* survey in 1988, this "is the key contradiction in sexual harassment in the 1990s. In every workplace we've surveyed, we find that a majority of employees don't have faith in corporate channels for complaint."

Of the Fortune 500 firms, 81 percent reported having sexual harassment training programs, compared with only 60 percent in 1988. Most executives believed their own companies are doing a good job on this problem.

Results for the *Working Woman* survey were based on a statistically representative sample of 9,680 responses from readers and responses from the human resources executives at 106 of the Fortune 500 companies.

The *Wall Street Journal* reported that Anita Hill's charges against Clarence Thomas brought much attention to the issue of sexual harassment and resulted in a significant rise in the number of sexual harassment claims well into 1992. The *Journal* said that General Motors reported a 50 percent increase in claims since the hearings because of "increased awareness" of the issue, although it reported no increase in the number of lawsuits. Ford Motor Co., Chrysler Corp., and Digital Equipment reported increased employee requests for training and prevention programs.

According to a random telephone survey of 400 people in the Chicago area in 1992, nearly a third of the women and a fifth of the men reported being sexually harassed at work. In the study, conducted by the Medill School of Journalism and Northwestern University, many of the respondents reported that they were verbally sexually harassed by their supervisor.

The report stated that "from the overall pattern of results, perceptions of what constitutes sexual harassment often appear to be linked to a person in a position of power behaving in sexually offensive ways to someone else lower in the company's organizations hierarchy." In 65 percent of the reported cases, a woman was harassed by a man, in 19 percent a man was harassed by a woman, and in 3 percent a woman was harassed by a woman.

The survey report also noted that the results translate into an estimated 300,000 women and 150,000 men who are victimized by sexual harassment in Chicago alone. "This is likely to be an underestimate of the problem," the report said, because adults with lower socioeconomic backgrounds are not as likely to define certain behaviors as sexual harassment.

Nine out of ten respondents said they are "fairly well

informed" about what sexual harassment is, and the same number said harassment can occur without physical contact. One-third of those surveyed said that "some women deserve the sexual harassment they experience."

Lawrence King, a partner in the San Francisco law firm of King & Green, told the Bar Association's Convention in 1992 that sex discrimination, especially sexual harassment, "is high on the priority list" of civil rights cases now. He said sexual harassment is happening more and that he believes there is a "subtle but pervasive kind of sex bias" in the workplace when it comes to making individual employment decisions.

The Equal Employment Opportunity Commission reported a 62 percent increase in the number of sexual harassment complaints compared with 1991. The agency said that sex discrimination charges are three times more likely to be sexual harassment claims than those of discrimination in hiring or pregnancy discrimination.

King said the emphasis on sex discrimination has changed and that it is not equal pay, but rather the glass ceiling, that women are now coming up against.

Another attorney, Stuart Linnick, a partner in Mitchell, Silverberg & Knupp of Los Angeles, emphasized training as the best tool for preventing workplace sexual harassment. He said an employer who is sued, but who has previously conducted proper workplace training, can say "What else could we have done?" Viewed this way, sexual harassment training is an investment, not an expense.

Survey Shows Offenders Are Punished

In a 1992 survey of 1,300 employers by Business & Legal Reports, Inc., 42 percent received a sexual harassment complaint from an employee in 1991. The survey also showed that in most of the cases the result was disciplinary action against the offender.

Employers in the manufacturing sector were slightly more

likely to have received a complaint than other types of business. They also were more likely to discipline offenders. Companies with more than 500 employees were most likely to have received a complaint (56 percent), while those with fewer than 100 employees were least likely to (21 percent).

Ninety percent of those responding have a policy statement against sexual harassment. Eighty-two percent said they rely primarily on written communications to disseminate their policies to employees.

Different Perceptions, Same Problem

Norman Werback, of Werback Rose, a management consulting firm in Dallas, Texas, specializes in sexual harassment prevention programs. Werback reported an incident in early 1993 of different perceptions of the same problem by different people in the same organization:

Werback said he was conducting a sexual harassment workshop for a high tech firm in the Southwest with the company's sixteen managers and their boss, the division vice-president. The male/female ratio was fairly even—nine men and seven women—and Werback said he was impressed by the honest discussion and interaction among the participants.

During the session, because of the topics that were raised, the vice president asked his employees to respond "yes" or "no" to three questions: 1) Is sexual harassment an issue at our facility [a location with approximately 150 employees]? 2) Do we [our facility staff] effectively deal with it? and 3) Is there a fear of reporting sexual harassment at our facility?

The vice president, obviously expecting different responses, was shocked at what he heard: 75 percent said sexual harassment is an issue at their facility, 73 percent said the facility staff does not deal with it effectively, and 63 percent said there is a fear of reporting instances of sexual harassment.

According to studies and surveys, these kinds of responses and the percentages responding this way is not the exception, but actually the rule. However, once the issue gains serious attention, all too often the result of a lawsuit or a major confrontation, attitudes do change.

In a poll of 160 New York-area executives by the law firm Jackson, Lewis, Schnitzler & Krupman immediately after the Thomas–Hill controversy, sexual harassment was shown to have suddenly become the third most critical workplace employment issue. In 1991, sexual harassment had ranked fourteenth. Benefits and job security were listed first and second, respectively, in the 1992 ranking.

Seventy-one percent of those surveyed expected the recent publicity about sexual harassment to boost harassment claims for a time; 45 percent believed claims would increase for the long term.

4

SECOND SHOCKWAVES:
INTERNATIONAL UNDERSTANDING
AND ACTION

I have come to the conclusion that if we have to look for a nation which has not violated women's human rights, I doubt we can find one.

Gertrude Mongella,
Former Tanzanian high commissioner to India

It's a worldwide disgrace. Half the Earth's population is relegated to permanent under-status.

Eleanor Smeal
President, Fund for the Feminist Majority

It was a typical cloudy, rainy day in Seattle last fall when I met with a representative from Tokyo to discuss how sexual harassment might be better dealt with in Japan. She kindly and quietly said how lucky she thought I was to be married, and to a nice man, since in her country life for women at work was made more difficult by being single.

In one job, she said, her boss repeatedly asked her to go for drinks after work. This didn't seem necessarily inappropriate to me, and I asked her why she saw his requests as wrong, that perhaps he only wanted to discuss business in a less formal atmosphere. She smiled and said he wanted to meet her in what are widely known as "sex hotels." Though her refusals did not result in direct, negative job consequences that she knew of, her work life was made continually uncomfortable by his pressure for dates and sex. This shy, quiet woman was 26 years old. Her boss was married and in his late forties.

When I mentioned that I knew sexual harassment in Japan was referred to as *seku-hara,* she looked distressed. She said she believed the term *seku-hara* actually serves to trivialize the problem, and that just the week before she had seen a businessman on the train reading an article titled "I Love Seku-Hara" and "Please, Seku-Hara Me." When she left my office, I think we both felt a bit wiser. We both had gained understanding from our meeting, but I felt a sadness as her cab drove away.

THE LEGAL FOUNDATION OF SEXUAL HARASSMENT

In order to understand the state of sexual harassment on a global scale, it is critical to not only understand the concept as presented in Chapter 2, but also how the concept is approached legally in various countries. Here is a brief overview of different legal foundations worldwide.

Of the twenty-three industrialized countries surveyed by the International Labour Organisation (ILO) in 1992, only seven have statutes specifically defining or mentioning sexual harassment. Those countries: Australia, at the federal level and in most states; Canada, at the federal level and in some provinces; France; New Zealand; Spain; Sweden; and the United States, at the state level only. In other countries, such as Ireland and Switzerland, sexual harassment has been specifically mentioned and defined by the courts. Some courts in Australia, Canada, the United Kingdom, and the United States, have addressed sexual harassment also. In most other industrialized countries, sexual harassment has been defined as an activity that is illegal in other ways, such as wrongful dismissal, tort law, or criminal law.

The original and most narrow definition of sexual harassment is q*uid pro quo* harassment ("this for that"), the direct abuse of power by a supervisor over a subordinate. The *quid pro quo* standard was first adopted in 1982 and 1983 by two U.S. Circuit Courts of Appeal. The courts also adopted a second, broader standard called *condition of work* or *hostile environment* harassment.

Quid pro quo harassment, as defined by the U.S. courts, encompasses all situations in which submission to or rejection of sexual conduct is made a term or condition of employment, or in which submission to or rejection of sexual conduct is used as the basis for employment decisions affecting the individual who is the target of such conduct. In the typical *quid pro quo* harassment case, the employee or prospective employee is approached by an individual with the power to affect the employee's future and is asked for sexual consideration in return for a job benefit or in order to avoid losing a job benefit.

Condition of work or *hostile environment* sexual harassment, as defined by the U.S. courts, consists of sexually related behavior that is unwelcome and demeaning and that creates an intimidating, hostile and offensive work environment. In the case *Henson v. City of Dundee,* the appeals court reversed the lower court's holding that the plaintiff must show some tangible job detriment in addition to the hostile work environment created by sexual harassment. The court said that although not every instance or condition of work environment harassment gives rise to a discrimination claim, a plaintiff who can prove a number of elements can establish such a claim.

Australia, Canada, New Zealand, Switzerland, the United Kingdom, and the United States, either by judicial decision or by statute, have endorsed the concepts of *quid pro quo* and *hostile environment* harassment. France has adopted only the *quid pro quo* definition.

However, it is important to note that certain protections have been provided against behavior defined as *quid pro quo* harassment, without that particular term being used, in Austria, Denmark, Germany, Greece, the Netherlands, Norway, and Sweden. For the most part, sexual harassment charges in these countries have been handled as wrongful termination cases in which the plaintiffs argued that they were illegally discharged—that refusing a supervisor's sexual demands is not a legitimate reason for being fired.

In Japan, a successful suit was brought in 1992 on the basis of *hostile environment* sexual harassment and the woman was awarded monetary damages. For many people, this was a new and extremely surprising court decision and award, given the cultural norms of Japanese society. The decision brought about a great deal of interest in the issue of sexual harassment in Japan. It seems fair to assume that if Japanese courts are willing to define hostile work environments as sexual harassment, *quid pro quo* harassment also would be considered illegal.

LAWS RELATING
TO SEXUAL HARASSMENT

The very words "sexual harassment"—as a phrase and as a legal and behavioral concept—are relatively new in the global vocabulary. Certainly the term as a legal concept had little meaning until the first cases in the United States in the mid-seventies defined such behavior as a type of illegal sex discrimination.

Since then, the term "sexual harassment," both legally and behaviorally, has passed from country to country, including Australia, Canada, New Zealand, and Japan. In some countries, the phrase is just beginning to come into use, while in others it still has not been defined at all.

Earliest Beginnings: the United States

According to Charles Clark in the August 1991 *CQ Researcher*, the foundations for the concept of sexual harassment fell into place in the United States in the 1960s for the following reasons:

- women began entering—and staying in—the work force in large numbers (in 1959, twenty-two million worked, constituting approximately 33 percent of the U.S. work force; by 1991, fifty-seven million women were working, accounting for almost 46 percent);
- the 1964 Civil Rights Bill was passed, expanding the employment discrimination section, Title VII, to cover sex discrimination; and
- the women's movement, availability of the birth control pill, and the sexual revolution began changing society's views of men, women, work, and family.

It actually took ten years after the enactment of the 1964 Civil Rights Act before U.S. federal courts heard the first cases in which sexual harassment was the primary complaint. In five of the first seven cases, the courts interpreted sexual harassment to be based on sex as a "personal matter" between the two individuals, and not as actions directed at or affecting groups of people. In *Corne v. Bausch & Lomb*, the court reasoned that the conduct complained of was based on a "personal proclivity, peculiarity or mannerism of the supervisor" rather than discrimination based on sex. In *Barnes v. Train* the court said the offensive conduct was because of the victim's sexual attractiveness, not her gender, and that "this is a controversy underpinned by the subtleties of an inharmonious relationship." In *Miller v. Bank of America*, the court ruled that the sexual advances were not employment related and that the law was not designed to "hold an employer liable for what is essentially the isolated and unauthorized sex misconduct of one employee to another." Apparently the courts feared a flood of legal actions around what they believed to be personal problems. In *Tomkins v. Public Service Electric and Gas Co.*, the court stated: "If the plaintiff's view were to prevail, no supervisor could, prudently, attempt to open a social dialog with any subordinate of either sex. An invitation to dinner would become an invitation to a federal lawsuit." Obviously, these cases were not successful in establishing sexual harassment as a form of sex discrimination.

However, in 1976, a case finally did establish a cause of action for sexual harassment (*Williams v. Saxbe*). The court ruled that the behavior in question only had to create an "artificial barrier to employment that was placed before one gender and not the other, even though both genders were similarly situated." And in 1977, another federal court of appeals, ruling on a previous case, *Barnes v. Costle (Barnes v. Train)*, said that *quid pro quo* sexual harassment did indeed constitute sex discrimination, since, "[b]ut for her womanhood ... her participation in sexual activity would never have been solicited ... [S]he became the target of her superior's sexual desires because she was a woman, and was asked to bow to his demands as the price for holding her job." Thus conditions of employment which were applied differently to men and women, like sexual harassment, were forbidden under Title VII as sex discrimination. These were major landmark decisions in beginning to address sexual harassment in the workplace in the United States, and in fact, for the rest of the world's workplaces as well.

Because these earliest cases in the United States involved claims that the plaintiffs had been deprived of tangible job benefits for their failure to succumb to sexual advances, the women had to show a clear relationship between the objectionable conduct (the harassment) and the negative employment consequences (being fired or demoted, given distasteful job assignments or poor performance reviews) that followed. If they could not show these tangible, negative consequences, then the harassing behavior was seen as isolated sexual misconduct, not a Title VII violation (*Hill v. BASF Wyandotte Corp., Neely v. American Fidelity Assurance Co., Davis v. Bristol Laboratories*).

During the final days of President Jimmy Carter's administration, in November 1980, the concept of sexual harassment was broadly expanded when the U.S. Equal Employment Opportunity Commission finalized its "Guidelines on Discrimination Because of Sex."

Soon thereafter, a U.S. appeals court decision in *Brown v. City of Guthrie* was the first to cite the EEOC Guidelines on Discrimination Because of Sex. The court quoted Section A, saying sexual harassment is a violation of Title VII when "such conduct has the purpose or effect of substantially interfering with an individual's work performance or creating an intimidating, hostile, or offensive work environment."

The case was the first in which a court considered the argument that sexual harassment created an "atmosphere of discrimination." While the plaintiff could not show a loss of tangible job benefits, she established that the harassment created a hostile, offensive and unbearable work environment.

Shortly after *Brown*, in *Bundy v. Jackson* in 1981, another federal appeals court ruled on the basis of the atmosphere of discrimination, citing the EEOC guidelines to support its opinion. The court interpreted "terms and conditions of employment" protected by Title VII to mean more than tangible compensation and benefits.

Some other U.S. courts did not follow the same pattern of the *Brown* and *Bundy* cases. One district court held that no action under Title VII for sexual harassment was available where the plaintiff did not show that her success and advancement depended on her agreeing to her supervisor's demands. The court observed that Title VII should not be interpreted as reaching into sexual relationships which arise during the course of employment but which do not have a "substantial effect" on that employment.

Nevertheless, in 1982 and 1983, in the cases *Henson v.*

City of Dundee and *Katz v. Dole*, two U.S. courts of appeal adopted a classification scheme for sexual harassment cases, identifying two types: *quid pro quo* and *condition of work* or *hostile environment* harassment.

Earliest Interest Worldwide

According to the International Labour Organisation, two factors influenced the larger—and recent—worldwide interest in sexual harassment. First, the massive influx of women into the labor force in the 1960s and 70s occurred not only in the United States, but on a global scale. This new and sudden influx of women into the labor force brought about two simultaneous, but seemingly opposite reactions to women at work. One was resentment and a perceived threat of women by men in traditionally male dominated work environments. In these cases the women were subject to overt discrimination, i.e. lesser-valued job assignments, lack of promotions, lower pay, and sexual harassment to cause embarrassment and humiliation. The second reaction was to exploit the presence of women and make sexual favors and submission to sexual behaviors conditions of employment, i.e. to keep from being fired, demoted, or otherwise adversely affected at work.

Secondly, the ILO said, legal decisions by U.S. courts in the late 1970s that recognized sexual harassment as a specific type of prohibited conduct, and not simply a violation of a more general legal sanction, caused researchers in the 1980s to focus on sexual harassment as a very specific behavioral problem in the workplace worldwide.

These decisions by U.S. courts also served to at least begin defining the parameters of modern sexual harassment law. While other countries have based their decisions on U.S. equal opportunity law, they have adapted them to fit within the framework of other types of law which may or may not relate to sex discrimination.

Various Countries' Laws Relating to Sexual Harassment

There are four types of laws that can apply to sexual harassment in the workplace:

- equal employment opportunity
- labor
- tort
- criminal

In some countries the laws overlap so that individuals are protected by more than one category of the law.

Equal employment opportunity laws

Equal opportunity laws explicitly forbid sex discrimination in employment (some specifically mention sexual harassment). These laws are regarded by most experts as the most effective in battling sexual harassment. Countries that have such laws are Australia, Canada, Denmark, Ireland, New Zealand, Sweden, the United Kingdom, and the United States. (These countries are among the twenty-three industrialized countries surveyed by the International Labour Organisation (ILO) in its 1992 study of sexual harassment.)

According to the ILO, most other industrialized countries have laws forbidding discrimination in employment on the basis of sex, but no court cases have been brought forth to test or interpret those laws. Since the words "sexual harassment" do not appear in these countries' laws, it is possible they would not interpret sexual harassment as discrimination. However, at this point, it is more likely they would define harassment as a type of discrimination.

Since equal employment laws apply to men and women, both sexes are protected from sexual harassment in those countries where the anti-discrimination law has been interpreted to include sexual harassment. Where the sexual behavior or advances are from a person of the same sex (a homosexual harassing another homosexual of the same gender; or a homosexual harassing a heterosexual of the same gender), U.K. and U.S. courts have held that this, too, constitutes sexual harassment. Sexual orientation of the harasser is irrelevant. With regard to sexual harassment that occurs on account of the recipient's sexual orientation, U.S. federal courts have ruled several times that this does not constitute illegal employment discrimination because sexual orientation is not a protected category under civil rights laws. However, to date, eight states have enacted state employment or anti-discrimination laws which include sexual orientation as a protected group in the workplace.

Labor law

Labor law, when defined broadly, can provide some protection against sexual harassment. However, its protection is often limited to *quid pro quo* type harassment since labor law is traditionally used to protect against constructive discharge (the employee was essentially forced to quit to escape the offensive behavior) or wrongful termination (the employee was fired for refusing to submit to unfair labor practices, i.e., requiring submission to sexual demands), both of which are related to employment contracts. In nearly all of the twenty-three industrialized countries surveyed by the ILO, this was the case (Austria, Belgium, Czechoslovakia, Denmark, Finland, France, Germany, Greece, Ireland, Italy, Luxembourg, the Netherlands, Norway, New Zealand, Portugal, Spain, Sweden, Switzerland, United Kingdom and the United States.)

These provisions of employment contracts are usually in terms of duties and obligations that employers owe workers and that workers owe their employers. For example, in Belgium, employers are required to respect the "propriety and decency" of their employees; in Italy, employers are responsible for their employees' physical and moral integrity;

in Portugal, the employer must provide good working conditions, both "physically and morally;" and in Switzerland, the employer must "protect and respect the worker's person and individuality" with due regard for the protection of the employees' "health and observance of morals."

In Spain and New Zealand, the labor laws specifically mention sexual harassment. Spanish labor law says that employees are entitled to protection from any verbal or physical offensive behavior of a sexual nature. According to the ILO, New Zealand's labor law is the most extensive of any country's dealing with sexual harassment, with the law spelling out the definition of harassment, the legal protections, employer liability, remedies, and grievance procedures. Many of the concepts in New Zealand's labor law are similar to those found in other countries' equal employment law or in the judicial decisions of those countries (Australia, Canada, the United Kingdom, and the United States). The difference is that sexual harassment in New Zealand is covered explicitly in its labor law as well as in its anti-discrimination laws.

In Switzerland, a particular labor law protecting working women has been applied to sexual harassment instances. In Canada, the labor code addresses the issue of sexual harassment, stating that all employees are "entitled to employment free of sexual harassment."

In all the countries where labor laws refer to employers providing healthy and safe work environments, such laws could be applied to sexual harassment—since it is behavior which does interfere with both health and safety at work. However, in most countries, such labor laws have not been widely used to stop and prevent sexual harassment.

Tort law

In addition to equal employment laws and labor law, tort law gives some protection to victims of sexual harassment. A tort is a legal wrong, other than a breach of contract, for which the court can provide a remedy, usually in terms of monetary damages. Tort law includes both acts of negligence, which result from carelessness or inattention, and also intentional acts that cause harm. Legal experts see sexual harassment as an intentional action that qualifies as an intentional tort. In Japan, Switzerland, the United Kingdom, and the United States, tort law has been applied to sexual harassment cases and could potentially be applied, in theory, in all countries (with the exception of Canada, where a particular statute is given as an exclusive remedy).

In the United States, there are a number of torts applicable to sexual harassment and a number of ways in which these avenues may be used. Most often, the plaintiff will co-join her anti-discrimination suit under federal or state law with a tort action, and file suit against the harasser, the harasser's supervisor, and the company. Thus in the United States the victim of sexual harassment has quite a variety of options to pursue—actions under state tort or contract law, as well as causes of action occurring under federal and state anti-discrimination laws. The available actions and remedies vary greatly from state to state.

Pendent state claims that have been heard by U.S. federal courts in recent sexual harassment actions include invasion of privacy, breach of contract, assault and battery, intentional infliction of emotional or mental distress, defamation, negligence, outrageous conduct, and intentional interference with contractual relations. These causes of action provide the plaintiff with recovery of punitive damages, as well as the compensatory damages of pain and suffering.

U.S. courts also have been expansive in the use of tort theories. In *Priest v. Rotary,* the court applied the tort of false imprisonment when a restaurant owner picked up a cocktail waitress and trapped her between his legs while he fondled her. In *Waltman v. International Paper Co.,* the court found invasion of privacy when a coworker placed a high-pressure air hose between a female employee's legs.

Criminal law

In severe cases, the victim may choose to file criminal law charges against the harasser. If so, then all legal action is based on criminal laws of the country, state, county, or city in which the harassment occurred, not on equal employment, labor, or tort law. In these cases, the victim does not receive compensation for physical, emotional or job related damages, but the harasser may be sentenced to prison. Criminal charges for sexual harassment do occur, but are rare so far.

France is the only country which has passed a specific criminal law relating to sexual harassment, with the law's intent to apply to any abuse of power in terms of requesting sexual favors (teacher/student relationships, landlord/tenant, etc.). Some argue that France limited its law to only the most serious sexual offenses out of fear of becoming involved in anything less than abuse of power. They believe that those responsible for the legislation did not want to be accused of outlawing what French culture deems appropriate—sexual and romantic behaviors in the workplace, at higher levels than acceptable in other countries, such as the United States.

Criminal laws of other countries that might be applied in sexual harassment cases include those that relate to taking advantage of someone in a position of economic dependency; sexual assault and battery; indecent assault; indecent behavior; and immoral conduct.

INTERNATIONAL ACTION

Three international groups—the European Communities, the United Nations, and the International Labour Organisation—have taken stances and steps toward the elimination of sexual harassment. While none of the three adopted any resolutions or documents which are binding on their member states, the resolutions they have passed are intended to give guidance to the members in preventing and eliminating sexual harassment in the workplace.

The European Communities

The European Communities, with its Council of Ministers, Parliament and Commission have probably been the most active international group on the sexual harassment issue. In February, 1976, to guide the actions of its member states, the council adopted a directive aimed at the equal treatment of men and women. While the directive does not specifically mention sexual harassment, it prohibits any form of sex discrimination related to employment, training, promotion, and working conditions. As a result of this directive, the EC has taken additional actions.

In 1984, the Council of Ministers adopted a resolution to encourage and promote "positive action for women," including elimination of unequal treatment at work, a "better balance between the sexes at work," and steps to increase the "respect for dignity for women at the workplace."

In 1986, the European Parliament adopted a resolution on violence against women with a section relating to sexual harassment. This section asked the commission to study the costs of sexual harassment and issue a directive to complete existing legislation. It asked the Council of Ministers to take steps to standardize member states' laws on sexual blackmail, and for national governments to reach a legal definition of sexual harassment. It also asked for action by trade unions and specified certain situations where sexual harassment might be most insidious—such as doctor/patient relationships.

In 1987, the commission published a report by Michael Rubenstein titled "The Dignity of Women at Work: A Report on the Problem of Sexual harassment in the Member States of the European Communities." The report stated that sexual harassment was a serious problem, existing legal remedies were inadequate, and few voluntary steps to address the problem had been taken.

In 1990, the Council of Ministers adopted a resolution on the protection of the dignity of men and women at work, and provided a definition of sexual harassment for acceptance by member states. The definition refers to "conduct of a sexual nature, or other conduct based on sex affecting the dignity of women and men at work," and explains the concepts of *quid pro quo* harassment (where "a person's rejection of, or submission to such conduct ... is used explicitly or implicitly as a basis for any employment decisions") versus *hostile environment* harassment (behavior which "creates an intimidating, hostile or humiliating work environment for the recipient").

In 1991, the commission adopted a recommendation and a code of practice, calling on member states to promote awareness of sexual harassment and its unacceptability, to take action in the public sector as an example to the private sector, to report back to the commission on progress within three years, and to give guidance to unions and employees on how to prevent and stop sexual harassment.

Trouble at the EC's Commission

While the European Commission has been pivotal in establishing new codes of conduct, a recent report was critical of the commission itself for not having its own house in order. A primary finding was that the movement of women to higher echelons or levels of management is "painfully slow," according to *European* newspaper.

The commission, headquartered in Brussels, employs approximately 13,000 workers, 46 percent of whom are women. However, the women are concentrated in support roles—in more than 80 percent of clerical positions and in language services, where they make up nearly 50 percent of interpreters and translators. Just 12 percent of the commission's 3,570 A-grade administrative staff are women, and the proportion of women in administrative staffs is expected to get worse, at least in the short run. This is because of the lack of women on waiting lists for these positions, lists that are "overwhelmingly male dominated." Among Directors General, only two of 53 are women. An internal report showed more than 45 percent of the female staff have training in management but did not explain their under-representation.

The head of Equal Opportunities in the Directorate General for Social Affairs, Agnes Hubert, said attempts to increase the number of women in top posts have been thwarted by the EC's competitive recruitment process. According to U.S. research, the first stage of the employment exam discriminates against women. A higher percentage of women fail at this beginning stage than any other. Of the more than one thousand people who passed the first stage in the last competition for general administrators, fewer than one out of five were women. "The figures speak for themselves," Hubert said. Many believe that once in the commission, women are promoted more slowly than men, though there has been an effort to move women ahead, sometimes in preference to men.

The commission has passed legislation for itself on maternity benefits and sex discrimination—including pay, pensions, recruitment, and sexual harassment. It also has adopted other measures on working time, part-time employment, and parental leave in an effort to improve working conditions for female employees.

The United Nations

United Nations actions are governed by the United Nations Convention on the Elimination of All Forms of Discrimination against Women, established in 1979, and the Nairobi Forward-Looking Strategies for the Advancement of Women, adopted in 1985. The convention provides that women have equal employment opportunities and the right to healthy, safe working conditions. The convention has been ratified by one hundred twenty-one countries, but many experts believe it has little enforcement power. The Nairobi strategies specifically address working conditions of women and sexual harassment.

In 1989, the Committee on the Elimination of All Forms of Discrimination Against Women, which monitors the convention, asked for information about violence and discrimination against women. In 1992, the committee recommended that effective legal measures be established to stop sexual harassment since such gender-specific violence would impair women in the workplace and could constitute a health and safety standard.

The U.N. Commission on the Status of Women, which monitors the Nairobi strategies, also is concerned with actions directed at stopping and preventing sexual harassment, specifically as a form of violence against women.

The International Labour Organisation

In 1985, the International Labour Organisation (ILO) adopted a resolution on Equal Opportunities and Equal Treatment for Men and Women in Employment, and included comments on the need for measures to stop and prevent sexual harassment in the workplace. At two official sessions, the 1989 Tripartite Meeting of Experts on Special Protective Measures for Women and Equality of Opportunity and Treatment, and the 1990 Tripartite Symposium on Equality of Opportunity and Treatment for Men and Women in Employment in Industrialized Countries, the importance of measures to stop and prevent sexual harassment were raised again.

Finally, in 1991, the International Labour Conference adopted a resolution regarding women workers of the world and urged the ILO to develop guidelines, training, and informational materials on sexual harassment and other issues of importance to working women. This work is to occur under the auspices of the Interdepartmental Project on Equality for Women in Employment and includes the ILO's most recent and comprehensive study on sexual harassment worldwide: *Conditions of Work Digest: Combating Sexual Harassment at Work, 1992.* The digest is part of the ILO's effort to disseminate information on the problem of harassment. The future plan is for additional research and awareness-raising seminars in certain developing countries and the preparation of a code of practice in 1994–95.

ATROCITIES WORLDWIDE

Sexual harassment sometimes seems a minor problem when compared with other issues that women of the world face. It would be unfair, and this chapter incomplete, without presenting a picture of the total, global problem for women.

In June 1993, the United Nations held a Global Tribunal on Violations of Women's Human Rights at the U.N.'s World Human Rights Conference in Vienna. Women testified about the harshness of life for women worldwide. They reported on domestic violence, murder, sexual slavery, wartime rape, female circumcision, human rights abuses in the family, war crimes against women, violations of social and economic rights, political persecution, and discrimination.

Gertrude Mongella, former Tanzanian high commissioner to India and one of the four judges who presided over the session, said: "I have come to the conclusion that if we have to look for a nation which has not violated women's human rights, I doubt we can find one." The judges requested the establishment of an international court to protect women's rights and the enforcement of a convention to eliminate discrimination against women. They also asked the U.N. General Assembly to establish an office for investigation of women's rights violations.

During the tribunal, the judges heard stories from India, where eight out of every ten women are abused (including dowry-related burnings); from Bosnia-Herzegovina, where about twenty thousand women have been raped by soldiers (the January 4, 1993, issue of *Newsweek* reported that thirty thousand to fifty thousand Muslim women and girls had been raped); and from Thailand, where there are an estimated eight hundred thousand prostitutes under the age of 16.

Geraldine Ferraro, a top U.S. delegation official, said African and other Third World women are "taking the lead" in spotlighting violence against women. "They're speaking up in anger." Others said that the tribunal itself and the increasing demands for more action show the rising influence of a global women's movement.

Violence Against Women Knows No Borders

Jessica Neuwirth, director of Equality Now, a New York-based international women's rights group, wrote the following commentary in *USA Today*:

> *In Bosnia-Herzegovina, 24 women—the youngest age 12—were abducted from their village months ago by Serbian soldiers, USA Today reports this week (8/11/92).*
>
> *Raped as many as 10 times a day, 12 of the women finally managed to escape a few weeks ago. At least one—a 17-year old girl—is pregnant as a result of the rapes. The 12 other women presumable remain captive—and still in danger of further abuse.*
>
> *This is the latest atrocity of violence against women to come to the world's attention—but,*

tragically, violence against women is systematic in countries around the world.

The international human rights movement must expand its agenda to oppose such violence against women, to oppose rape and other human rights violations which disproportionately harm women, with the same force and skill we use to defend other fundamental human rights around the world.

The need is clear and urgent. Consider these incidents that have occurred in the past year:

- *Kenya, July 14, 1991: 300 schoolboys at a boarding school in Meru attack the girls' dormitory, first cutting the power line, then battering down the door. Seventy-one teen-age girls are raped; 19 girls, in their attempt to escape, are trampled to death in the stampede.*

  Joyce Kithira, vice principal of the school, explains afterward that "the boys never meant any harm against the girls. They just wanted to rape."

- *India, Oct. 20, 1991: In tears a young girl tells a flight attendant who asks her why she is crying that she is 10 years old and her father has forced her to marry the 60 year-old Saudi Arabian man sitting next to her, Yahya M.H. al-Sagih. He had rejected her older sister as dark and ugly and purchased her for the equivalent of $240.*

- *Ireland, Jan 27, 1992: A 14-year-old Irish girl tells her parents that she has been molested and raped by her best friend's father. Three days later, her pregnancy is confirmed. She threatens to kill herself rather than give birth, but the High Court issues an order for-*

bidding her to leave the country for nine months, preventing her from traveling to England for an abortion. A month later, the Supreme Court of Ireland revokes this order, but only because doctors confirm that she is capable of suicide if forced to carry the pregnancy to term.

These are only a few instances of abuses that result in the degradation, enslavement, injury and death of girls and women around the world—not occasionally but every day. Every single day.

In the United States, a woman is raped every six minutes. More than 4 million women are beaten and several thousand women murdered every year by their male partners.

More often than not, batterers, traffickers and rapists are not ever prosecuted for crimes they're thought to have committed.

In many countries, in fact, their behavior is reinforced by official and quasi-official policy; their activities are not even considered criminal. Despite governments' systematic failure to protect women from this violence, it has not been addressed as an international human rights issue.

The international human rights movement can help change the climate of indifference by working to stop these human rights violations. Inaction is often defended with arguments that the abuses are "nongovernmental" or "culturally relative" or "personal" as opposed to "political."

But such distinctions don't mean much to the women who must endure these abuses. The pain they suffer is the same.

Governments have a fundamental obligation

*to protect their citizens equally. Let's remember
the forgotten gender and address these human
rights violations by putting names and faces to
women raped and beaten in Bosnia and to all the
world's victims of gender violence.*
*Most importantly, let's act now to end violence
against women.*

Distressing International News

December 6, 1993, was the fourth anniversary of the day gunman Marc Lepine killed fourteen women at the Canadian
University of Montreal's Ecole Polytechnique. The day is now
a federally recognized National Day of Remembrance and
Action on Violence Against Women in Canada. The day is associated in Canada to the expression of mounting concern
about abuse of women.

According to Salem Alaton in Toronto's *Globe and Mail*,
"Men are the dominant victims of war, occupational death and
homicide while remaining overwhelmingly the perpetrators
of violence." Alaton reports a number of alarming statistics
that are reprinted here. Since sexual harassment, particularly
severe sexual harassment, lies on the same continuum as
other male/female abusive behaviors, it is appropriate to look
at these distressing numbers, from Alaton and from Alice
Vachss's book *Sex Crimes*:

Around the World

- Percentage of children in the U.S. who
  are victims of sexual offenses 19
- Percentage of U.S. women who say they
  have been sexually assaulted some time
  in their lives 27
- Percentage of wives who are regularly
  battered in poor districts of Bangkok 50

- Percentage of wives who are battered in rural New Guinea 67
- Percentage of all reported crime in Peru that is wife assault 70
- Percentage of Austrian homicide victims who are women and children when the murderer is a family member 90
- Number of women in Beijing who have attended seminars on their rights in relation to spousal abuse 90,000
- Number of women in Africa whose clitoris has been altered or removed .... 80 million
- In India, number of police-recorded killings in 1987 of brides in dowry disputes 1,786
- Number of aborted fetuses at a Bombay clinic, out of 8,000 that were female 7,999
- Money spent in India for medical care of firstborn daughters, as a percentage of that spent on firstborn sons 38
- Ratio of boys to girls receiving the benefit of hospital treatment in an impoverished Bangladesh community 50-to-1

In Canada

- Percentage of female assault victims who are attacked by a current or estranged partner 43
  - Of males by a female partner 3
- Percentage of female homicide victims killed by a current or estranged partner 38
- Number of female victims of violent crime per 1,000 population 77
  - Of males 90
- Percentage of those charged with violent crime who are male 91

- Percentage of those charged with
  serious crimes who are male 90
- Percentage of spousal assault charges
  against men 93
- Percentage of wife assault occurring
  during a first pregnancy 40
- Percentage of wife assault occurring
  while children are present 50
- Percentage of battered women who say
  their partner also battered their children 26
- Percentage of women who say they
  have been sexually harassed at work 37
- Average number of minutes between
  sexual assaults (including rape) 17

In the U.S.

- Average number of minutes between
  rapes in the United States 6
- Number of rapes reported in 1990 102,555
- Number of convictions from reported
  rapes in 1990 18,024
- Percentage of rape convictions
  compared with reported rapes .... Under 20
- Average time served for a rape
  conviction .... Less than 3 years
- Percentage of female homicides
  committed by men 90
- Percentage of female homicides
  committed by woman's partner 50
- Number of days between husband
  or partner murdering female partner
  in Massachusetts .... 22 days

Alaton says that since all studies show that violent males have typically been brutalized themselves, "it seems that men, from many vantages, need the changes that will make for a society that is not abusive of women."

Equality of the Sexes Takes Time

While many people believe women are making a great deal of progress in combatting the problems they face because of their gender, the facts do not confirm this belief. According to a March 1993 United Nations report, women will need another thousand years to catch up to the political and economic clout of men. The International Labour Organisation, in a forty-one country study, reported that at the current rate of progress, women will hold equal managerial posts with men in five hundred years and then reach equal political and economic status four hundred seventy-five years after that.

The report cites the "invisibility of women in public life and consequently in political, economic and professional activity." Other findings are:

- Women hold 41 percent of management jobs in the United States, with 11 percent high-ranking and 3 percent top level.
- Women hold 40 percent of management posts in Australia and Canada; 8.3 percent in Japan; 4 percent in South Korea; and 1.4 percent in Bangladesh.
- Greece and Paraguay had a drop in female managers.
- Only six of the one hundred seventy-nine members of the United Nations have a female head of state.
- Worldwide, women hold 3.5 percent of Cabinet posts.

Eleanor Smeal, president of the Fund for the Feminist Majority, said: "It's a worldwide disgrace. Half the Earth's population [is] relegated to permanent under-status."

5

GLOBAL REVERBERATIONS: COUNTRY BY COUNTRY

Everywhere around the world, study after study, survey after survey reveals the same thing—sexual harassment is a serious problem for women ...

Susan L. Webb,
*Shades of Gray
Training Program*

Not everyone agrees with the changes that come about when the problem of sexual harassment is addressed. Journalist Charles Bremner wrote in the *London Times* that "the French laugh at what they see as the puritanical zeal which is purging America of its pleasures great and small, from sex to mayonnaise. Thanks to the progressive enthusiasm of the Socialist government, however, some cherished French traditions are about to succumb to American-inspired reform."

Bremner discussed two new additions to French law—one dealing with sexual harassment, and one forbidding smoking in certain public places. In response to the ban on smoking, he quoted Genevieve Dormann, a Paris writer, who wondered why they do not "ban aperitifs and ... while they are at it, deprive the French of the pleasure of farting as well." In response to the sexual harassment law, even the secretary of state for women's rights dissented, saying she deplores the excesses of American sexual correctness, where "even the slightest wink can be misinterpreted." Her women's ministry advises women who receive unwanted sexual attentions to respond with a "good slap in the face."

This chapter contains an overview of the problem of sexual harassment in many countries throughout the world. While the initial plan was to include—for each country—information on the numbers of victims of harassment, the legal status of the issue, and certain cases or stories illustrating the problem, that turned out not to be possible. In some countries this information was simply not available. What is presented is information that was currently available, even though in some cases it is only bits and pieces.

Australia

As early as 1983, some courts had interpreted anti-discrimination legislation to include sexual harassment. In 1984, the first laws specifically mentioning sexual harassment were adopted by the federal government, as well as the states of Victoria and South Australia. Since 1984, Western Australia, Queensland, and the Australian Capital Territory have adopted laws dealing specifically with sexual harassment.

One of the first cases in the country, considered a landmark, occurred in New South Wales in 1985. The plaintiff was awarded $35,000 for being subjected to sexual harassment. The amount of the court's award was considered substantial and brought a great deal of attention on the part of employers to the issue of sexual harassment.

The federal Human Rights and Equal Opportunities Commission, according to a 1982 survey by the International Labour Organisation, found that most sexual harassment victims are young and work in businesses employing fewer than one hundred people. Of the complaints that went to public hearing, 75 percent involved women under age 20; for most of the women, it was their first job. The women were primarily in clerical and retail positions. During 1990–91, sexual harassment complaints comprised just over 36 percent of all sex discrimination complaints made under the federal Sex

Discrimination Act of 1984; state commissions also reported significant numbers of complaints during the same period.

Recent stories indicate that the problems Australia faces have an all too familiar pattern. In December 1992, the Australian government ordered "offensive" scenes cut from a new advertising campaign promoting tourism in Queensland. The action came after complaints were received that the commercials violated the government's own policy on women. The commercials included a close-up shot of a model wearing tight, ripped jeans being pinched on the behind and another shot of a woman's G-string clad buttocks being sprayed with suntan oil.

Australia's minister of tourism, who originally stood by the campaign, ultimately directed the Queensland Tourist and Travel Corporation to edit out the scenes, which were part of a $500,000 "Yo! Way to go!" campaign. The tourism minister said he thought the scenes were "a bit over the top," and that his actions followed a discussion with Australia's premiere and advice from the director of the government's Women's Policy Unit and women's advisor to the premiere. He said the discussions concluded that the scenes contravened Australia's Stop Violence Against Women policy. In response, Peter Laurance, chairman of the Queensland Tourist Corporation, said the government was being "hypersensitive."

Many people were alarmed by the results of a survey in 1992 of Australia's young people. According to a September 4, 1992, article in the *Brisbane Courier Mail*, 29 percent of 125 fourteen-year-old boys surveyed said they would hold a girl down and force her to have sex if she "led them on." Twenty-one percent claimed not to know that such violent behavior was wrong. Ten percent of the boys said that forced sex was acceptable if the couple had been dating a long time.

On the other hand, the same article said other reports indicate that many Australian adult men are quite clear on limits that should be set. The day after the report on teenage attitudes about forced sex, the organization Men Against Sexual Assault (MASA) marched in most Australian cities to draw attention to male responsibilities for changing behavior and attitudes. MASA says it has a three-part agenda—being pro-feminist, affirming the belief that men can change, and opposing homophobia. The organization says that in addition to its pro-feminist stance, it also challenges women who treat all men as potential rapists by emphasizing that men have a responsibility to reduce the incidence of rape and harassment by not staying silent.

According to MASA, the organization's stance against homophobia recognizes the most complicated elements in the elimination of sexual violence against women—that women's fears of men grow out of men's fears of women, of other men, and of themselves. MASA says wife-beating and gay-bashing are interrelated—that any gentleness or "feminine" behavior is regarded as negative, weak, or homosexual. To be the opposite—tough, sometimes violent—becomes the valued alternative.

Journalist Humphrey McQueen, in his article in the *Weekend Australian*, also reported a study in Australian public sector which showed that men who gave evidence supporting women's allegations of harassment or abuse were more likely to suffer than were the accused. The offenders "sent the witnesses to Coventry, applying psychological pressure until they resigned."

Austria

No laws exist in Australia specifically mentioning sexual harassment in the workplace. While the Equality of Treatment Act, covering only the private sector, forbids sex discrimination in employment, no court cases have used this law to address sexual harassment. The Salaried Employees Act could be applied to sexual harassment since it says that "the employer is required to take those measures necessary to protect the moral standards of the employee, appropriate to the worker's age and sex," but no cases related to sexual harassment have been pursued under this act either.

The Federal Ministry of Labour and Social Affairs has proposed an amendment to the Equal Opportunities Act to address sexual harassment as a form of sex discrimination. Expansion of the Equality of Treatment Act to public sector employers also is under consideration.

The Ministry conducted a study of sexual harassment in 1986 with the following results: of the 1,411 women interviewed, almost 31 percent reported serious instances of sexual harassment. Of those, almost 3 percent said they were forced into sexual contact with threats to their job or employment status; almost 7 percent said they were offered or promised tangible job benefits in exchange for sex; about 17 percent were asked to have sexual intercourse; almost 17 percent were touched on the breasts; and almost 18 percent were touched or fondled. The study said women in service industries are especially prone to be victims of harassment.

In a 1987 case in the District Court of Innsbruck, a woman said she was subjected to sexually suggestive remarks and explicit sexual conversation about sexual acts. The court ruled that this was a violation of the woman's intimate sphere of privacy, her sexual integrity, and an affront to public moral, but the words "sexual harassment" were not used.

It is also possible that in severe cases the Austrian penal code would apply to criminal acts that could also be defined as sexually harassing behaviors.

Belgium

While there are no specific laws in Belgium explicitly mentioning sexual harassment, interest in the problem has been evident for some time. In 1984, the Ministry of Employment and Labour conducted a survey and found that 41 percent of the women and 21 percent of the men who responded said they had experienced sexual harassment at work. The study also showed that single, divorced, or separated women, and women under thirty were most likely to be sexually harassed.

In 1986, the Secretary of State for Social Emancipation initiated a national educational effort to raise awareness about sexual harassment at work. In 1988, the Ministry of Employment and Labour issued a booklet about the potential legal protections against sexual harassment. In July 1989, the minister requested that the National Labour Council speak to the issue of harassment. This council is an organization in which trade unions and employers work together to find solutions to labor-related problems. The council issued a statement saying that collective bargaining contracts could be used to address sexual harassment and calling for preventative steps to be taken to eliminate the problem.

Existing laws that might be applied to sexual harassment cases include: the Economic Reform Act, which prohibits sex discrimination and says that "every worker shall be assured of equality of treatment in all provisions and practices related to conditions of employment and dismissal;" the act respecting contracts of employment, which specifies that "an employer and worker shall show respect and consideration for each other;" the Civil Code, which places obligations on all people to compensate for injury they have caused to others because of irresponsible conduct; and the Penal Code, which forbids immoral conduct, indecent assault, corruption of minors, and assault and battery.

Brazil

According to Thomas Kamm in his *Wall Street Journal* article titled "Besieged Brazilian Machos Battle Advance of the

Amazon Feminist," a conference was recently held in Brazil, organized and attended by men as the founding act of the Brazilian Macho Movement. One founding group member said it is now necessary for Brazil's machos to take the offensive because "it's a disappearing species, so we have to preserve the last ones."

The group said its purpose is to combat the extremes of feminism, because in the name of equality, women are losing their femininity. They used slogans such as "The best feminine movement remains that of the hips" to express their views.

Another member said, "They say there's discrimination, so they revoke laws banning women from being truckers, construction workers or miners. This is working against women. Who wants to go home to a wife who smells of cement and has big muscles?" His wife is a former secretary who "pilots the stove rather than a truck ... that's more appropriate."

At the same time, however, conference attendees said that a true macho is a gentleman, though perhaps sexist, who believes decisions should be left to men. Macho men should open doors for women, they said, give them seats on the bus, bring them flowers, and even write poems or cry. One attendee said he even believes women should have the last word, as long as what they say is, "Yes, sir."

Many Brazilian women were outraged at the men and the conference's philosophy. A woman journalist said the men "represent the worst in Brazilian society ... I hope [they] have no success."

Canada

Interest and action on sexual harassment has been ongoing and increasing for a number of years in Canada. There is no shortage of stories, surveys, and reports of the same kinds of inappropriate sexual and gender-related behaviors as seen in other parts of the world. Surveys of more than 2,000 people, conducted as early as 1981 by the Canadian Human Rights Commission, showed that 20 percent of women respondents said they had been sexually harassed. Yet more than ten years later, only 55 percent of the companies surveyed by management consultants Towers, Perrin and the Hudson Institute said they have a formal sexual harassment policy. Nine percent said they were planning to institute a policy.

Many believe that even these efforts at policy development are only a matter of the companies and organizations being forced into taking action. The policies "did not come out of the goodness of their hearts," said Michael Takla of the Towers, Perrin firm. The "big impetus" was the 1987 Canadian Supreme Court decision that held the Department of Defence liable for the actions of a supervisor who sexually harassed an employee.

A more recent study, conducted by the Angus Reid-Southam News of more than 1,500 people, showed that almost 40 percent of Canadian women say they have experienced sexual harassment at work. Most of the victims said they have done nothing about it because they have little faith their complaints will be taken seriously. Thirty-seven percent of women respondents and 10 percent of men said they have experienced harassment. Among young women, 44 percent said they have been harassed. Fifty-nine percent of those who've been harassed said they did nothing about it.

In Ontario, approximately 8 percent of women said they have either been sexually harassed or abused by their doctors. The study, conducted in late 1991 by Canada Health Monitor and Price Waterhouse Management Consultants, began a nationwide debate over the amount of sexual abuse by physicians—a debate that is continuing still today.

The types of harassment and abuse described by the Canadian women were not minor. In the survey, the patients were asked whether, during an examination or consultation, the doctor "watched the patient dress or undress, or made sexual comments about the patient's body or underclothes, or made comments about the patient which were sexually demeaning, or criticized the patient for her preference of a sexual partner, or made comments about the patient's potential sexual performance." Seven percent answered "yes." The second question asked of the patients was whether any of the following behaviors had occurred during a visit to the physician: "sexual contact or activity of any kind, initiated by the doctor or patient, including kissing, genital-to-genital contact or oral-to-genital contact; touching of genitals or another sexualized body part for any purpose except for appropriate examination and after asking the patient for permission." Of the women responding, 2 percent said yes to this question. In the meantime, a number of physicians have been suspended and/or fined for such inappropriate conduct and medical boards and disciplinary bodies have continued to deal with this serious issue.

Canadian Definitions of Sexual Harassment

While there are many similarities between Canadian and U.S. definitions of sexual harassment, both in terms of behavioral and legal definitions, the legal structure in Canada is unique. According to the Supreme Court of Canada, all labor relations issues are within the jurisdiction of each of the provinces, unless a federal problem is directly involved. Therefore, with regard to sexual harassment, each territory and province administers its own human rights law or code and each has its own Human Rights Commission. The federal government has a human rights law protecting federal government employees and those people employed in federal projects.

This means that on the federal or provincial level there are a total of thirteen human rights acts or codes, all forbidding discrimination in employment on the basis of sex, but only the provinces of Manitoba, Newfoundland, Ontario, and the Yukon Territory specifically mention sexual harassment.

Nevertheless, most Canadian Human Rights Tribunals have

used the prohibition of sex discrimination in cases involving sexual harassment and interpreted sexual harassment to be a type of sex discrimination. The first court ruling in this manner was in 1980. Since then the Supreme Court of Canada has relied on both Canadian and American experts and also ruled that sexual harassment is sex discrimination. Additionally, the Canadian Labour Code addresses sexual harassment specifically. While criminal laws could be applied to the most serious forms of behavior that also could be classified as sexual harassment, these laws are not usually used to deal with harassment in the workplace.

The Canadian Human Rights Act refers to sexual harassment without giving an exact definition, stating "it is a discriminatory practice ... in matters related to employment, to harass an individual on a prohibited ground of [sex] discrimination." The various provinces have similar codes stating that sexual harassment is unwelcome sexual conduct or comments, or sexual solicitation and that harassment is intended to mean behavior that a person should "know or ought to reasonably know are unwelcome."

The Canadian Labour Code defines sexual harassment as "any conduct, comment, gesture or contact of a sexual nature that (a) is likely to cause offence or humiliation to any employee; and (b) that might, on reasonable grounds, be perceived by that employee as placing a condition of a sexual nature on employment or on any opportunity for training or promotion."

The Canadian Supreme Court defines sexual harassment as "unwelcome conduct of a sexual nature that detrimentally affects the work environment or leads to adverse job-related consequences for the victims ... When sexual harassment occurs in the workplace, it is an abuse of both economic and sexual power ... Sexual harassment in the workplace attacks the dignity and self-respect of the victim both as an employee and as a human being."

The Canadian Human Rights Commission states sexual

harassment consists of "verbal threats or abuse, unwelcome remarks ... leering or other gestures [and] unnecessary physical contact."

Quid Pro Quo and "Poisoned Work Environment" Harassment

Quid pro quo harassment and harassment that poisons the work environment both have been identified and recognized by Canadian Boards of Inquiry and are specifically identified by a number of factors that are similar, though not identical, to those used by U.S. courts. For behavior to be *quid pro quo* harassment, "the conduct must have verbal or physical sexual overtones; it must be unwelcome and unsolicited; it may be intentional or systemic; it need not be persistent, depending on the severity of the conduct; and the sexual harassment may or may not have adverse job-related consequences."

As for "poisoned work environment" harassment, one court ruled that "conduct that makes the work environment hostile by reason of constant taunting, verbal exchanges, or statements directed at a person's gender is discrimination on the basis of sex." In these cases, as in U.S. cases, frequency and severity of the conduct are taken into consideration, and "work environment" is deemed a condition of employment.

Specific attention has been focused by women's groups, the media, associations, and other interested groups on sexual harassment in the medical profession, school systems (teacher/student and student/student), the legal profession and judicial system, the military, corrections facilities, theater and the arts, and churches and religious institutions.

In Canadian Sports and Schools

Early in 1993, Canadian interest turned to the sexual harassment faced by women athletes. In the February 8 *Globe &*

Mail, Mary Jollimore reported that the Coaching Association of Canada published a paper on sexual harassment in sport by Helen Lenskyj, an associate professor at the Ontario Institute for Studies in Education in Toronto.

Lenskyj said, "The harassment problem is not new. For example, a former physical education student at an Ontario university in the 1970s reported the coach of the women's swimming team was known to have a serious drinking problem and was often 'drunk and obnoxious' in front of students … He was notorious for bum pinching and other intrusive touching ['hands all over' the female students], and for walking into the locker room when the women were changing. The department's way of dealing with him was to require him to take a year's sabbatical."

In another story, Sandi Kirby, associate professor at the University of Winnipeg, asked a female athlete why she retired from sports at age 19. The student replied that her coach had been sexually harassing her since she was 13, and she thought that if she stayed in the sport it would mean continuing to put up with the harassment.

Lenskyj said young female athletes are particularly vulnerable to sexual harassment and most feel powerless to stop it. This pattern appears to be the same, regardless of the area or field where harassment occurs. She said the athletes "fear repercussions. They've made a choice to go into a sport … and don't want anything to threaten that … they tolerate it … they turn a blind eye. They have to survive in a hostile environment so they develop defense mechanisms." Typically, the defense mechanism, as in other areas where sexual harassment occurs, is to do nothing, to remain silent, or to try to ignore it.

Ann Hall, a professor in the physical education department and chair of the women's studies program at the University of Alberta, said sports are just far behind the rest of society and that harassment has been pushed under the table. "What will bring sexual harassment in sport into the open is that it's being brought out into the open everywhere else," she said.

Another disturbing trend is sexual involvement between coaches and the athletes they coach, usually male coaches and female athletes. Many believe that such relationships are inappropriate even between consenting adults, and that sports governing bodies should develop prohibitions against such relationships similar to those prohibitions in the workplace (particularly supervisors and their own subordinates).

In the Canadian Legal Profession

Officials of the Law Society of Upper Canada approved in May 1992 a comprehensive sexual harassment policy tailored especially for legal firms. In development for two years, the policy was distributed to the managing partners of all Ontario law firms in the hope they would adopt it or a similar policy. A committee on women in the legal profession conducted the research for the policy.

The policy suggests that law firms commit to providing "a collegial working environment" in which all employees are treated with dignity and respect. It also says the policy should be applied equally to all employees from staff to senior partners. It adds that firms should do all in their power to support staff members subjected to harassment from clients, opposing counsel, or judges.

In the Canadian Armed Forces

In May 1993 the Canadian Defence Department released results of a study of 4,055 people surveyed the previous fall. The study showed that nearly one-third of the country's military personnel reported being harassed at work and stated that immediate measures must be taken to address the problem. The "findings clearly indicate that improvement is required in the current Canadian Forces approach to personal harassment," the study said.

Women respondents were most likely to be victims of harassment, with almost 27 percent reporting sexual harassment, almost 33 percent reporting personal harassment, and almost 32 percent saying they had been the subject of "abuse of power." Men also reported being harassed, but in lower numbers: 2 percent said they were sexually harassed; 20 percent said they experienced personal harassment; and 29 percent cited abuse of authority.

Defence Minister Kim Campbell, who has been criticized for ignoring the problem of injustice to women in the military, said the 30 percent figure was low compared with some civilian fields of employment in which as many as 50 percent of women report harassment. However, she said, "The point is that Defence's policy is zero incidents. We don't want any sexual harassment."

Toronto Firm Tough on Harassment

As of November 1992, under a new policy of Toronto Hydro, employees can walk off a job immediately if they feel they have been harassed. The company says the policy is a groundbreaking effort to eliminate harassment in the workplace.

According to Rob Fairley, president of Local 1 of the Canadian Union of Public Employees, twenty specially trained representatives of employees and management will review each complaint within twenty-four hours. A determination usually will be reached within three days.

"We don't use the words 'integration' and 'segregation' in Canada," Fairley said, "but twenty years ago, of the five hundred blue collar workers at Toronto Hydro, four hundred ninety-nine were able-bodied white males and one was a visible minority. There were no women. Now, of our six hundred workers, about sixty are from visible minorities and ninety are women."

Fairley said that while some people might be skeptical of the policy or fear it will end good-natured joking, the "respect at work policy will result in a workplace that's more fun for more people." He added that if "every joke an individual knows is racist, sexist, homophobic, or at the expense of someone with a disability—it's certainly time to come up with some new material that doesn't degrade anybody."

Under the new policy, unacceptable conduct includes unwelcome remarks, jokes causing awkwardness or embarrassment, leering, unnecessary physical contact, sexual solicitations, or refusal to work with someone because of gender, sexual orientation, race, disability, religion or ethnic background. Toronto Hydro General Manager John Brooks said he expects the program will "save thousands in the long run," although the company has not done cost estimates.

In Law Enforcement

Also in late 1992, a former Metro Toronto Police constable testified before a tribunal that she suffered a nervous breakdown as a result of treatment by male colleagues while she was an undercover narcotics officer. The officer told the police disciplinary tribunal that her picture was taken with a Polaroid camera by a fellow police officer while she urinated in a cold, dimly lit parking lot during a break in a drug "drive through."

She said that in January 1991 she was with a group of officers who had a rendezvous at a parking lot in a shopping plaza in Etobicoke. Some of the officers, with their backs to her, relieved themselves soon after they got to the area, she said. This practice is fairly common since there is often not time to find restroom facilities.

The woman, who had been on the squad for three months, said she crouched down behind a parked car to "not be observed" and used the bathroom herself. While she was urinating, one of the officers came up to surprise her and took her picture. During that night and the next day the picture was shown, displayed, and finally tacked on a bulletin board. She says she did not report it to her supervisor because he was one of the officers who had displayed the picture the night before and had been laughing. "I was in the drug squad doing something I really wanted to do," she said, adding that another woman who preceded her on the squad had been let go at the request of the officers. She did not want that to happen to her. "But they got rid of me in the end, didn't they?" she said. Her attorney said there are at least ten other complaints that the tribunal should be considering and that the police investigation and the tribunal's hearing is a "painfully inadequate response." The officer also filed a civil action against the Metro Toronto Police and thirteen other officers.

In the meantime, ten of the Metro police officers filed a $2 million countersuit against the female officer, saying their reputations have been damaged as a result of the public exposure the case has received. The claim said the men have "been exposed to contempt, ridicule, and embarrassment, which has negatively affected their reputations in the estimation of fellow officers, senior officers, and the community at large."

Canadian Steelworkers Support Women

The Canadian Steelworkers union voted unanimously in May 1992 to support efforts to fight violence against women. The union said it will bargain for the right of women to refuse work if they are being harassed and will develop workplace safety audits for female employees. The union also said it will play a broader social role in raising public awareness about violence against women.

The policy, issued at the union's national policy conference in Hamilton, Canada, stated that 25 percent of all women are sexually assaulted in their lifetime, 10 percent of women are assaulted by the men they live with, and that between 50 and 90 percent of women are sexually harassed in the workplace. The policy said that "although the actual number of men who act violently against women is in the minority, most of us—men and women—fail to act and speak out," and that this effort will begin the speaking out process.

The union said common excuses for harassment or abuse are: "We just treat her like one of the boys," "When I come home from work, I don't want to have to hear the kids screaming," and "I saw the way she looked at that guy. Does she think I'm stupid?"

Inquiry Into Violence Against Women

In January 1992 the Canadian government opened an inquiry into violence against women, despite accusations of sexism by the inquiry's opponents. The inquiry panel of nine members had a budget of $10 million and planned to visit more than one hundred communities to develop a national plan for fighting the problems of wife-beating, sexual assault, and other forms of abuse of women.

Inquiry spokeswoman Nicole Bourget said, "I believe it is the first committee of its kind that has this mandate anywhere in the world." The panel was set up by the Canadian women's minister, Mary Collins, after the outcry that followed the 1989 murders in Montreal of fourteen female students by an alleged woman-hating gunman.

Bourget said that each year in Canada one out of every ten women is beaten and one hundred women are murdered by their husbands or boyfriends. One in four women is sexually assaulted at some time in her life.

Bourget said the panel members intend to research the root causes of the violence and to propose wide-ranging solutions that could involve many options—from better education for judges to improved street lighting.

Peter Raeside, a men's issues columnist for the *Vancouver Sun* newspaper, was one of the panels critics. He said he believed that at least three or four men should have been appointed to the panel, rather than only the one who was selected. "It doesn't seem to be very equitable. It doesn't seem to be very balanced."

Raeside also said that the government's approach to the violence problem is superficial. "I think it [violence] is more a societal problem than just a men's problem. It's a massive problem that's been covered up in families for generations," he said. Bourget dismissed the criticism, saying "I think there are more important issues to look at than there's only one man on the panel ... The issue is violence against women."

Still Problems Remain

On the other hand, things don't always look so positive in Canada. In one case, Judge Inger Hansen of Kitchener ruled that a man who admitted making sexual advances to a female employee had a reasonable belief that the woman was consenting because she giggled when she protested. The man was acquitted of sexual assault.

The man admitted putting his hands in the woman's pockets and moving them toward her upper thighs, poking her in the breast with a pen, and unhooking her bra—incidents that occurred during a three-month period at a Mega Pizza outlet.

The judge said that the man, who was the store manager, had reason to believe that the woman consented to such behavior because she giggled on some occasions while she said no. The judge called the behavior "inappropriate and reprehensible," but said she believed the manager meant no harm and would have stopped had he known the woman wanted no further advances.

Chile

Even Chile's federal mining minister was shocked to discover that women are working in the underground mines in his country. At several mining locations, women have begun to break down barriers in one of the world's most conservative countries and in one of the most conservative, and some say sexist, work environments. Many men still believe that women bring bad luck to the mine itself or that the mother lode will dry up when women enter the shafts. Chile is one of Latin America's most traditional countries, making the integration of women into nontraditional professions slow.

In Chuquicamata, a bleak, dirt-blown mining community in Chile's Atacama Desert, a group of women miners, geologists, and mechanics works and discusses attitudes: "It's attitudes like his [the federal mining minister] that have kept us out of the mines and other professions for so long," said one female mechanic who works repairing nearly forty-foot high rock-hauling trucks.

Chile has undergone a foreign investment boom in its gold and copper mines and, facing a shortage in mining professionals, women are now being allowed to enter the profession. At Chuquicamata, the world's largest open-pit copper mine, women have been hired as geologists, engineers, mechanics, and miners. This is a very recent occurrence, despite the fact that Chilean universities have been graduating female mining professionals for almost four decades. Today, in the mining ministry's department of geological studies, nearly half the two hundred and fifty professionals and researchers are women.

One woman miner said, "Men simply didn't accept me. It was hard for the first few years because I constantly had to prove to the men that I knew what I was doing. Now if the men don't like me, at least they have gotten used to me." The eight hundred women who work at the mine have worked in the hospitals and schools, but for the first time, are now working underground. Codelco, the government company that operates the mine at Chuquicamata and three other locations, has more than twenty-five thousand employees, but still no women executives. Only a few are in management positions.

Two years ago, the women at Chuquicamata organized the Corporation of Women Copper Workers, the largest women's organization in Chile with a membership of five hundred.

This effort was their way of challenging and changing the traditional roles of women in mining. The organization began as a community and social group but now takes an active role in policy decisions at the mine, organizing workshops and seminars on health, the environment, labor psychology, and women's rights. The lobbying of the group helped elect the first woman to one of Codelco's unions and the company now automatically deducts alimony payments from a man's pay if he refuses to pay his former wife.

Women at Chuquicamata said sexual harassment there is not a problem because the men know it would be cause for immediate dismissal. This is provided for under a clause in the union contract. The women who work underground are seen as a good, but tough, group of women who work the same shifts as the men and often share the same dormitories.

At La Escondida, a $900 million copper mining operation in northern Chile, women work as engineers and metallurgical specialists, operate computers in the production plants, and drive large cranes. The company has an equal opportunities policy and a training program to encourage women to acquire new skills for use in nontraditional occupations. At El Teniente, the biggest underground copper mine in the world, women work underground as geologists and engineers.

China and Taiwan

At the same time the Thomas–Hill controversy was making headlines in the United States and around the world, another sexual harassment case was making headlines in Taipei, Taiwan. On October 19, 1991, thirteen China Airlines female flight attendants anonymously issued a joint allegation charging the director of the aviation medical center with sexual harassment. According to newspaper reports, the flight attendants said the forty-seven year-old physician forced them to undergo breast examinations as part of the standard airline employee check-up, even though such exams are not a requirement of the physical exam. The women also said the doctor conducted the breast exams without a nurse present, and in such a way that the women were uncomfortable and offended.

In another incident a month after the flight attendants' complaint, a group of nurses at National Taiwan University Hospital in Taipei signed a statement declaring their refusal to work with one of the hospital's osteopaths. Newspapers reports said the nurses claimed the doctor frequently used obscene language and behaved in a lewd fashion toward the nurses. The hospital mediated the situation and the nurses agreed not to boycott the hospital after the doctor made a formal apology to the hospital director and to the nurses' representative. The nurses said they planned to continue to watch the doctor's behavior.

Quietly "Eating Tofu"

This was the first time such a claim has been made publicly. In the past, the term "sexual harassment" was not often heard in Chinese society. The closest equivalent in Chinese language is the slang term "eating tofu," which refers to verbal or physical insults with sexual connotations. Women who experienced "eating tofu" were expected to view it as harmless and to keep it to themselves in order to save face.

Helene H. Lin, an associate professor at Soochow University in Taipei, said that in the past sexual harassment has been overlooked or not recognized as offensive. Lin believes that acceptance of sexual harassment has been encouraged and perpetuated for generations because of social norms which view women as men's property and expect women to behave in a passive, submissive manner. As a result, Lin said, women often have "swallowed the insults quietly. Today, we hear more about sexual harassment not because more men behave that way, but because our society is more open about sex. Only a few years ago, the topic was taboo."

However, in 1990 some progressive women's groups began to speak publicly about sexual harassment in the mass media and public seminars. Two such organizations, the Modern Women's Foundation and the Awakening Foundation, said they were motivated by the many phone calls they received from frightened and angry female victims of sexual harassment.

Ninety-five percent of victims said they felt terrified, disgusted, or resentful, but the action they were willing to take varied widely. More than 17 percent said they would either try to settle the matter quietly or quit their jobs; 10 percent said they would laugh and try to act as if nothing had happened; almost 8 percent said they would report the harassment to their supervisor; and 65 percent said they would speak up or try to embarrass the harasser immediately, and in front of other people.

New Attitudes of Chinese Women and Men

The assistant to the commission of Taipei's municipal police force, Ma Jen-Hua, said Chinese women are now beginning to see the need to protect and claim their civil rights. "Women are receiving higher levels of education, joining the work force, competing with men, and becoming financially independent. While women's needs were traditionally neglected by their dominant male counterparts, in recent years our society had begun stressing full equality between genders. That helps raise the consciousness of many ... " he said. As a result, male behavior that was considered to be acceptable in the past is now becoming unacceptable.

Chen Li-jung, the woman responsible for supervising the Modern Women's Foundation survey, said many women were impressed by Anita Hill and her ability and courage to tell her story to the U.S. Congress and in front of the national media. She believes that this motivated many women to begin to speak out, not only in China, but around the world, and also caused many people to begin to look at and analyze their own behavior towards others.

As in all countries, upbringing, occupation, education, and age influence the way individuals perceive or define sexual harassment. This is especially so in countries with strong traditions and narrow roles and values. Yet, in November 1991, when the *United Daily News*, one of Taiwan's leading newspapers, asked 620 career women to define sexual harassment, 80 percent of the respondents said it meant touching a woman's legs, buttocks, lips or cheeks; 45 percent said it included talking about sex; 38 percent said discussing a female employee's figure or body; 34 percent said telling off-color jokes; and 42 percent said aggressively and repeatedly asking for dates constituted sexual harassment.

Chinese men's definitions of sexual harassment also vary widely, and this too depends on their age and social upbringing. According to the March 1992 issue of *Free China Review*, many older men have never considered the topic and feel at a loss when asked to discuss it. One Taipei metal company president, over age fifty, said sexual harassment is too new a topic for discussion and laughingly added that "the topic is for younger generations."

Another man, somewhat younger, said sex often is discussed at work and usually involves a joke, so women should not be upset by it. He did add that if such talk is malicious, the harasser "should be punished." A third man said he believes that only physical contact should be considered a punishable offense.

Male and Female Victims

Most victims of sexual harassment in China are women, but a few male victims have been reported as well. Professor Lin of Soochow University said the new social phenomenon of male harassment victims is because of the changing attitude of many men and women toward relationships. "Some women are becoming more aggressive and they're not afraid to take the initiative in a courtship," Lin said. Sociologist Ma Jen-hua said socioeconomic status often determines who plays the dominant role in a relationship and that when a woman has more money or authority than a man, she has more opportunity to take advantage of him, as men often do of women.

Male and female victims of sexual harassment in China still have few places to go for help, though. There are no institutions to help with the problem, other than a few women's civic organizations.

Chinese Law

As for civil law, Taiwan's Social Order Act, passed in June 1991, somewhat addresses sexual harassment, but provides for very light punishments. The law states that persons found guilty of verbal, physical, or other obscene behavior will be sentenced to a maximum of three days in jail, or pay a fine of up to US$230.

Women also may seek redress for sexual harassment under other laws, but no law specifically addresses sexual harassment. For example, under ROC criminal law, a woman could charge her boss with sexual coercion if he tried to force her to trade sexual favors in return for job benefits; if he actually forced her to submit, he could be charged with rape. However, even with these laws, sexual harassment cases seldom go to trial.

According to Vivian Chen, an attorney and member of the Taipei Bar Association's Women's Safety Study Committee, there are many reasons that sexual harassment cases don't find their way to court. First, she says, there is no clear precedent in Chinese legal history and the definition of sexual harassment is still unclear. Second, evidence is hard to collect since there may be no physical evidence, unlike a rape. Third, when a victim does bring charges, she may face what is referred to as a "little rape" by being subjected to unwanted publicity and criticism and to hostile and humiliating questions from prosecutors. Furthermore, Chinese tradition is against using legal means and confrontations in an effort to keep reputations intact and to avoid bringing on bad luck.

With regard to labor law, no present statutes provide protection for victims of sexual harassment. This was confirmed in December 1991 by the Taipei city government's Department of Labor decision in the China Airlines case. The department decided that sexual harassment causes only psychological damage or "invisible injury," and therefore cannot be truly called an occupational injury.

The Women's Safety Study Committee is lobbying for a new law which would specifically address sexual harassment. Many people believe such regulations should be included in Taiwan's Equal Employment Opportunity Law, as other countries do. The committee also recommends that businesses include sexual harassment in their policy statements and guidelines on employee conduct.

Unusual Solutions Sometimes Come About

A recent response to sexual harassment in China is the opening of a kung fu college, established and run by a former poet, Wang Geng. According to Wang, "I wish people would take us seriously ... We have people waiting at our door to pick quarrels with the women whenever they step foot outside just to see if they can fight."

Wang and his brother opened the Nanking Brothers Public Relations Company in 1992 with the intent of training women in secretarial and public relations skills. That focus changed, however, when his students began encountering serious sexual harassment on the job.

Wang decided to teach kung fu to women so his students could defend themselves and also be employed as bodyguards. Soon, he said, hundreds of women lined up to enroll.

One young woman student, age 27, said she has been molested by men at dance halls, in karaoke bars, and even walking down the street in broad daylight.

A technology company in Jiangsu province has employed ten of Wang's female bodyguards, and the Shanxi military region has indicated a need for several female guards to work in its business operations.

Bringing About Real Change

Free China Review states that ending sexual harassment "will require changing the long-standing social customs and economic inequalities between genders that promote such behavior. According to sociologist Ma Jen-hua, only when the socioeconomic status of a large number of women in Taiwan nears that of men will incidents of sexual harassment taper off. Says Ma, 'Then women will become even more expressive about their real feelings and needs, and men will have more risks to consider before taking advantage of women.'"

France

Most experts agree that sexual harassment as a political issue in France emerged a result of the development of Canadian and U.S. law during the 1970s, the efforts relating to sexual harassment by the European Communities in the 1980s, and finally, the uproar caused by the Thomas–Hill controversy in the early 1990s.

French interest in the issue first showed in October 1985, when the Secretary of State for Women's Rights publicly condemned sexual harassment in the workplace. Then in May 1988, the Secretary of State for Women's Rights sent an official commission to Quebec to gather information and data on women's issues in the work environment. In March 1989, an international meeting was held in Paris to address the issues of sexual harassment and abuse of authority in the workplace.

First Sexual Harassment Case

In January 1992, in the first case of its kind in France, a supervisor was sentenced to jail for sexually harassing one of his female employees. Both lawyers and feminists called the decision a landmark that would have an important effect on workplaces throughout the country.

The court at Lille imposed a three-month suspended sentence on Jean-Paul Droissart, 42, after he admitted harassing a 21-year old telephone operator by fondling and stroking her. He was fired from his job after the allegations were made public and began undergoing psychiatric treatment.

The judge in the case said it was "hardly the affair of the century," and ruled that the man had not tried to use his position to threaten the woman's employment. But the Lille branch of the Union of French Women, who brought the case to court, said the case was significant because it brought attention to a problem that has long been ignored in France. The defendant was prosecuted under an article of the Penal Code that came into force just the month before, allowing for jail sentences of up to ten years in prison for anyone using their authority to attempt to obtain sexual favors.

Josiane Sion, the union's representative in Lille, said no one had taken the problem of sexual harassment seriously before, and that until recently such prosecution would have been impossible. Sion said sexual harassment in France is widespread, though.

Isabelle Lapeyronie, a lawyer for the union, said: "In our country there is sometimes a tradition of sexual innuendo that means that women who complain about this kind of behavior are often not taken seriously." The union has represented women since the end of World War II.

In the years immediately after the war, France legislated equal pay and working conditions for men and women.

Although such equality has not been achieved, some believe that there exists in France a tradition of powerful women in the workplace, such as Prime Minister Edith Cresson, as well as the traditional macho image of men. French sociologists say that the drive to strengthen legislation on sexual harassment comes from the United States and also from the need to bring French legislation in line with that of other countries in the European Community.

New French Sexual Harassment Law

French laws relating to sexual harassment have been moving rapidly and are still in a state of flux. However, at present, the latest effort to address sexual harassment is in the new Penal Law Article 222-32-1, which specifically makes sexual harassment by supervisors illegal. The law was approved by the National Assembly in late 1992 and scheduled to become part of the penal code in 1993. The law is designed to prohibit abuse of authority, and therefore includes only harassment of subordinates by supervisors, not harassment by coworkers. However, the law's section dealing with abuse of authority is not limited to the workplace. Under the law it can be applied to other areas where one person has authority over another.

The new law states "that the act, by anyone abusing authority that is conferred by his or her position to pressure [someone] with the intention of obtaining sexual favors, is punishable." It is interesting to note that a number of French legislators wanted to use the term sexual "aggression" rather than "harassment," because of the dictionary definition of harassment meaning repeated behaviors. They saw the term "sexual harassment" as a North American term and were concerned that it would not cover those egregious behaviors that occurred only once. As a compromise, the title of Article 222-32-1 was voted to be "sexual harassment," but neither the words "sexual harassment" or "sexual aggression" actually appear in the text of the law. This apparently satisfied legislators who wanted to make sure that harassing behaviors could include those that are repeated as well as those that occur only one time. Under the newest penal law, sexual harassment can include a fine of up to 100,000 francs (about US$18,000) and/or up to one year in prison.

The new law is a direct result of the Thomas–Hill controversy in the United States, which experts say initiated debate about the use of power or position to extract sexual favors at work. Some say many French men behave as if they still believe they are the natural heirs to "le droit de cuissage"— the squire's right to spend the wedding night with the new brides of his estate. However, French government officials assert that the new law is the toughest of its kind in Europe and goes far beyond a conduct code written by the European Community. That code was sent to employers, labor unions, and employees in the community's twelve member nations to help educate people about the problem.

The new French law is in addition to an earlier amendment in the penal code that made sexual harassment punishable by a jail sentence of up to ten years. The newest law is important because it gives the movement against sexual harassment full government support and will be added to the labor code.

The new law has certain limitations and applies only to sexual harassment by superiors in the workplace—not to sexual harassment by coworkers. Reportedly this is to differentiate between sexual extortion and office flirtation. Some believe this is merely a concession to sexist French attitudes that too liberally allow sexual behavior—some of it unwanted—in the workplace.

Veronique Neiertz, the Secretary of State for Women's Rights, criticized U.S. attitudes, in which "the slightest wind can be misinterpreted." Her ministry's advice to women who feel harassed by coworkers is "a good slap in the face."

The French Labour Code includes sex discrimination as an illegal employment practice, but there have been no cases in which the courts have interpreted the code to forbid sexual harassment.

Civil law also could be applied to sexual harassment since it provides that all people are liable for willful or negligent conduct which results in injury to others. But like the Labour Code, no court cases have interpreted tort law to include sexual harassment at work.

Again, a summary of the current state of the French Penal Code as it relates to sexual harassment is as follows: The provision prohibiting assault and battery has been interpreted to cover sexual harassment and allows for punishment by a fine from 500 to 20,000 francs and/or two months to two years in prison. The penal provision relating to indecent behavior also has been interpreted to include sexual harassment, and allows for punishment by a fine from 6,000 to 60,000 francs and/or three to five years in prison. For cases in which there are exceptional circumstances, punishments can be raised to a fine of 12,000 to 120,000 francs and/or five to ten years in prison. Under the newest penal law, approved by the National Assembly and scheduled to be adopted in 1993, punishment can include a fine of up to 100,000 francs (about US$18,000) and/or up to one year in prison.

The Numbers

A recent poll in *Le Point* magazine shows that French women see harassment differently than American women. In a survey including various scenarios, 20 percent of the women who responded said they would not consider themselves harassed if they were asked to undress during a job interview. Forty-seven percent of the women said it was harassment if a male manager asked a woman to spend the weekend with him to discuss her promotion, but 45 percent did not think this so. (Among men, 43 percent said this was harassment, 51 percent said it was not.)

Marie-Victoire Louis, leader of an association fighting violence against women in the workplace, said many are unhappy with the new penal law's limitations. "In the name of progress, we're being disarmed against other forms of harassment," she said, by not addressing coworker harassment as well. A French journalist said, "All too many men think they are being charming when they're being a pain."

Many French have pushed to amend the labor laws as well as the penal code to address sexual harassment of employees by their supervisors and to make prosecution even easier. According to a recent Lou Harrris opinion poll, 21 percent of French employees have been sexually harassed in the workplace or have witnessed such harassment. Another poll showed that harassment usually occurs by a supervisor harassing a subordinate, whether the supervisor is male or female.

Complaints of sexual harassment sound the same in France as elsewhere: sexual proposals and gestures, continued sexual advances after refusing overtures, and a generally uncomfortable, offensive work environment. In one survey, 12 percent said the sexual advances they were subjected to were accompanied by actual threats.

Germany

In a 1992 survey by a German women's magazine, 68 percent of the women responding said they were sexually harassed on a regular basis at work. However, 44 percent of their male colleagues who responded said that they did not consider their own behavior offensive.

In 1990, the Ministry of Youth, Family, Women and Health conducted the first significant study of sexual harassment at work. The survey found that sexual harassment is a serious problem in the workplace, particularly in terms of the impact on victims: 6 percent of the women responding said they had resigned from a job because of sexual harassment. As for the impact on alleged harassers, only 6 percent had received a warning from their employer, 1 percent had been transferred, and fewer than 1 percent had been fired.

Currently there are no federal German laws which specifically address sexual harassment, although the federal law does prohibit discrimination in employment on the basis of sex. To date, however, no court cases have interpreted prohibited discrimination to include sexual harassment. On the state level, only the State of Berlin Anti-Discrimination Law mentions the issue of sexual harassment, and even this law is limited only to those employed by the state. It defines sexual harassment in familiar terms as being "particular unnecessary physical contact, unwelcome comments of a sexual content, unwelcome remarks, suggestive comments or jokes about a person's appearance or body, display of pornographic literature and sexual propositions."

Nevertheless, some courts have ruled that several articles of the German penal code, the Civil Code, and Labour Law do currently apply in certain sexual harassment cases and that these provisions could be applied to other cases. For example, under the Civil Code, non-discrimination of men and women is prohibited in such areas of employment as recruitment, hiring, firing, pay, promotion, job assignment, and related conditions of employment concerning the health and safety of employees.

Under the Penal Code, sexual abuse of minors is prohibited, especially when the abuser is in a position of authority; offenses against sexual privacy are prohibited; and inducing another person to engage in sexual acts is also illegal. But while it could be argued, as in many countries, that sexual harassment is a criminal offense, few German women complain or go to court.

Attitudes and laws may be changing, though, in part because of the unification of Germany, which brought 3.6 million women in eastern Germany into the work force. Under communism, these women were offered ample day care and real career opportunities in middle management, and they expect the same under a unified Germany.

A striking gender gap at the top of most Germany companies also is creating pressure for change. A survey of Germany's 626 biggest companies showed that there are only 12 women—compared with 2,286 men—on the managing boards. Women hold just under 6 percent of all jobs down through middle management, although they account for almost 42 percent of the total work force.

In July 1993, German Chancellor Helmut Kohl's government proposed a comprehensive statute designed to guarantee equal rights for women in the workplace. The statute includes what would be Germany's first law specifically meant to protect employees from sexual harassment on the job. The law is expected to be passed.

The law's sexual harassment clause would give public and private sector employees the legal right to file a complaint with superiors, who could then take the matter to labor court. If convicted, a person could be warned, transferred, or dismissed. Currently sexual harassment cases are rare in Germany. When complaints do occur, many companies deal with them by dismissing the person who files the complaint.

Ireland

Since 1985, sexual harassment has been defined by Irish case law as a form of sex discrimination in the terms and conditions of employment, covered by the Employment Equality Act of 1977. Sexual harassment also is addressed under the Unfair Dismissals Act of 1977. Unfortunately, one of the most recent and notorious sexual harassment stories involved alleged sexual harassment of a young Irish woman by a male U.S. citizen living in New York.

In this case, the young woman, Deborah Rocks, was just 18 and living in her native Ireland in 1983 when she answered a newspaper advertisement seeking a nanny for a U.S. family.

Rocks had grown up in a home with no running water or telephone and found the opportunity to be a nanny for the three children of a record producer and his wife, Bill and Maureen Civitello, to offer the promise of a glamorous life.

Rocks agreed to a salary of $50 a week to care for the children and to clean the four-bedroom house. In the first three months, she said, she was not paid at all, and was repeatedly told that the Civitellos "just didn't have it." She also said that Mr. Civitello made repeated sexual advances, despite her continual protests. She said she didn't know what to do or who to tell because she was afraid she would lose her job and be turned out on the street.

Rocks said she essentially had no money, no transportation, and, if she quit her job, she would have had no home. She was "totally isolated" since the Civitellos also told her to stop telephoning her mother in Ireland. When she finally left the family, they still owed her $950, she said, and finally paid her $300.

The Civitellos deny any wrongdoing and said the lack of payment to Rocks was because they were in dire financial trouble at the time. Mr. Civitello denied any sexual advances or impropriety.

After leaving the family, Rocks sought counseling with New York therapist Nancy K. Brown, who said, "I work with battered women ... this is a classic." Brown said Rocks "had this idea that 'This is expected of you, didn't you know?' She felt disempowered, embarrassed, alone, and isolated."

Rocks, who is now married and living in New York, is a college student and mother of two children. She said "Looking back, I think, You should have done something!" But back then, "things were different. I was numb. I thought there was nothing I could do."

Irish Laws

Under the Employment Equality Act of 1977, the employer is

forbidden from discriminating on the basis of sex in all terms and conditions of employment. The Labour Court recognized sexual harassment as a form of discrimination in the first court case addressing the issue in 1985. The court ruled that "freedom from sexual harassment is a condition of work which an employee of either sex is entitled to expect" and that the court would find "any denial of that freedom as discrimination." To date, most sexual harassment cases have involved wrongful termination and constructive discharge. This act applied to both public and private sectors.

Under the Unfair Dismissals Act of 1977, no explicit mention is made of sexual harassment, but the act states that "the dismissal of an employee shall be deemed to be a unfair dismissal unless," considering all the circumstances, "there were substantial grounds justifying the dismissal." This provision could be applied in cases where the employee is terminated for refusal to respond to sexual advances or for complaining or undertaking legal action against such harassment. The act also could allow for termination of employees who engage in sexual harassment of other workers.

Numbers

The Employment Equality Agency issued a report in 1990 stating that thirty complaints of sexual harassment had been received that year, with fourteen of the complainants saying they had been fired from their jobs. The agency stressed in its report that sexual harassment is frequently not sexual in terms of actual sexual interest or desire, but is really about an abuse of power. The agency also reported on the psychological damage that women suffer when subjected to sexual harassment and hostile work environments.

Israel

In 1987, Dr. Nitza Shapira-Libai, a professor at Tel Aviv University, conducted one of the first studies on sexual harassment in Israel. The study showed that 40 percent of female government employees reported being sexually harassed, with 21 percent saying they were harassed on a weekly basis. Seventeen percent said they had not been harassed themselves, but were aware of coworkers who had been. Many believe it was this survey that led to passage of equal employment legislation.

Israeli Law

The Equal Opportunities in Employment Law, passed in 1988, forbids both sexual harassment and discrimination in the workplace. Under the law, the victim must show that she suffered injury as a result of the harassment; that she quit because of the harassment; that she was subject to sexual blackmail or coercion with employment benefits conditioned upon her response to the advances; or that, as a result of rejection of her supervisor's advances, she was fired, demoted, refused raises, given poor job assignments, or passed over for promotion, i.e. *quid pro quo* harassment.

The law also applies to the army and in education settings, particularly in cases of the superior taking advantage of a subordinate. For example, under the law, a female student could file a complaint against her professor if she felt her grades were conditioned upon her response to his sexual advances.

However, many Israeli women feel the Equal Opportunities law is only a step in the right direction, and a small step at that. Rachael Benzamin, who founded the Israel Women's Network hotline for women with questions about sexual discrimination and harassment, said society is still too accepting of harassment as "the way it is" and is supposed to be. She said too many woman also feel that way and are still not aware of what their rights are and how to file complaints.

Yehudit Knoller, an attorney who is a member of the legal staff of the women's network, said the battle for the hearts and minds of judges is crucial because their attitudes and beliefs determine the outcome of cases. She said, "Based on the few claims that have reached the courts, the results are not encouraging ... Even though the legislature has made its position clear, its effect hasn't been felt in the field."

Two Different Outcomes to Critical Cases

Evidence that judicial attitudes impact individual cases is apparent in opposite outcomes of two recent cases. In one case, a senior advisor to the minister of tourism was charged with seven counts of sexual harassment. A secretary testified he would discuss his sexual prowess with her and often invite her to spend the night with him when he was in Jerusalem. When she asked him if she would be allowed a car allowance as part of her job, he said, "When you open your legs, you will get a car allowance."

The man was eventually convicted on one count only, for demanding sexual favors from an employee in exchange for a car allowance. He was fined NIS 15,000 and given fifteen months probation. Many believe the penalty was ridiculously lenient. Furthermore, the judge in the case continually insinuated that the secretary may have been sending mixed signals to the alleged harasser, thus encouraging his behavior.

In the second case, a professor who was formerly the director of the Health Ministry's Research Institute for Environmental Health, was accused by two women scientists at the institute of locking his office, drawing the blinds when meeting with them, fondling them, trying to remove their clothes, and even masturbating in front of them. He was eventually acquitted.

The judge in the case said he could not believe that any woman would sit in a locked room while her boss masturbated without at least banging on the door or yelling out to other employees. The judge also believed that because one of the women accepted a ride home with the man and sat and talked with him in a "quiet place" indicated that she was not revolted by his behavior and that her relationship with him was more than simply professional.

Attorney Knoller said: "There is no substitute for increased awareness, especially among women, who must press their claims ... The more claims that accumulate, the more likely it is that the legal system will respond."

In the Army

Many Israeli experts believe that if 40 percent of the civilian population experiences sexual harassment, then the numbers in the military must be much higher, though, to date, no surveys support this belief.

Shapira-Labai said, "We are talking about a framework that puts men and women together in close quarters, often for long periods, in locations far from home and the authorities. The dependence, both physical and in terms of her status as a young woman soldier, on her superior officers is almost total. It is a setting very conducive to sexual harassment."

The Israeli army has dealt aggressively with harassment. Women soldiers who believe they have been sexually harassed may report directly to the Commander of the Women's Corps, thus avoiding having to use the often ineffective chain of command. Charges of sexual harassment are quickly investigated by military prosecutors and women soldiers are often reminded by their officers to come forward with any complaints.

The army also has adopted a policy of publicizing the complaints as well as the punishments meted out to those found guilty of harassment. Shapira-Libai said she believes that publicizing the punishment serves as a deterrent to potential harassers because it sends a clear message that such behavior is forbidden, that "it is not a compliment, but in fact traumatic, for the woman."

Harassment of Newcomers to the Country: the Olim

Among the most vulnerable to sexual harassment are immigrants. Since they are desperate for jobs and because they are not familiar with the acceptable norms of sexual behavior, they often find themselves in difficult situations.

Dalit Kinar, a spokesperson for the Rape Crisis Center in Haifa, said, "It is clear that the olim are an easy target for sexual harassment because in most cases they don't have money or any other job options, and they understand neither the language nor how things work here."

Nevertheless, few Soviet newcomers report incidents of sexual harassment by their employers or coworkers because "there are no crisis centers [for reporting] in the former Soviet Union ... They are not accustomed to reporting this type of thing," said Miri Seger, a coordinator of the rape crisis center in Jerusalem. Seger also said that many newcomers simply do not understand that the sexual proposition of an employee by an employer is not acceptable behavior in Israel.

Seger believes the unwillingness by Soviet immigrants to report such incidents also stems from a basic distrust of authority, as well as the fact that they do not know where to go or how to file a complaint. She said, "They were afraid to turn to the police in the Soviet Union, and they bring that with them here."

Old Attitudes Persist

While changing laws may seem slow to some, changing attitudes can be even slower. Many believe that the widespread attention the Thomas–Hill controversy gained in Israel indicated a change in attitude and awareness. Rena Shashua-Hanson, chair of the legal staff of the Israel Women's Network in Jerusalem, said, "I think a very clear warning has been sent to bosses that they'd better think twice before making advances to subordinates. The subject of sexual harassment is no longer a topic for gossip, but has become a public issue."

As with family violence, there is a tendency to believe that sexual harassment is not as pervasive in Israel as in the United States, even though studies show differently. Still, in many cases, there is the tendency to believe that if sexual harassment occurred, the woman must have asked for it, by her dress or other provocative behavior. Still others, particularly men, believe that sex games are a fringe benefit of the job, despite the fact that women in one survey felt that even lewd suggestions or jokes constituted serious sexual harassment

As in other countries, surveys in Israel show that women who are most likely to experience sexual harassment are those seen as most vulnerable, weak, or dependent: young women at their first jobs or those who don't have tenure or seniority; unmarried women, and women who are the sole support of their families.

Italy

While Italy's Constitution states that citizens of both sexes are equal, reports are that the process of adopting legislation to achieve true equality has been long and arduous. Sexual harassment is not mentioned specifically in any Italian law, nor has it been defined by the courts, but there are at least two ways in which the problem might be approached legally.

In 1977, the Equal Opportunities Act was passed to ensure equal treatment of men and women in the workplace. The act forbids discrimination because of sex and states that such discrimination includes acts or behaviors which negatively impact workers, even when the discrimination is indirect. The act was strengthened by a 1991 provision that requires affirmative action to promote equal treatment of men and women at work. So far, only a few court cases have interpreted this act to provide protection from sexual harassment.

The Italian Civil Code has certain provisions that cover labor relations, and states that "just cause" is required for termination of an employee. Therefore a victim of sexual harassment could claim that she was terminated without just cause if termination occurred because of her response or lack of response to sexual advances.

In one interesting case, a woman was fired for complaining of unwanted sexual advances by her supervisor because, the company said, by making such a complaint she brought public embarrassment to her employer. The company claimed that she violated her duty to maintain confidentiality and trust on behalf of her employer. The court found that the company did not have "just cause" for terminating the woman.

In 1991, in a second case, the court ruled that an employer does have "just cause" for terminating an employee for sexually harassing another employee, but that the punishment must be in proportion to the infraction. The court said the determination of appropriate punishment must be made on a case by case basis.

In a third case, the court ruled that the Civil Code also establishes the responsibility of an individual to compensate a person he or she damages by intent or negligence. Combining this obligation with the Constitutional right of people to a fundamental right to health, a woman was awarded damages for sexual harassment at work.

Certain provisions of the Penal Code could apply, such as sexual abuse by a public official, sexual assault and battery, and harassment and disturbance of others.

Japan

Recently it was reported in a number of newspapers around the world that a group of female employees at a major Tokyo brokerage had sent a message on the company's computer screens to men who had spied on the women while bathing at a company function. "Dear Colleagues at all branches: Ten male employees stood with their faces pressed against the window, naked, and peeped inside when we female employees were taking a bath. This is unforgivable!" The company said it is considering strict punishment against the men. However, the company also said such use of company equipment by the women was highly inappropriate. Any protest such as this is very unusual for Japanese women and indicates a growing awareness of sexual harassment and increased unwillingness to continue to put up with such behavior.

According to the International Labour Organisation, a group called the Sexual Harassment in the Workplace Network conducted the first survey on sexual harassment in Japan in 1989, interviewing 70 women who said they had been harassed at work. Of the 70 women, 40 said they have left their jobs because of the sexual harassment (including 12 who said they were fired). Most of the 30 women who remained employed said they experienced verbal abuse or negative financial consequences in addition to the harassment. It was found in this survey that married men in positions of authority were most likely to be the harassers.

In 1990, Santama No Kai, a Japanese women's organization conducted an even larger survey—this of some 6,500 working women, of whom 3,131 said they had been sexually harassed. The results: almost 24 percent were harassed by their bosses; 14 percent were harassed by a superior; almost 19 percent were harassed by someone with more job experience; almost 16 percent were harassed by coworkers; and almost 7 percent were harassed by customers or clients.

The Tokyo Metropolitan government reports it has handled hundreds of sexual harassment complaints and has sent employees to the United States to gather information and study the problem of harassment. The problem of "seku-hara," from the American term sexual harassment, is of serious concern in the Japanese workplace today. According to Governor Shunichi Suzuki of Tokyo, "The Tokyo Metropolitan Government makes it an annual practice to send abroad a number of experienced officials for the purpose of having them research public administration in foreign countries. More specifically, they study the systems and practices of government administration as well as areas of expertise and other related matters. The results thus obtained are utilized to improve and streamline the operation of our metropolitan administration."

One employee was sent to the United States in 1993 to study the social system of women in the workplace, including, and with emphasis on, sexual harassment.

Crucial Court Case

Currently, there are no laws that specifically mention or prohibit sexual harassment in Japanese workplaces. However, in April 1992, a Japanese woman, identified only as Miss H., won the first sexual harassment case to be brought to trial in Japan, though the case was brought under the Civil Code.

In this important case, the judge of the District Court of Fukuoka found that the woman's supervisor had indeed damaged her reputation and made her working environment so uncomfortable that she was forced to quit (constructively discharged) by spreading rumors about her sex life. The court's ruling was crucial since it defines as illegal sexual harassment that often is considered the less harmful—*hostile environment* harassment. This gives rise to the belief that the courts would certainly rule as illegal any case of *quid pro quo* harassment. Government consultant Masaomi Kaneko said her office has been swamped with calls from companies seeking advice on how to recognize and prevent harassment since the Fukuoka case.

Yukiko Tsunoda, a lawyer in the case, said, "This is the first case in which verbal comments by a man have been found to constitute sexual harassment ... it is a big problem in Japan, and we hope this will send a signal to men that they have to be more careful." The news media presented the case as a startling triumph for Japan's small feminist movement, and many projected that the action would have far-reaching effects in Japanese culture.

In Japan, the women's movement is small compared with movements in other countries, and there have been few positive outcomes in the legal arena regarding sexual harassment. Only within the last three years has sexual harassment gained attention in Japan and become one of the major issues Japanese feminists have supported. Both women's groups and women responding to surveys indicate that sexual harassment is an important problem and that sexual approaches by men—ranging from suggestive remarks to outright touching—are the norm in Japan. About 40 percent of Japanese workers are women, but most are in traditional jobs, primarily clerical positions, and are known as "office ladies."

The defendants in the Fukuoka case were ordered to pay the equivalent of $12,500 to the woman. The names of all parties involved, including the plaintiff, who is a 34-year-old woman, were withheld to protect their privacy. The female employee, a single woman, alleged in her suit that one of her supervisors had spread rumors about her, saying that she had a reputation for being promiscuous. When she tried to get him to stop spreading the rumors she was advised to quit her job at the small publishing company in the city of Fukuoka. According to an interview with *The New York Times* in 1989, the woman said she had taken her complaint to two arbitrators, a man and a woman, who told her that she should be flattered by her supervisor's attention. The woman reported that "They said, 'These rumors are better than no rumors at all.' "

This was not the first sexual harassment case in Japan, but other cases have involved ambiguous verdicts. In a 1991 case, a woman was awarded damages after saying that a man had assaulted her on a business trip. Another woman received damages after she said a colleague had threatened her when she refused to go to a hotel with him. However, these earlier cases were won by the plaintiffs because the defendants did not show up in court. In the Fukuoka case, the man was defended aggressively and his actions were not direct threats.

Nevertheless, sexual harassment is still seen by many in Japan as a trivial issue. Some bars have even adopted "seku-hara" as the name of their establishments. However, after the Thomas–Hill controversy in the United States, the Japanese press did caution Japanese businesses with operations in the States to exercise caution.

Be Careful of American Women!

Tokyo-based Komatsu, the world's second-largest maker of construction equipment, distributed a forty-eight page book-let in late 1992 called the "Business Manners Bible" to four hundred new employees. The booklet explains the dos and don'ts of the subtleties of Japanese manners.

For example, the booklet states that the depth of a person-'s bow of respect depends on the particular situation: fifteen degrees for coworkers, thirty degrees for customers, and forty-five degrees "for important guests or to express apolo-gies or thanks." It also discusses chopstick manners, saving face for your boss, and even where to sit on the train if travel-ing with your boss (always let your boss have the window seat, of course).

But one of the most interesting quotes is about dealing with women: In the section on sexual harassment, the book-let says the best course is to avoid such dangerous topics alto-gether. "Be careful about European and American women: They are especially sensitive."

Then the booklet addresses what to do when you meet your male boss and he is accompanied by a woman you don't recognize. "If the woman is about the same age, she could be his wife, while if the woman is young, she could be his daughter. If he acts like he doesn't notice you, you'd better act like you didn't notice him."

Japanese Laws

While no laws specifically mention or prohibit sexual harassment in Japanese workplaces, there are a number of ways in which sexual harassment could be addressed. The Equal Employment Opportunity Act, for private sector employees only, was passed in 1985 with the aim of equality for men and women in all aspects of employment—recruitment, work assignments, promotion, training, benefits, retirement, hiring, and firing—but the act has no enforcement provisions and has not yet been applied to any sexual harassment cases.

The Labour Standards Act, also applicable to private sector employees only, prohibits discrimination against women in pay and salary and could be applied to cases in which sexual harassment resulted in wage discrimination.

Japanese Civil Code does not refer specifically to sexual harassment, but as demonstrated in the Fukuoka case, can be applied to certain harassment situations. The court relied on the section of the code which says that "a person who intentionally or negligently violates the right of another is bound to make compensation for damages arising therefrom." Other sections that might apply to sexual harassment are those dealing with unfair termination, the individual's right to enjoyment of private rights, or injury to a person's reputation.

Those aspects of the Penal Code which might apply to sexual harassment are those dealing with indecent acts, compulsion or inducement for illicit intercourse, or intimidation of another. Sexual harassment is not specifically mentioned.

The Cultural Change in Japan

Only recently have we begun to read and hear about a profound shift in attitudes concerning the status of women in

Japanese society. Perhaps no single issue better crystallizes the essence of that question than the matter of sexual harassment in the workplace.

To appreciate the significance of this shift in attitude it must be kept in mind that for centuries Japanese society has maintained rigid sex roles for men and women. Assigned roles from birth, neither men nor women previously found reason or opportunity to challenge Japanese society's strict code. However, starting about ten years ago, serious challenges began to be raised about the appropriateness of a male-dominated culture.

Traditionally in Japan, work outside the home has been almost exclusively a male domain. Women who had jobs outside the home were understood to be interested in working only long enough to find a husband. Then, after marriage, the expectation was that the woman would stay at home to tend the house and raise the children. Now, the Japanese work force is 45 percent female. Another factor to note: the average age of a new bride in Japan is 25.7 years, while in the United States it's 23.6 years.

Through the export of goods and money, Japanese corporations have established a potent presence in every major market in the free world. Owing in no small part to Japan's phenomenal economic might, Japanese women have been able to travel the world over and see for themselves how women elsewhere are living. Many have come home to challenge the status quo.

One such woman is journalist Mikiko Taga, who, reporting on her experience living abroad, said, "In the United States, I learned the word 'sexual harassment,' but I had already seen many examples of it in the Japanese company where I once worked." Today in Japan, sexual harassment has a name: *Sekuhara.* It is the Japanese transliteration of the English words. But the fact that this term has no direct Japanese language equivalent demonstrates how far-removed this concept is from customary Japanese values.

Behaviors traditionally practiced by men against women that are being challenged include "fanny-patting" and questions such as, "What color panties are you wearing today?" or, "Are you a virgin?" There also is the not infrequent episode of a woman being pulled on the lap of a male boss or coworker. This conduct, so common in Japanese business offices, prompted one columnist for the popular weekly magazine *Themis* to matter-of-factly assert that an executive ought to be able to ask his secretary what color underwear she is wearing that day.

Being expected to accept such treatment without rancor is second only to the expectation that the "office ladies" or "OL's," regardless of status, serve tea to the men. It is a standard requirement and a glaring example of discrimination against women. One young woman on the management career track at a major bank complains that her male supervisors think of her in terms of a woman first—perhaps as a *geisha* rather than as a banker.

Journalist Kumiko Makihara, correspondent for *Time* magazine in Tokyo, relates that she is often referred to as a *josei kisha*, or "woman journalist." On one occasion, when she objected to an executive's joking suggestion that she sit on his lap, she informed him that it was a form of sexual harassment. The executive disagreed, maintaining that, "Japanese women like to be told these things."

In the Japanese corporate structure, the powers that be are far more comfortable seeing women in the role of "OLs" serving tea, acting as official greeters and working as low-level clericals. Getting to the *sogo shoku,* or main career track leading to executive level positions, is rare for women. For some who make it the prize is hardly worth the price to keep it. The young banker mentioned earlier provides a case in point. It was not enough that she had to perform as well or better than her male counterparts. She also made her own tea and made copies of her own documents so as not to appear "stuck-up" to the "OLs." Despairing of the entire arrangement, she quit.

Upon the announcement of her decision, her male colleagues assured her that "this will lead to your happiness." It is this socio-cultural backdrop that makes the action discussed earlier of Miss H. so remarkable and that may usher in a new era for women employees in Japan.

Also, through vigorous efforts by Japanese feminists, lawyers and journalists, the fact that sexual harassment can be challenged is being communicated through conferences, articles, surveys and studies. On October 7, 1989, the Tokyo Bar Association conducted an unusual experiment. For six hours, twenty-five lawyers took turns answering telephone complaints about sexual harassment on the job. One hundred thirty-eight calls came in; of these, fifty-three callers said they had been pressured for sex. Some apparently had given in. Also reported were two rapes and eight attempted rapes.

Shizuko Sugii, a representative of the Tokyo Bar association, said, "Although women's status is improving, a lot of issues are escaping attention. Right now there is no law forbidding trivial behavior, like making a crude or offensive sexual comment to a woman in the office. That is something we want to change." In addition, several news organizations have sponsored surveys and conferences highlighting the fact that in the United States employers can be sued if they to fail to maintain a workplace for female employees free of objectionable behavior, language and graphic depictions.

Many books and articles from the United States and Europe have been translated and distributed and are serving to raise the consciousness of Japanese women on this issue. Mikiko Taga, the journalist mentioned earlier, has recently published a series of articles in *Lucky Seven*, the largest women's weekly magazine in Japan. In them she details her findings during her recent tour of the United States, during which she interviewed prominent women experts on the issue of sexual harassment.

Other groups also are beginning to show interest in this issue. The largest labor union in Japan recently held a conference and plans a survey of its members. And, the Tokyo Labor Relations Bureau is now collecting data on claims of sexual harassment.

Definitions of sexual harassment are becoming more precise. Generally, sexual harassment is defined as any behavior that denigrates, embarrasses or compromises women in the office or at the after-work cocktail lounge. These after-work cocktails are standard procedure and any employee expecting to make it onto the executive career track is expected to partake. But many men, signaling what is an apparent backlash, are claiming that the issue of sexual harassment is nothing but another passing fad imported from the United States.

The tradition of after-work cocktails is especially tricky in Japanese offices, since work occupies so large a place in the life of professionals. These cocktails are standard procedure. Daniel Burstein, author of *Yen,* the bestseller describing America's descent into mediocrity and Japan's ascent to global dominance, offers this example of life inside Nomura Securities Co., Ltd.: "Nomura is a cradle-to-grave establishment. New recruits frequently live in company-provided dormitories. In return for the arduous commitment Nomura men are expected to make—so arduous they don't have time for dating girls outside the office—are the company's staff of OL's. 'Nomura girls' are graduates of the best universities, but they will get little chance to put their education to work."

Indeed, historically senior department personnel see it as a part of their responsibility to see that the new recruit soon finds a mate. The young ladies in the office are the prime candidates. After a few years of doing clerical work, serving tea and functioning as official greeters of visitors, marriage to one of the young upwardly mobile executives is presumed to follow, and thereafter managing the home and raising the children. Confucianism is still a real force in Japan, directing women to serve their fathers, husbands and sons.

According to Mikiko Taga, author of *Single Mind,* a landmark study of sexual harassment in her native Japan, at a very

early age society sets in motion the series of initiations inform-
ing both boys and girls of their respective "places" in the hierarchy. During her junior high school years, boys names were
listed ahead of girls' on all rosters. Taga reported that, "In
Japan, women's liberation does not exist." After spending five
years in the United States, Taga has found that many Japanese
women are choosing to go abroad, where carving out a career
for themselves is less personally and professionally grueling.

In his well-received book, *Trading Places,* Clyde V.
Prestowitz, Jr. captures this sentiment when describing a brief
exchange with the wife of a ranking Japanese diplomat sta-
tioned in Washington during their going-away party: " … I
remarked to his wife that she must be glad to be going home
after so many years. Her immediate and emphatic reply, 'not
at all,' wasn't what I had expected. She explained that in the
United States she had great freedom. 'Here I'm alive,' she said.
'I accompany my husband to parties and am included in the
life of the embassy and of the city. In Tokyo I'm excluded.' "

Taga, author of four books and mother of two, sums it up
best: "America is a paradise for women. Japan is a paradise for
men."

The "arduous" work commitment to which Burstein
referred is a life of fourteen- to sixteen-hour days—a day that
begins with an early morning hour-long train commute into
Tokyo from an outlying suburb. Few people anywhere in the
world work as long or as hard as do the Japanese. After a full
day in the office, followed by an obligatory round or two of
drinks, it's back on the train for the long ride home. Arriving
at home around nine or ten o'clock, these men are able to see
their children only a short time before the children are off to
sleep. For young women seeking to enter the race to the top,
such a life style can be daunting—especially, if she plans to
get married and have children.

While many men claim that the issue of sexual harassment
is just another passing fad imported from the United States,
others, like Shoichiro Irimajiri, former president of Honda

America Manufacturing, Inc., acknowledge that "the times, they are a changin'," as the old saying goes. Irimajiri, noting the vast difference between Japanese and American women's perception and interpretation of sexual harassment, said, "Until you experience this you don't really understand the cultural differences fully."

Another primary reason for the attention now being paid to this issue is the passage by the Japanese Parliament five years ago of the Equal Employment Opportunity Law. Most assuredly a step in the right direction, the new law prohibits discrimination against on the basis of sex. But many thoughtful women wonder about its effectiveness since it carries no penalties for violation. Time will tell whether it truly is an effective tool.

History of Legal Changes in Japan

The Japanese Constitution, adopted in 1946, bans discrimination in political, economic or social relations because of race, creed, sex, social status or family origin. After the adoption of the Constitution, the Civil Code and laws related to elections, education, and labor were revised to bring them into line with the requirements of equality of the sexes. At this time, women were granted the right to vote and hold office, public schools were made co-educational, and women were allowed to enroll in universities and colleges that previously excluded them. In 1947, the Labor Standards Act was passed requiring equal pay for men and women performing the same jobs and establishing maternity leave for women.

After World War II, articles of the Civil code pertaining to family relations also were drastically changed. The Code was revised to abolish the *ie* system—Japan's traditional family system—and the discriminatory practices inherent in it. The revisions guaranteed married women the same rights as men in terms of property disposition, inheritance, and divorce.

The old Civil Code, enacted in 1898, strengthened the *ie*

system. Under this code, the approval of the head of the family had to be obtained when marrying; men under 30 and women under 25 had to get the consent of their parents to get married. The code also stated that a married woman must have her name entered in her husband's family register and must defer to his choice of domicile.

The postwar reform of the Civil Code abolished the *ie* system and stated that mutual consent of the people getting married is the basis for marriage for adults (those 20 years and older) and that only marriages involving minors (under 18 for men and under 16 for women) needed parental approval.

The new Civil Code firmly established the principle of equality between husband and wife. Under the prewar code married women were denied any legal rights with regard to property; the husband was to be deferred to in all areas of authority by the wife and children; the husband was given the right to manage his wife's property; and wives, but not husbands, were required to maintain chastity. The new Civil Code clearly abolished all provisions of the old code that ran counter to sexual equality.

More Recent Changes—The Good News

Since 1975, declared International Women's Year, and the following United Nations Decade for Women, from 1975–85, additional changes were made in Japanese law addressing the imbalances between men and women. For example, changes in the Civil Code gave women the right to continue to use their surname after marriage, gave women the right to 50 percent of the inheritance from her husband's death (with the children splitting the other 50 percent), and changed the laws governing the nationality of children of international marriages, so that a child no longer was required to have a Japanese father in order to be a Japanese citizen. And finally, in 1985, the Equal Employment Opportunity Law was passed.

However, according to *Japanese Women Yesterday and*

Today, one of a series of booklets published by the Japan Foreign Press Center, while "major advances have been made in elevating the status of Japanese women ... traditional views retain a strong hold on the people. As a result, women's attitudes are characterized by the co-existence, and sometimes clash, of the new and the old. Attitudes also vary depending on whether a woman lives in a major city center or the countryside, was born before or after the war, and is a full-time homemaker or has a career outside the home."

Merry White, Associate Professor of Sociology at Boston University, wrote in *Home Truths: Women and Social Change in Japan*, that it is Japanese women themselves who are forcing the taboo issues out into the public arena, that they are changing the face of public policy, of the economy, and of the workplace. "Most strikingly," she said, "they have brought questions of social class and diversity into the public eye, and forced the realization that Japan is heterogeneous and stratified. As examples, White discusses women whose mothers had never left their neighborhoods except for funerals and weddings and who are now in the labor force, at least part time, or off on weekend trips with friends, or taking up hobbies that were formerly considered off-limits to women. The trend is called *onna tengoku*, "women's heaven."

The latest statistics show that women are now 40 percent of the Japanese work force. Many feel the Equal Employment Opportunity Law validated their aspirations for equal treatment at work. Sixty-eight percent of all employed women are married, most with children, and more than 50 percent of mothers have jobs outside the home. While children remain a high priority for women in Japan, White said, women are increasingly demanding the right to be mothers and to have rights in the workplace—such as flex-time, job sharing, child care, and family leave time—and with increasing intensity—the right to work environments free from *seku-hara*.

The Bad News

Most agree that in the late 1980s in Japan, when stock prices and corporate profits soared, there also were rising opportunities for women. A woman, Mariko Mitsui, was leader of the largest political opposition party, and strong-minded career women appeared more and more frequently in adverting throughout the country. Some of the larger companies had even begun to discuss and consider a "fast-track" career system for women's advancement up the corporate ladders.

However, according to the media as well as reports from individuals from Japan, opportunities for women have gone the same way as Japanese fortunes the last few years—down. Mitsui, who is now an ex-member of the Social Democratic Party, has for many people, become a symbol of the ongoing discrimination against women.

As a member of the Tokyo National Assembly, Mitsui set up the city's sexual harassment complaints office and stopped the municipal government from financially sponsoring beauty pageants. At the same time, she was severely criticized by male party members, and she said she has recently been the target of sexual harassment by a fellow council member. After she resigned from the council in early 1993, she said, "I thought the Social Democratic Party would have a liberal atmosphere, but it was just another male hierarchy."

While most Japanese companies claim that women have the same employment opportunities as men, there are a number of reasons to doubt the commitment of these companies to equal employment. First, there is a reluctance, only recently noted, to hire female graduates. Second, there has been very little impact of *sogoshoku,* the career tract launched by image-conscious companies in 1986 that was supposed to give women the same promotion opportunities as men. Third, is the finding by Japanese women, that in addition to the rigid corporate hierarchy, they still must fight the strict cultural roles required of them.

Recruit Research recently conducted a study of 1,700 companies with the following findings: almost 88 percent of the companies have female employees serving tea to coworkers; almost 71 percent have female employees clean the desks in the office; and only about 33 percent allow women into policy-making meetings and discussion. Other findings: only about 23 percent of the companies offered management opportunities to women—something that company managers said is the fault of women and their failure rate.

A manager for Seibu Department stores said: "Of course the basic ideal is for men and women to be equal, but social roles are different, and this affects daily office work as well." Seibu is a leading retailer known for its use of women as managers. However, if a client comes in and the secretary is unavailable, it is still the women who are required to make and serve tea.

Mitsui was quoted, saying of Japanese men, "They're just not brought up to think that women can be partners or rivals."

"It's Time to Get Serious, Japan"

Mikiko Taga is a free-lance journalist on women's issues, other social issues, and education. After graduating from Ochanomizu University, she worked as a magazine editor before going free-lance. Her works include *Single Mind* and *Cornered Children.*

I spent two days with Ms. Taga last winter discussing the issue of sexual harassment in Japan and the United States. She graciously granted permission to reprint this article in its entirety from *Look Japan,* June 1990.

I lived in New York from 1983 to 1988. While there I heard and read, in magazines and newspapers, about how American women were conducting a resolute fight against sexual harassment in the office. It reminded me of my own unpleasant experiences while working in a Japanese com-

pany for two years.

When I returned to Japan in 1988 I introduced the concept of sexual harassment to the Japanese public in a book
entitled "Single Mind." I was anxious about the Japanese
public's reaction to sexual harassment because they had
never heard about it before. In Japan, there is a gray line
between business and private life. Would Japanese people
understand the concept, I wondered?

It turned out that my apprehensions were unfounded.
Book reviewers took up "Single Mind," and the mass media
quickly seized upon the topic. When the experiences of the
general public were solicited, the response was incredible. It
was clear that sexual harassment—seku-hara in
Japanese—had been around for a long time in Japan.

Soon after the book was released, the Second Tokyo
Lawyers' Association held a one-day telephone counseling
session on October 7, 1989. Between 10 AM and 4 PM they
received 138 calls from around the country relating to sexual harassment.

Soon after, a female employee of a publishing company
in Fukuoka Prefecture sued the company in August 1989,
claiming that she had been forced to quit her job because of
sexual harassment. She asked for total damages of $23,000.

This was the first case of sexual harassment taken to
court in Japan. I went to the Fukuoka District Court in
November to view the first hearings. The case attracted the
largest number of hopeful viewers in the history of the
court. I was impressed by the way the plaintiff held her head
high, unashamed that she should be suing a company for
something unheard of in the company-is-God Japan. She
stated her feelings and opinions clearly and powerfully. She
did not seem to be depressed.

I noticed one particularly interesting thing. The accused
had an all-male defense team, while the plaintiff's lawyers
were all women. It was little more than a stand-off between
the sexes. Moreover, 90 percent of the audience was women,

which again I thought was strange.

Japanese women's magazines were generally sympathetic to the subject and featured the case in a serious vein. Japanese women instantly understood what sexual harassment meant and soon expressed their anger.

Men's magazines, on the other hand, reacted slowly. When they did react, it was with callous humor. Some of their headlines:

"Talking dirty soothes personal relationships in the office;"

"Touching a woman's behind is just another way of expressing closeness with staff;"

"Touching women who wear tight clothes is undercover investigation."

If these pathetic jokes were not enough, I learnt of a "seku-hara" coffee shop and a "seku-hara" bar in Tokyo where a TV station filmed the goings-on in these establishments. A women in a very brief mini-skirt and low-cut blouse pretends to be working in the office. She makes phone calls at her "desk" while men live out their fantasies as male "staff."

The new business advertises: "Come and enjoy touching women in an atmosphere of safety! If you do it in the office, you'll just get caught immediately." The TV director asked me to comment, but I was too dumbstruck to reply.

There is no doubt that the meaning of "sexual harassment" in Japan in considerably different from that in other countries. People make fun of it here in cartoons and TV skits.

I gave a speech at the Foreign Correspondents Club in March this year. Some of the questions touched upon sexual harassment and "White Day," a day that Japanese men are supposed to give women underwear in return for their gift of chocolate on Valentine's Day. (yes, in Japan women give men chocolate).

The foreign journalists wondered why Japanese women

did not protest against department stores that displayed colorful women's underwear, why they did not get angry at this new form of sexual harassment (the imbalance between the harmlessness of Valentine's Day candy and the suggestiveness of men giving women intimate apparel). I could well understand the foreigners' amazement at Japanese women's seeming incapacity to protest. I was ashamed of the immaturity of Japanese society.

The expression "sexual harassment" was chosen as the most "fashionable" word in 1989. This is not something that I wanted to see happen. Rather, I wanted to see the introduction of a stringent new law that would remove sexual harassment from the office, once and for all. What Japan should do is to add a revision to the Equal Employment Opportunity Law, like the guidelines that the American-based EEOC established in 1980.

When American women said "no" to sexual harassment, they were supported by large numbers of men. This is because men wanted to protect their own wives and daughters. Sadly, Japanese men show little such concern. Compounded by the fact that many Japanese female employees take little responsibility for their own freedom in the office, it is obvious that much needs to be done before men will begin to realize the error of their ways.

The concept of "sexual harassment" shocked the Japanese because it broke a social taboo, one that had existed for many, many years. Anti-sexual harassment movements have started in many countries and I am confident that the gathering momentum in Japan is a part of this world-wide trend.

Concern with seku-hara must amount to more than a here-today-gone-tomorrow fad.

Still More Progress Needed

In early 1992, the *Mainichi Daily* newspaper reported that a

50-year-old woman was fired from her job after she refused a drink from her union boss. She is suing for damages. A spokesman at the Fukuoka District Court in southern Japan said a suit had been filed January 28 for $31,700 in work related damages.

The newspaper reported that the women was offered a drink of sake, a rice wine, by the union boss at a year-end party in December, but the woman refused the drink saying she had a cold. Shortly afterwards, the boss called off the party and sent everyone home when he saw the woman accept a drink from another employee. She was then dismissed from the union and lost her job because of a labor-management rule which requires that workers be union members. She had worked at the company for ten years prior to her termination.

The union boss said, "She has challenged the solidarity of the union with her rebellious attitude."

Most Recent Happenings

In late 1992, Kiyomi Kikuchi filed suit against her former boss for sexual harassment as the first plaintiff in such a case in Japan to make her name public. Afterwards, she said she received more than 300 supportive phone calls and letters from all over the country. Kikuchi asked for ¥5.85 million (about $52,000) in damages and an apology from her former employer. She claims that on visits to clients he would proposition her to go to a hotel with him or try to kiss her on their way back from dinner.

Kikuchi's case follows the landmark decision of April 1992 in Fukuoka District Court. Two other such cases in addition to Kikuchi's have been filed since. Because of these cases, increasing numbers of public and private initiatives and events are being organized to increase awareness of sexual harassment throughout Japan.

The Netherlands

According to the *London Times*, in late 1991, the Dutch decided to work on changing men's attitudes about women by launching an advertising campaign designed to reduce sexual violence against women. Using the motto "Sex is natural but not a matter of course," a series of television spots and magazine advertisements were directed at males age 15 to 35. Marie Jose van Bave, the campaign's spokeswoman said, "We want to make men aware of the unsolicited side of their sexual behaviour and the stereotypes upon which this is based. We also want to prevent sex crimes by getting youths and men to realise their responsibility."

The campaign cost approximately two million pounds and will run until mid-1995. Its purpose is to prevent all forms of sexual abuse, from rape to verbal attacks. The magazine ads use clever plays on words to deliver what are hoped to be hard-hitting messages against men who expect sexual favors. "If she agrees to go to the cinema, it doesn't automatically mean you can play the leading role," one slogan states.

The campaign is based on research showing Dutch men still see women as conforming to one of two stereotypes: the "flighty type" who takes sexual harassment as sort of a compliment, and the "decent sort" who is easy prey for sexual jokes and remarks. The government also wants the public to be more aware of all types of sexual abuse, including unsolicited intimacy and verbal attacks.

Recent research showed that one in three Dutch women has experienced some form of sexual abuse. Government studies show that 20 percent of teenagers had experienced sexual violence more than once.

Dutch Law

While there are no specific provisions in Dutch legislation that relate to sexual harassment, some provisions of the Civil

Code on employer and employee rights have been interpreted by the courts as applying to sexual harassment, particularly in wrongful termination cases. Other provisions, listed in the laws that follow, could potentially be applied to sexual harassment cases as well, but as of this time, sexual harassment has not been defined either by statute or by case law.

The Men and Women (Equal Treatment) Act applies to both public and private sector employers and forbids discrimination in employment on the basis of sex. This law provides no specific remedies to victims of discrimination other than a declaration of legal nullity, and therefore it has not been applied to sexual harassment cases.

The Civil Code applies to contracts of employment in the private sector. In part, it says "The employer/employee is generally required to do or refrain from doing everything that a good employer/employee in identical circumstances should do or refrain from doing," and it is this provision that has been applied by the courts in sexual harassment cases. The courts have allowed victims of sexual harassment to submit requests for termination of their employment contracts because of sexual harassment by supervisors, coworkers, and by non-employees as well. Potentially, the employer also could submit a request for immediate termination of an employee's contract where the employee was harassing another. The Civil Code also allows for an employee, where no other legal avenues are available, to take direct legal action. This section applied to both public and private sectors.

The Working Environment Act requires that public and private sector employers provide safe and healthy work environments for employees, and thus it could potentially be applied to acts of sexual harassment.

The State Civil Servants Regulations requires employees to conduct themselves "in a manner befitting a good civil servant." This includes not using rough or indecent language of other forms of "delinquency" of which sexual harassment could be included.

The Penal Code has provisions against sexual aggressions, acts such as violations of decency and assault, and these have been applied by the courts to instances of sexual harassment in the workplace.

Recent Action

The Dutch government passed a resolution on May 22, 1992, to include a specific provision on sexual harassment at work in the Working Conditions Act. This provision is expected to become part of the act in 1993, following Parliament's approval. The provision obligates employers to stop and prevent sexual harassment in the workplace, holding them responsible for non-compliance.

New Zealand

Court decisions in New Zealand have primarily dealt with sexual harassment in terms of wrongful termination or constructive discharge claims, though there are at least three other ways in which it could be or has been addressed.

The Human Rights Commission Act of 1977 forbids discrimination on the basis of sex, but does not specifically mention sexual harassment. However, a tribunal decision on 1985 did rule that sexual harassment is a type of sex discrimination forbidden by the act in all areas of employment. The tribunal ruled that the act forbids discrimination, and therefore harassment, by the employer, managers, supervisors, and coworkers against men and women who are job applicants or employees in public and private sectors.

The Employment Contracts Act of 1991, which replaced the Labour Relations Act of 1987, states that sexual harassment is a kind of personal grievance which an employee can bring against his or her employer. It specifically mentions sexual harassment (as did the earlier Labour Relations Act in

1987), and discusses harassment in terms of conduct by the employer, managers, supervisors, coworkers, customers, and clients. The act defines sexual harassment by stating "an employee is sexually harassed ... if that employee's employer or a representative of that employer (a) makes a request of that employee for sexual intercourse, sexual contact, or other form of sexual activity which contains (i) an implied or overt promise of preferential treatment in that employee's employment; or (ii) an implied or overt threat of detrimental treatment in that employee's employment; or (b) by (i) the use of words (whether written or spoken) of a sexual nature; or (ii) physical behaviour of a sexual nature, subjects the employee to behaviour which is unwelcome or offensive to that employee (whether or not that is conveyed to the employer or representative) and which is either repeated or of such a significant nature that it has a detrimental effect on that employee's employment, job performance, or job satisfaction."

While there is no criminal law in New Zealand that specifically mentions sexual harassment, and criminal laws are not usually used to deal with harassment in the work environment, some provisions of the Crimes Act of 1986 could be applied. One such provision that deals with indecent assault, or inducing another person to have a sexual connection by an express or implied threat to make improper use of power or authority to the detriment of that person, could apply to sexual harassment at work. This law covers employers or anyone acting on behalf of the employer and includes both the public and private sectors.

Spain

It has been widely reported that some legislators in some European countries believe that the United States, and those countries who have followed the U.S. example with regard to sexual harassment laws, have gone too far, and have in fact engaged in what they refer to as "desexualization" of the country and the culture. The French Secretary of State for Women's Rights indicated her desire to ensure that French law avoided the "American excesses" of perceiving all sexual advances as potential criminal offenses.

These beliefs exist more so in the Mediterranean countries, where socializing usually involves more physical contact than in the United States or Northern Europe. In these more southern countries, there is an opinion that flirtation and sensuality are part of the fun or spice of life and should not be limited. At least some say so, but many of the comments simply show the continued lack of understanding of what sexual harassment really is and how it impacts its victims.

Coro Mira, in charge of women's affairs in Spain's largest labor group, said in an interview in *The New York Times,* "Compliments about the way a woman looks are not generally considered bad taste here. If a woman were offended by compliments, she'd have a hard time claiming harassment. It's an accepted part of our culture."

On the other hand, Purificacion Gutierrez Lopez, head of the Women's Institute in Spain, said in the same article that the problem had always existed. "But the fact that it is now recognized and talked about means we have started dealing with it. So far, though, Spanish women are only just beginning to understand that sexual harassment is an offense."

The problem gained public attention in Spain in late October 1992 when accusations of sexual harassment and sexual aggression were made against a well-known television announcer, Alfredo Amestoy. The harassment allegedly occurred during a business trip. The public prosecutor asked for a year's imprisonment as punishment; Amestoy denied any wrongdoing.

Although discussion of the problem is now more open and apparently on the increase, few women file complaints. One female office worker in Madrid said sexual harassment is everywhere. "And it's worse in a recession because women are afraid of losing their jobs if they speak up."

While two in-depth studies of sexual harassment have been conducted in Spain—in 1986 by the Women's Department of the General Worker's Union, and in 1987 by the Women's Institute—results were not available. Studies throughout Europe, however, show that from 20 to 70 percent of working women say they have been sexually harassed.

Spanish Law

Spain's Constitution states that there shall be no discrimination on the basis of sex. In March 1989 the government adopted a provision to protect against sexual harassment and included the provision in both the Worker's Charter and the Civil Servants Regulations.

The Worker's Charter, which applied to private sector employers, specifically states that "all workers shall enjoy [the right] to respect for his privacy and proper consideration of his dignity, including the protection against verbal or physical offense of a sexual nature." The Charter allows the employer to suspend or terminate employees for disciplinary reasons and for employees to request termination of his or her contract for such reasons as "substantial alterations to his or her conditions of employment which adversely affect his or her personal dignity." Employees may also be terminated for "offensive behavior by word or deed towards the employer, [or other] persons working in the undertaking."

The Civil Servants Regulations state that "all civil servants shall enjoy the right to respect for his or her privacy and proper consideration for his or her dignity, including protection against any verbal or physical offense of a sexual nature." The regulations also state that discrimination in employment on the basis of sex is illegal and that any supervisor who knowingly allows such misconduct by subordinates has engaged in serious misconduct. It is possible to apply these regulations against sex discrimination to acts of sexual harassment.

While the Penal Code does not specifically mention sexual harassment, certain behavior could be covered. This could include crimes against physical injury or impairment of physical or mental health, of sexual aggression by force or intimidation, of acts, words, or deeds that dishonor, discredit, or degrade another, or of intentionally offending another person by words or actions.

Sweden

While there are no Swedish laws which specifically address sexual harassment, the issue has received attention for a number of years. The first court case which included some claims of sexual harassment was brought by the Equal Opportunities Ombudsman to the Labour Court in 1983. This case, and the following information, was reported by Ninni Hagman to the International Labour Organisation in their 1992 study of sexual harassment.

In this case, a man who was to be appointed to the position of office manager was said to have bothered or harassed at least seventeen women, with these women complaining of his unwelcome and humiliating sexual conduct. In his new position as office manager he would be in charge of an even greater number of women. The Ombudsman lost the case.

In 1984, at the National Federation of Social Democratic Women's conference, a number of women realized through discussion of one of the agenda items called "erotic peace zones," that sexual harassment was a problem for many women in Sweden. After the conference, many women began contacting the Equal Opportunities Ombudsman or their trade unions.

In 1986 the Labour Court ruled that the termination of a woman who was allegedly sexually harassed was a violation of the Employment Security Act, so the issue began to gain momentum. At that time the Equal Opportunities Ombudsman also undertook a study of sexual harassment of women with the resulting Frida Report presented to the Ministry of Labour in 1987. As a result of this study and other actions, the Equal Opportunities Act of 1991 was passed. The act states that the employer must take affirmative action to stop and prevent sexual harassment in the workplace.

Swedish Laws

While the Equal Opportunities Act does not provide a specific definition of sexual harassment, many examples were used in the legislative pre-work in the development of the act. This work discusses molestation of sexual nature, punishable under the Penal Code, sexual insinuations that are unwelcome and which cause discomfort to others, unwelcome sexually suggestive actions or remarks, or sexually explicit pictures which may humiliate women, especially in a predominantly male work environment.

The act says "an employer may not subject an employee to harassment because the latter has rejected the employer's sexual advances or lodged a complaint about the employer for sex discrimination" and the employer "shall endeavor to ensure that no worker is exposed to sexual harassment." It requires that employers with ten or more employees prepare and submit an annual plan for promoting and ensuring equal opportunities and that this plan include a survey of the actions taken at work to stop and prevent harassment on account of sex or as retaliation for filing a discrimination complaint. Annual progress reports on the plan are also required. This act applies to employers or anyone acting on behalf of the employer and covers both the public and private sectors.

Switzerland

To date, little information is available on sexual harassment in

Switzerland. According to the International Labour Organisation, the National Commission for Women of the Swiss Union of Public Service Employees estimated in 1987 that because of sexual harassment, 7 percent of its female members said they have lost their jobs; 2 percent were fired; and 5 percent resigned from their jobs.

Currently, there is no Swiss federal law prohibiting sexual harassment, nor is there an equal opportunities law forbidding sex discrimination in employment. However, since 1981 Article 4 of the Federal Constitution has addressed the issue of equal treatment of men and women in the family, education, and employment. In addition, the Swiss penal code, the Civil Code, and the Code of Obligations contain portions that could be applied to sexual harassment in the workplace.

In one case, *Pfleger v. Muhlebach S. A.*, in Geneva, November 1991, the court defined sexual harassment in terms of "persons who in their position of employer, supervisor, or collaborator, take advantage of their position or influence in an enterprise to harass an employee or a job applicant of the same sex or of the opposite sex, by unwelcome propositions, immoral comments, images, objects, gestures or undesired behavior ... with the goal of directly or indirectly obtaining sexual favours in making understood either verbally or tacitly that the acceptance or refusal of such favours should or could constitute a decisive criterion for the signature, content, means of application or the continuation of an employment contract, or ... with the goal, or with the result, of poisoning the existing or future work environment." The court went on to say that in determining whether or not sexual harassment has occurred, the behavior should be considered from the "perspective of the victim" and not that of the alleged harasser—i.e. the "reasonable woman" ruling issued by the United States Ninth Circuit Court of Appeals only a few months earlier.

The Labour Act was intended to obligate the employer to provide for health, safety, and morals of women workers, and in that protection, limited the employment of women in certain areas of work. This act could be applied to sexual harassment where it caused unsafe, unhealthy, or immoral conditions. Article 33 of the Act was used to win a court case against a male supervisor who harassed a female employee.

The Code of Obligations contains several articles designed to protect workers' in the work environment, though no specific mention is made of sexual harassment. Like the Civil Code, which states that a person who is subject to "a violation of his or her personality can undertake legal action against those persons who commit the act," the Code of Obligations required the same of employers for their employees. Sexual harassment could be considered a "violation of personality" and be covered by both codes. In the *Pfleger* case, the court ruled that the violation of fundamental rights, such as sexual harassment, does constitute a wrongful act on the part of the employer, and is covered by the Code of Obligations.

Several articles of the Swiss Penal Code could be applied to sexual harassment, including: wrongfully inducing a woman to engage in sexual intercourse; indecent assault by violence or serious threat; protection against immoral purposes; abuse of a woman's dependence; and infringement upon a person's decency.

Strange Methods

In an August 1992 issue of the *London Times,* a short article appeared: "Stockholm: For an experimental year from July 1, police in four Swedish regions are to equip women subject to persistent sexual harassment with free alarms, mobile telephones and even bodyguards, a police spokesman said. (Reuter)" While this certainly appears to be an interesting approach, nothing more was reported about this unusual method of combating harassment.

The United Kingdom

Britain's Equal Opportunities Commission reported that as of June 1992 complaints about sex discrimination in the workplace increased by 40 percent compared with the previous year. The commission said the increase was because of the continued rise in the number of women going out to work, increased expectations among younger women and the higher profile of the commission itself. Joanna Foster, who chairs the commission, said the recession also had a part to play in the rise. "Organizations are getting leaner and some are getting meaner."

There were more than nine thousand complaints about employment issues in 1991, compared with sixty-five hundred the year before. The primary areas of complaint included recruitment, pregnancy-related issues, and less favorable terms of employment in general. Sexual harassment complaints were up 35 percent from 317 to 427. Foster said the numbers showed that sex discrimination is still a big problem in the workplace. "Yet while expectations of fair treatment are higher than ever before, redress is more difficult to obtain because of the complexity and cost of taking legal action."

Foster said if the government is serious about its Citizen's Charter, it needs to consider amendments recommended by the commission to strengthen and simplify the equality laws. She said a simple start could be made by revising tribunal and court procedures to remove barriers causing delays. The average length of time taken for a case to reach employment appeal tribunals is two years in England and Wales.

In addition, growing numbers of men are alleging sex discrimination as they apply for jobs in areas traditionally dominated by women. Most of the complaints are related to recruitment practices, with allegations that companies are unwilling to hire men to work with word processors, as secretaries and machinists, or as nurses and care assistants. Thirty percent of complaints to the commission in 1991 about recruitment practices were from men.

General Status of Women in the United Kingdom

J. Mole, in his book *Mind Your Manners: Managing Culture Clash in the Single European Market*, reported that women comprise 45 percent of the United Kingdom's work force—the largest percentage of any of the member countries in the European Communities. This, he said, is despite the fact that female employees in the United Kingdom have the lowest maternity benefits and negligible child care facilities.

A 1992 survey by the Institute of Directors of its members showed that 75 percent of the female company directors believe women are discriminated against and that a third of these women said they had personally experienced discrimination, especially in the early stages of their careers. The chief causes of the discrimination were said to be male attitudes at work and the employers' failure to take into account the child care and domestic responsibilities of their employees.

According to *The Independent*, in March 1992, women in the United Kingdom still remain almost invisible at the top of public and private businesses and institutions, despite some legislation to help them advance. There are no female House of Lords judges or Cabinet ministers, and only one permanent secretary in the civil service—Barbara Mills, Director of Public Prosecutions. Only one out of every 200 company directors are female, although more than 40 percent of private-sector employees are women. *Labour Research* magazine published a 1992 report showing that while women account for 49 percent of all non-industrial civil servants, fewer than 7 percent are at the level of under-secretary of above.

U.K. Legal Approaches to Sexual Harassment

While sexual harassment is not mentioned specifically in any British law, it has been held to be illegal in certain court cases

involving the Sex Discrimination Act of 1975, which addresses discrimination of the basis of sex or gender. Sexual harassment also has been ruled illegal under the Employment
Protection (Consolidation) Act of 1978, which provides protection against unfair dismissal for employees with two or
more years of continuous employment. The first court decision in the United Kingdom to interpret sexual harassment as
a form of sex discrimination was in 1986.

In one case, involving the Sex Discrimination Act of 1975,
the court ruled that while sexual harassment usually involves
repeated, unwanted conduct, there are some circumstances
under which one incident, if sufficiently serious, could be
considered enough to constitute sexual harassment. The
court said sexual harassment is "a particularly degrading and
unacceptable form of treatment and that harassment may be
verbal or non-verbal.

In order to show that the Sex Discrimination Act has been
violated, claimants must show they suffered a "detriment"
because of their sex. However, "detriment is defined to mean
a disadvantage that can include either a tangible job loss (*quid
pro quo harassment*) or a negative work environment that "a
reasonable employee could justifiably complain" (*hostile
environment harassment*). The courts also have said that
each instance of sexual behavior or harassment must be examined "in the context of each person."

The Sex Discrimination Act of 1975

This act prohibits sex discrimination (interpreted by the
courts to include sexual harassment) in recruitment and hiring; all terms and conditions of employment—promotion,
transfer, training or other benefits, facilities or services; termination; and any negative or detrimental treatment of an
employee. The courts have interpreted the act to include sexual harassment by supervisors and coworkers, and indicated
that employers may be held strictly liable for even employee

to employee harassment: "anything done by a person in the course of his employment shall be treated ... as done by his employer as well as by him, whether or not it was done with the employer's knowledge or approval." The act also applies to non-employee agents of the employer and could be interpreted to include harassment by clients if the employer intentionally or negligently placed an employee in a position where they would be sexually harassed by the clients (i.e. this subjects the employee to a "detriment based on sex").

The Act applies to sexual discrimination of both men and women and applies to both public and private sector employers. It also has been applied to a case of sexual harassment of one homosexual by another homosexual.

Other Applicable Laws

The Employment Protection (Consolidated) Act of 1978 was applied to a sexual harassment case in 1978, when the court said that "persistent and unwanted amorous advances by an employer to a female member of his staff" would be considered grounds for constructive discharge.

As for criminal law, none in the United Kingdom mentions sexual harassment, but those statutes prohibiting assault and battery, indecent assault, or false imprisonment could be applied in some cases. However, as in many countries, it is unusual for sexual harassment cases to rely on criminal law.

Under common law, the employer has the responsibility of providing a safe workplace, so tort claims for negligently permitting sexual harassment have been brought against employers. To date, however, such claims have been settled prior to trial and no rulings have been made.

U.K. Police Chiefs Launch Drive Against Harassment

According to the February 1993 *London Times,* Britain's chief constables believe sexual harassment of female police officers by their male counterparts is much more widespread than previously thought and must be eliminated. The chiefs launched a new campaign to stop sexual harassment of female officers, warning that any such conduct would lead to tough penalties. The Association of Chief Police Officers issued the warning and said it was prompted by research in seven police forces across the country. The recent research showed that sexual harassment, ranging from physical abuse to crude language, was experienced by many female officers.

Bill Skitt, chief constable of Hertfordshire and chairman of a police equal opportunity commission, said, "It is a much more common problem than was previously considered to be the case." But many believed that work within the police force had brought some improvements.

In 1992, research conducted in the Hampshire force showed the extent of the problem to constables. They agreed to conduct a wider survey among scores of policewomen in the six other forces. John Hoddinott, chief constable of Hampshire and vice-president of the association, said after its quarterly meeting in January that the research did show evidence of sexual assault and physical misbehavior as well as other types of sexual harassment.

John Burrow, chief constable of Essex and president of the association, said policewomen represent only 12 percent of a force of more than 120,000 officers, and thus a very clear statement of support is needed to aid those women who are subjected to sexual harassment. In addition to such policy statements, police discipline codes and informal counseling plans are also in place to encourage victims to come forward.

Office Sex Pests

A leaflet issued by the U.K.'s employment department in March 1992 urged employers to take a tougher stance against sexual harassment. The leaflet deals with "bottom pinching, innuendo, and intimidation" and says that sexual harassment "can seriously affect the confidence of your employees and consequently how well they do their jobs." The leaflet was sent to one hundred thousand companies.

Guidelines on sexual harassment are issued for U.K. employers to ensure consistency with the European Commission's recommended code of practice. The code defines sexual harassment as "unwanted conduct of a sexual nature, or other conduct based on sex affecting the dignity of women and men at work." It recommends drawing up a company policy and explains the procedures to be followed after a complaint is made. The guidelines follow a survey earlier this year that said victims are more likely than their harassers to be forced to switch jobs.

According to the *Times,* many large firms and organizations already have a working code in place. Ken Best, the Post Office Equal Employment Opportunities Manager, who is in charge of his organization's policy, said the policy "was introduced in 1989 and we have seen more cases since then, probably because it is easier for women to come forward. It has put sexual harassment on managers' agendas and forces people to take it seriously."

Brenda Wilkinson, Women's Officer for Brighton borough council, introduced the borough's code in 1990. She said, "We concentrated on creating a network of sympathetic women—and it was women that came to us rather than men—so that there was always someone to go to."

In a further move to improve equal opportunities in the civil service, government departments will have to set targets for the number of women to be appointed to different grades of jobs. The government wants to increase the number of women appointed to science and engineering posts, as well as increase representation in the senior levels of civil service.

From London

In June 1992 an industrial tribunal in London awarded a

woman $9,000 in compensation for being fired when she complained of sexual harassment. Donna Van Den Berghen, a 21-year old legal secretary, complained that at a company Christmas party, penis-shaped chocolates were served and that a trainee lawyer repeatedly put his arm around her and squeezed her breasts.

The woman said that after she complained to her supervisors, her coworkers became angry and "sent her to Coventry," ostracizing her, until she was finally fired some months later. She said that when she complained of the fondling at the party, she was told she should have dealt with it.

The alleged harasser was an attorney with the London firm of Nabarro Nathanson, where both he and the female employee worked. The firm denied any harassment or discrimination.

More From the United Kingdom

Most Europeans now agree that just as ideas of sexual equality came across the Atlantic from the United States to the Continent more than twenty years ago, the new debate about the problem of sexual harassment also came from the United States. While many Europeans, particularly men, reportedly believed that the Thomas–Hill controversy in the United States was feminism "run amok," the case also caused governments, labor unions, women's organizations, and employers to look more closely at the problem. When they did examine the issue of sexual harassment, the numbers showed it to be just as much of a problem in Europe as in the United States.

According to Denise Kingsmill, a London attorney who specializes in sex discrimination cases, "Widening awareness has a lot to do with the Thomas case. Ten years ago, it was difficult to explain to people what sexual harassment was and whether it existed. Now I discuss the many subtle ways that harassment occurs."

Michael Rubenstein, an American who edits the *Equal Opportunities Review* in London, said that approximately half the sexual harassment complaints brought by women in Britain are sustained. "Tribunals here tend to believe people who claim to have been harassed. In the United States, the question is asked: did she provoke it?" he said.

U.K. law limits monetary damages to £10,000 (about US$16,000), but the Industrial Tribunal also can recommend suspension or transfer of an offender. A woman employed by the London Fire Brigade won $40,000 in damages when she brought a criminal case for assault involving verbal and physical abuse of a sexual nature by a coworker.

According to Alan Riding in the December 3, 1992, *New York Times*, "Courts and ombudsmen in many countries are increasingly ruling in favor of women when cases come to trial, even though most are settled out of court." However, he goes on to say that one reason cases in Europe have not received much attention is because so far, no charges have been brought against any prominent personalities.

The United States

Although the legal issue of sexual harassment in the United States is based on Title VII of the 1964 Civil Rights Act, it was not until 1976 that the federal courts recognized sexual harassment as a form of sex discrimination. The court in *Williams v. Saxbe* ruled against previous decisions that sexual behavior or harassment was a "personal matter" between the two individuals, or a "personal proclivity, peculiarity or mannerism" of the supervisor. The court said that conditions of employment that are applied differently to men and women, such as sexual harassment, are prohibited under Title VII as a specific type of sex discrimination in employment. This was a very significant ruling for beginning to address the issue of sexual harassment in the United States, and as we now know, throughout the world.

One of the earliest, if not the earliest, sexual harassment

surveys was conducted by *Redbook Magazine* in 1976 with startling results. Of the approximately 9,000 women who responded, 88 percent said they had personally experienced sexual harassment and half had been fired or knew someone who had been fired for sexual reasons. While the survey was criticized for its methodology (as many of the studies are, not necessarily for scientific reasons, but because people do not like the results), and because many people believed that the results were skewed—saying that those who had been harassed were the women most likely to respond to the survey—it nevertheless served to bring attention to the problem.

Within a year, interest and public discussion increased. Three of the first people to begin to openly explore and discuss the issue of harassment were Lin Farley in her book, *Sexual Shakedown: The Sexual Harassment of Women on the Job* (1978) in which she defined the problem and told story after story of women who experienced harassment at work; Catherine A. McKinnon writing in *Sexual Harassment of Working Women: A Case of Sex Discrimination* (1979) and arguing the legal remedies; and anthropologist Margaret Mead in an article titled "A Proposal: We Need Taboos on Sex at Work," still widely quoted today. Since then, study after study, and survey after survey, has been conducted in the United States, each with essentially the same results.

Studies and Surveys

The Merit System Protection Board's most recent study indicates that sexual harassment in the federal workplace is as prevalent as it was in 1980. The board repeated its 1979–80 landmark study. According to the 1988 study, 42 percent of the women and 14 percent of the men said they had experienced some form of unwanted sexual attention between 1985 and 1987. The 1980 study showed 42 percent of women and 15 percent of men were sexually harassed in the period 1979–80, percentages nearly identical to the latest numbers.

The board sent questionnaires to approximately 13,000 federal employees and received responses from 8,523 in the 1988 study, as compared with 23,000 surveys and a response of 19,500 in the 1980 study—both considered large sample groups. The 1988 survey repeated many of the questions asked in the first study and found that while sexual harassment has different meanings for different people, the employees are more likely now than in 1980 to label particular behaviors as harassing.

Specifics of the 1988 report: unwanted sexual teasing was the most common form of harassment, encountered by 35 percent of women respondents and 12 percent of men; pressure for sexual favors was reported by 9 percent of women and 3 percent of men; coworker harassment was more common than harassment by supervisors, with 31 percent of women and 22 percent of men reporting harassment by an immediate or higher-level supervisor; the most common response by victims of harassment—52 percent of women and 42 percent of men—was ignoring the behavior or doing nothing (only 2 percent filed complaints); and asking or telling the harasser to stop was said to be a response by 44 percent of women and 25 percent of the men.

The Merit System Protection Board estimates, based on the study, that more than 36,000 federal employees quit their jobs because of sexual harassment during the period 1985 to 1987, with 8,000 women quitting their jobs during 1979–80. The board said the cost totaled $36.7 million in recruiting, rehiring, and retraining expenses. Further expenses, the board stated, were the costs of sick leave—$26.1 million—and lost productivity—$76.3 million—from those employees who stayed on the job despite being sexually harassed. The result was a total cost of $139.1 million in 1979 versus $189 million in 1988 because of sexual harassment in the workplace.

In a 1988 survey of Fortune 500 companies by *Working Woman* magazine, results showed 90 percent of the companies had received sexual harassment complaints, more than a third had been sued, and nearly one-fourth had been sued repeatedly. The typical large firm will lose $6.7 million per year from lost productivity, absenteeism, and turnover from harassment. A second survey by the magazine in February 1992, showing that more than 66 percent of the women who responded said they had been sexually harassed; more than 33 percent said they knew someone who had been harassed.

The *National Law Journal* released findings from its 1989 study showing that 60 percent of women attorneys responding said sexual harassment at work is a major problem—unwanted sexual attention, touching, pinching, comments, looks, gestures, and sexual remarks from supervisors (36 percent), colleagues (30 percent), and clients (32 percent).

In 1990, a *Working Smart* magazine survey indicated that, of the women responding, about 51 percent experienced sexual harassment; almost 50 percent were harassed in the last two years; almost 48 percent said harassment was overt; and 32 percent reported it. In 1991, a Pentagon survey of 20,000 military personnel revealed that 64 percent of women and 17 percent of men said they had been sexually harassed. Also in 1991, the U.S. Navy's survey of 6,700 enlisted people worldwide indicated that 75 percent of women and 50 percent men said harassment occurs within their commands. (Information on additional and more recent studies and surveys is in the chapter on the United States.)

U.S. Legal Approaches to Sexual Harassment

The 1964 Civil Rights Act, the federal legislation, prohibits discrimination in such areas as housing and public accommodation based on someone's race, color, religion, national origin, or sex. Title VII of the act forbids discrimination in any and every aspect of employment—hiring, firing, pay, promotion, job assignment, training, apprenticeships, orientation, and even the general work atmosphere. As mentioned previously, sexual harassment, while not specifically mentioned in the

1964 act, has been interpreted by the federal courts to be a prohibited type of sex discrimination in that it places barriers before those of one gender and not the other.

Under the federal law, harassment can be a violation of the act if committed by the employer, managers, supervisors, coworkers, and certain non-employees, such as customers, vendors, clients, or sub-contractors. The law also has been interpreted to include sexual harassment of employees of the same gender, i.e. unwanted homosexual sexual advances, since the recipient was harassed on account of his or her sex or gender. The recipient's sexual orientation does not matter. The court called this type of harassment the "obverse side of the coin" to heterosexual sexual harassment in *Wright v. Methodist Youth Services.* The law does not protect employees from harassment on account of their being homosexual, since, the courts have ruled, sexual orientation is not a protected category under federal employment law.

Case law also has addressed several forms of indirect sexual harassment. As far back as 1983, in a case handed down in the fall, *Toscano v. Nimmo*, by the District Court for the District of Delaware, the court held that the Veterans' Administration had unlawfully discriminated against a female employee when a supervisor at one of its hospitals promoted a coworker with whom he was having an affair over an employee with whom he was not sexually involved. The court found that the promotion of the coworker was based on the receipt of sexual favors, and consequently, unlawful sex discrimination against the non-promoted employee who was unable to obtain the promotion because of the supervisor's improper conduct.

Another form of indirect sexual harassment that the U.S. courts have recognized is that which is not directed specifically at an employee, but which creates a hostile, offensive work environment by its very existence. This may be the case where pin-ups are on office walls, abusive language is used so as to be overheard by those it offends, or behavior is directed at one person which is degrading and offensive to others.

Title VII of the 1964 Civil Rights Act applies to public and private employers with fifteen or more employees and is enforced by the Equal Employment Opportunity Commission, which also is responsible for investigation of complaints and issuance of interpretive guidelines for defining and understanding the issue. EEOC issued the first Guidelines on Sexual Harassment in 1980, defining harassment as a type of discrimination. Although EEOC's Guidelines are not legally binding, the U.S. Supreme Court has stated that the guidelines "constitute a body of experience and informed judgments to which courts and litigants may properly resort for guidance" and suggests that courts defer to the guidelines in their decisions.

The 1991 Civil Rights Act

Prior to 1991, under federal equal employment law such as Title VII, remedies such a mental suffering or punitive damages were not allowed. The original intent of these laws was to restore the individual to the status he or she enjoyed prior to the discrimination (or harassment), i.e., to make the individual "whole" again. Such "make-whole" remedies included back pay, reinstatement to the job, granting of a promotion, or attorneys' fees.

However, the federal 1991 Civil Rights Act now allows for expanded remedies for pain and suffering, including compensatory and punitive damages. The 1991 law places caps or limits on the amounts of damages which can be awarded: $50,000 for firms with up to 100 employees, $100,000 for those employing more than 100, and $300,000 for companies with more than 300 employees. Firms with fewer than 15 employees are exempt from the law. The caps apply to cases involving sex discrimination or harassment; no caps exists for discrimination of other protected groups.

Title IX of the Education Amendments of 1972

In February 1992, the U.S. Supreme Court ruled that sexually harassed students may sue to collect monetary damages from their schools and school officials. The court said Congress intended to let students try for monetary damages and compensation when it passed Title IX of the Education Amendments of 1972. The law bars sexual bias in educational programs receiving federal funding, thus including nearly all educational institutions. Lower courts had ruled that Title IX allows alleged victims of intentional sex discrimination and/or harassment to sue only for "injunctive relief" or halting an illegal practice.

Individual States' Laws

In addition, employees who are the victims of sexual harassment may also be entitled to bring claims against their employers for violating state anti-discrimination statutes. At the present time, 40 states (all except Alabama, Georgia, Louisiana, Mississippi, North Carolina, North Dakota, Texas, Tennessee and Virginia) have statutes banning sex discrimination in private employment. In many of these states, the state courts or agencies responsible for administering the statutes have interpreted them to prohibit sexual harassment. Actions brought under these state anti-discrimination statutes or under common law causes of action, may entitle plaintiffs to recover damages not otherwise recoverable under Title VII or one of the other federal statutes.

The victim of sexual harassment has the option of pursuing a variety of actions under state tort or contract law in addition to causes of action occurring under federal and state anti-discrimination law. The available actions and remedies vary greatly from state to state. Pendent state claims that have been heard by federal courts in recent sexual harassment actions include invasion of privacy, breach of contract, assault and battery, intentional infliction of emotional or mental distress, defamation, negligence, outrageous conduct, and intentional interference with contractual relations. These causes of action provide the plaintiff with recovering punitive damages as well as the compensatory damages of pain and suffering.

In the United States, it is unusual for criminal laws to be used to protect against sexual harassment. However, in the most severe cases, where criminal charges are filed against the harasser, the legal action is based on criminal laws of the state, county, or city in which the harassment occurred, not on equal employment law. In these cases, the victim does not receive compensation for physical, emotional or job related damages, but the harasser can be sentenced to prison. Criminal charges for sexual harassment do occur, but are rare in the United States.

PART THREE:
FROM THE UNITED STATES

6

PUSHING LIMITS IN THE UNITED STATES

Winners in the "unbelievable boss" category included one in Cleveland who told his secretary to take his stool sample to the doctor's office; a boss in Tampa who asked his secretary to ar-range his vasectomy; and a paralegal's boss in Washington, D.C., who told her he had a direct line with God. One day he told her he had "divine sperm" and she needed the sperm to be "saved."

9 to 5 Annual Good,
Bad & Unbelievable
Boss Contest

The limits of defining and eliminating sexual harassment in the workplace are indeed being pushed in the United States. But as in most countries, news about sexual harassment in the United States consists of some good, some bad, and some downright ugly.

THE BAD

Some of the more distressing yet interesting stories come from Texas. According to *Time* magazine, the latest fad on Texas golf courses is topless tournaments. A December 21, 1992, article noted that one Ft. Worth topless club has arranged three such tournaments in recent months where golfers, usually businessmen entertaining clients, pay $150 each for dinner, all the beer they can drink, a golf cart and a bikini-clad "caddie." During tournaments, players can buy a $10 "cart dance" striptease performed on the green. Because of complaints from residents near a city course, the topless club now holds tournaments only at a private course thirty miles outside Ft. Worth.

In Dallas, one of the newest upscale topless clubs, The Men's Club, advertises itself as "the best business climate in town," a place for businessmen (and businesswomen) to entertain clients amid plush fixtures and nearly naked women. Similar clubs pride themselves on providing amenities for business people, ranging from conference rooms to fax machines and secretarial help. In addition, owners say, the clubs provide a setting for relationship building among business people and their clients.

Many legal scholars and business experts predict that such climates are conducive to lawsuits as well as business deals. According to experts, the problem is that many women are uncomfortable doing business in places like The Men's Club, no matter how upscale the amenities. Such discomfort can cause them to exclude themselves from business opportunities enjoyed by their male counterparts. On the flip side, should women be determined (or required) to do business in such an environment, means, or implies, that tolerating an uncomfortable sexual work environment is "part of the job."

An Atlanta topless club owner said: "These people (customers) aren't actually sitting in the club working through the details of a contract ... you can't get away from the fact that business relationships are developed on the golf course and hunting trips—and in adult entertainment clubs."

That is exactly the problem, said expert Wendy Crisp, national director of the National Association for Female Executives. "Women are getting into the (traditional) men's clubs and they're out there on the golf course. So men are constantly looking for a place where they can be away from women and behave in a way women consider sophomoric and men consider bonding. It establishes relationships that are extremely difficult to be included in. There's a continual circling of the wagons."

Norman Werback, a principal in the Dallas workplace-consulting firm of WerbackRose, said the practice of using topless clubs is "a potential source of lawsuits against companies that condone it. If a company, by reimbursing expenses, supports its people doing business in topless clubs under the guise of that's where their clients like to go, in essence they're saying that a man must be the one who handles the business. And the law says business can't be directed towards one gender and not the other."

Club owners and managers say topless clubs that cater to business people offer a sophisticated environment that female executives should feel comfortable in. Others believe legal liability should be of concern to any business that condones use of such clubs for business purposes.

Jane Dolkart, a law professor at Southern Methodist University, said, "Whether just going to a topless bar is enough for a sexual harassment suit is debatable. More likely, it would be part of an allegation of hostile environment rather than the sole factor in bringing such a suit."

Werback said some companies have stopped reimbursing business expenses from topless clubs, even though identifying such expenses can be difficult. Topless bars often use nondescriptive names on their charge slips such as Prive Corp. rather that Cabaret Royale, or TMC rather than The Men's Club. Even so, companies are becoming more aware of the situation and taking steps to address it.

Conoco Inc. began paying more attention to how such expenses are handled after one employee charged $22,600 at a Houston topless club two years ago. "I've turned down expense accounts from some of my people … it's not the type of expense that I felt would reflect well on Conoco," said Jim Felder, Conoco's manager of public relations.

Crisp, from NAFE, said companies should establish definite policies to curb the use of topless clubs for client and business meetings. "After all," she said, "a company really doesn't want it known that their entire midwestern sales force had topless women sitting in their laps."

And more from Texas includes Leander City Councilman Morris "Pop" Robertson, who lost his office because of sexual harassment in mid-1992. He denied having kissed female employees and said he would rather kiss his dog. Robertson said he would appeal, even after more than twelve witnesses testified against him.

The witnesses said Robertson prodded women and made lewd contact with a citizen who then complained about him. Witnesses also claimed that he used racial slurs and profane language about city employees and that he offered to resign in return for money.

After he was found guilty of the harassment, but before he was ousted from office, Robertson, 82, walked out of council chambers, placed a notice of appeal on the dais, and said, "We'll see ya'll in court."

In Other States

Lest anyone think that Texas is the worst, or only "bad" place where sexism and sexual harassment runs rampant in the United States, consider this: Cleveland-based, 9 to 5, the National Association of Working Women, recently released the results of its annual competition for bosses who are "good," "bad," and simply "unbelievable." Ellen Bravo, national director of the organization, said, "The National Boss Contest gives working women the opportunity to honor good bosses and skewer bad bosses."

9 to 5 was founded twenty years ago as an advocacy group for women workers, especially those working in offices, Bravo said. The boss contest attracted thousands of entries from all over the country. Judges included Cathy Guisewite, author of the comic strip "Cathy," and Beecher Eurich of Ben & Jerry's Homemade Ice Cream Co.

Winners in the "unbelievable" category included: the boss in Cleveland who told his secretary to take his stool sample to the doctor's office; the Tampa, Florida, boss who asked his secretary to arrange for his vasectomy; and a Washington, D.C., paralegal's boss who told her he had a direct line with God. The paralegal said her boss told her one day that he had "divine sperm" and she needed the sperm to be "saved."

Winners in the "bad" category included a boss in Torrance, California, who fired his secretary on National Secretary's Day after she complained about poor treatment, overwork, and sexism in the office. She had been employed at the company for four years. Also in the bad category was the management of a mortgage company in Sundance, California, which fired several women after they complained of sexual harassment by one of the managers. However, when the manager quit the company, he received a nice severance package and had his attorney's fees paid by the company.

In the "good" category was the management of Business Volunteers for the Arts of Philadelphia, which worked out an agreement that allowed an administrative assistant with serious liver disease to continue working—benefiting everyone by saving both the employee and employer money and time.

General Electric's medical systems division in Milwaukee also was cited in the good category for developing flexible work hours for a female production worker so she could be with her son while he was receiving bone cancer treatment.

THE GOOD: PUSHING AND DEFINING THE LIMITS

Despite the horror—or humor—of the previous stories, many new concepts, as well as U.S. court decisions, have been a positive force in pushing the limits to eliminate workplace sexual harassment. Other rulings and regulations have served

to limit or define existing concepts. Those of most interest
are given in the following pages.

Non-Employee Harassment

Non-employee harassment—sexual harassment of employees
by people who are not employees—is rampant, said L. A.
Winokur, writing in the *Wall Street Journal*. Such harassment
can lead companies into a maze of legal and moral issues.

While many women are harassed by customers, suppliers,
vendors, or sub-contractors, they often take the "grin and
bear it" approach because they feel there is an economic
interest at stake for them as individuals as well as for the company. Women professionals and sales representatives whose
jobs require them to come into contact with people outside
the company, and women who are in non-traditional fields
(inspectors in construction environments, for example), are
particularly vulnerable to non-employee harassment.

Since the Thomas–Hill controversy, many companies have
developed policies and procedures for dealing with sexual
harassment. But still, Winokur wrote, "most managers are surprised to learn they have a responsibility to protect their
employees from non-employee harassment."

While federal and state governments and courts have just
begun to address this issue in significant numbers, the issue
has been known for many years. In cases that have arisen, governments, regulatory agencies, and the courts have made it
clear that complaints about such harassment can be brought
before them. The EEOC's Guidelines on Sexual Harassment,
for example, define sexual harassment as unwelcome sexual
conduct that is a term or condition of employment or which
creates a hostile, offensive work environment. The guidelines
do not specify where the harassment must take place.

Furthermore, Section E of the Guidelines explicitly states
that the employer may be held responsible for the acts of non-

employees with respect to sexual harassment of employees in the workplace where the employer is or should be aware of such behavior and fails to take immediate and appropriate action. Liability will more readily be imposed if it can be shown that the employer had the ability to control or prevent the harassment from occurring.

One of the first cases in which an employer was held liable for the harassing actions of non-employees also involved employee dress requirements. In *EEOC vs. Sage Realty Corp.*, the court held that an employer was liable for sexual harassment for insisting that an employee wear a sexually provocative uniform despite the fact that (1) the employer knew that the wearing of such uniform made the employee the target of repeated offensive comments and lewd propositions by customers of the employer; and (2) the nature of the uniform did not aid the employee in her work duties.

In another case, the New Jersey Casino Control Commission fined two Atlantic City casinos, Caesar's and Trump Plaza, for transferring minority and women dealers from a customer's game and replacing them with white male dealers. The transfers were made after the customer allegedly made racial, ethnic, and sexist slurs against the women and minority dealers while playing craps.

In November 1990 Caesar's was fined $250,000 for the offense, and in June 1991 the Plaza was fined $200,000 for the same practice. In October 1991 the commission permanently barred the customer from any of the casinos because of his alleged mob association. According to the Newark, N.J., *Star-Ledger*, the customer is "an allegedly foul-mouthed high roller with reputed mob connections." The customer denied the charges of mob association and the casinos are appealing the commission's fines.

Elsewhere, Gold'n Plump Poultry, a poultry processor based in St. Cloud, Minn., sued the U.S. government in late 1992, alleging that a government food inspector had sexually harassed eight female employees at the company's Cold

Springs, Minn., plant. The suit alleges that Gold'n Plump Poultry notified the U.S. Department of Agriculture of the harassment but the agency did not take appropriate action to remedy the situation. The suit asks the federal government to remove the inspector from the plant because EEOC guidelines state that employers can be held responsible for non-employees' sexual harassment of the company's employees.

In the suit, USDA food inspector Tim Mater was alleged to have sexually harassed eight employees during the previous two years. Despite Mater's admission of some of the complaints, and the company's complaint to USDA, the federal agency refused to remove him from the plant. Mater is alleged to have thrown chicken parts at one employee's chest, made sexual innuendoes and jokes, and propositioned one employee. He also is alleged to have visited several workers' homes at unusual times and to have called them at their homes. The suit asks that Mater be removed from the plant and that he not be assigned to any other facilities owned or operated by Gold'n Plump or its parent company, Jack Frost, Inc.

The complaint states that when employees complained to the company, the company investigated the charges and filed complaints with USDA. The company said that USDA took no action on the 1990 complaint until another complaint was filed in early 1992. It was then that Mater met with company management and USDA officials, admitted to some of the allegations, and subsequently took a one-week leave of absence. When the USDA told Gold'n Plump that Mater would be reinstated, the company filed the suit.

Steven W. Wilson of Briggs & Morgan, a Minneapolis-based law firm for Gold'n Plump, said the company had little choice but to file suit because EEOC's guidelines state that the employer may be responsible for the acts of non-employees with respect to sexual harassment of its employees if the employer knows of the conduct and fails to take corrective action.

Wilson said the complaints against Mater put the company in an unusual position since he was not a Gold'n Plump employee. At the same time, if it did not take action, the guidelines indicate that the company could be held liable for the alleged sexual harassment.

Assistant U.S. Attorney Robert Small said that the government's answer to the suit has not yet been filed, but that Mater has been removed from the plant and an investigation by USDA is pending.

Sexual Harassment As A Class Action Suit

Usually, sexual harassment cases are filed by an individual plaintiff, a small number of plaintiffs joined in one suit, or a small number of plaintiffs filing separate suits. For a woman, or several women, to be able to file a sexual harassment suit on behalf of a class of people—all the other women who were in the group subjected to harassment—is a new, interesting, and potentially explosive occurrence that could greatly expand the number of people entitled to damages and the dollar amounts awarded.

In 1992, a U.S. District Court in Minnesota granted women who work for a mining company the right to file a class action sexual harassment suit. The mining company, Eveleth Taconite of Cleveland, had argued that sexual harassment claims cannot be made on a class basis. It stated that reactions to profanity, pornography, or other potentially offensive material are highly individualized.

U.S. District Judge James M. Rosenbaum disagreed. He said the question "is not how an individual class member reacted, but whether a reasonable woman would find the work environment hostile." While class action suits have been used in racial or sexual discrimination cases, it is believed that this ruling allowing a sexual harassment class action suit is unprecedented.

This case covers all women who applied for or have been employed by Eveleth's mining operations since December 30,

1983, until the time of the trial. The plaintiffs allege sexual harassment ranging from open display of photos of nude women to sexually explicit graffiti and posters on the walls and in the lunchroom, lockers, desks, offices and elsewhere.

At the trial in May 1993, the federal judge ruled that Eveleth's mines are a hostile environment for all hourly women workers. Judge Richard H. Kyle in Minneapolis said the Duluth, Minn., company's mines are a "sexualized, male-oriented and anti-female atmosphere."

Since the company has now been found liable, the next step is for the court to decide damages for the one hundred to two hundred women who are part of the class action. Judge Kyle ruled that it is up to the plaintiffs to show that they were at least as affected as a "reasonable woman" by the harassment. In other discrimination cases, the burden of proof is on the company to show that it did not discriminate.

This case is important because sexual harassment cases are usually filed on behalf of individuals; the 1991 ruling that this could be tried as a class action was unique. Class action cases are considered somewhat difficult in sexual harassment cases because the nature of class action requires that the group of plaintiffs be "similarly situated," and it may be difficult to show that all the women in the workplace were similarly harmed by the misconduct.

Eveleth said no sexual harassment occurred at the plant and that it expects to prevail on appeal. Company representatives also said that any complaint of harassment is immediately investigated and corrected.

A court-appointed special master will recommend which of the class members are entitled to damages and how much they should receive. Paul C. Sprenger of the Washington and Minneapolis law firm Sprenger & Lang, which is representing the women, said the damages "could be multimillions." In addition, two of the women said they experienced post-traumatic stress syndrome because of the harassment, preventing them from working. They are seeking additional damages.

Workers Charge Ads Contribute To Hostile Work Environment

Eight female employees of Stroh Brewery sued the parent company in Detroit in May 1992, alleging sexual harassment and lack of job advancement. The suit asked for compensation in the six figures and for Stroh to drop sexist advertising. While such allegations of harassment are not unusual for women working in traditionally male work environments, the suit against Stroh states that the company's media campaigns contribute to the alleged workplace harassment.

The employees alleged that the "conduct of Stroh is so extreme and outrageous that it passes the bounds of decency and is utterly intolerable in the civilized community." They also said that Stroh's produced "sexist, degrading promotion posters and advertisements."

The women said they were subjected to both verbal and physical confrontations by male coworkers and supervisors, causing them severe mental and physical distress. The women's attorney, Lori Peterson, said the company's advertising helped create a climate in which sexual harassment was more easily tolerated.

George Kuehn, senior vice president of Stroh, said that the company "for upward of ten years has maintained and enforced a definite policy against discrimination, including sexual harassment."

The lawsuits were filed against the company and several male employees and asked for compensatory damages in excess of $50,000 on nine to eleven causes of action.

The suit asks for Stroh to stop using women as sexual objects and that one series of television ads, featuring bikini-clad women known as the Swedish Bikini team, be discontinued. While initially the connection between the advertising campaign and sexual harassment in the workplace may not be clear or may appear trivial to some, consider what the women said occurs at work:

- One of thirty women among the three hundred thirty employees at the St. Paul Stroh Brewery Co. claims she has been subjected to a "barrage of sexual harassment, discrimination, and intimidation;" among her list of forty allegations of obscene and threatening behavior are charges that photos of nude, spread-eagled women were left in her work area and that obscenities were written about her on the bathroom wall.

- A former Stroh machinist, said male employees "grabbed her on the rear end" and that she was told, as a Native American, that "squaws are only good for one thing."

- A Stroh bottler claims she was called a "bitch" and "a dumb Mexican spic."

- Another bottler, alleges that a male employee "displayed his pubic hair and grabbed my head and pushed it down to his crotch."

Stroh denies allegations of sexual harassment and says there is no connection between ads and workplace behavior. A company representative said the company has a "very definite and strong policy" against sexual harassment and that the company has "maintained and enforced" this policy for more than ten years.

Lori Peterson, the Minneapolis attorney who represents the women, disagreed with Stroh's statement. "You can't tell me a company is interested in ending sexism in its plants when it spends millions of dollars a year promoting it," she said. "When the women first came to me telling me how powerless, sick and devastated the harassment made them feel, I asked to see what they said was on all the walls."

In response, Peterson said, the women brought in material that Stroh has produced: posters of women in baseball and football uniforms cut to the navel with breasts exposed, and ads showing rear views of women in bikinis that read, "Why the average beer commercial has more cans that bottles."

According to the attorney, Stroh has stopped the bikini ads and offered a cash settlement to the women, but they turned the offer down because it did not deal with the company's overall campaign and did not offer sexual harassment training and education for supervisors. "It would be derelict to only take money and leave women to work in a hostile environment that shows no signs of change" Peterson said.

According to Ellen Bravo, co-director of the Milwaukee branch of 9 to 5, the National Association of Working Women, challenging an advertising campaign is important because "it says that corporate culture and image help shape the behavior of people who work there." Bravo, who has counseled women on sexual harassment for the past twenty years, said that after the Hill–Thomas controversy, 9 to 5 received more than two thousand phone calls from women with stories of harassment. Bravo added that "using women to sell products cheapens the work done by competent, hard-working women who are just as much in need of a job as men."

Marlene Sanders, a former television network correspondent and author of *Waiting for Prime Time: The Women of Television News*, said the commercial exploitation of women adds a "sexual component to women in the workplace. If men believe these ads, they will treat women as sexual objects rather than as coworkers." Sanders teaches journalism at New York University and is director of Women, Men and Media, a non-profit organization that monitors women's media images.

Almarie Wagner, senior vice president for administration and development at the Metropolitan Chicago YMCA, said the attitude of top management "reflects all the way down the line. Advertisements that appear to support looking at women as something less than equal subtly sanction direct bias."

1991 U.S. Civil Rights Act Expands Boundaries

According to experts at a recent seminar in Washington, D.C., jury trials and increased damages (which are now allowed under the Civil Rights Act of 1991) for intentional sex, religion, and disability bias will change civil rights enforcement and de-emphasize the role of EEOC.

One speaker, Jeff Norris, a partner in the Washington, D.C., firm of McGuinnis and Williams, said the act's significant changes in terms of damages "turns on its head" the prior law's philosophy of restorative, make-whole relief for victims. Norris said the basic shift to remedies for pain and suffering will have serious consequences for employers regarding the costs of litigation. Other experts believe the act also will mean increased responsibilities for human resource managers.

Experts at the conference also said that the settlement value of cases will change and that EEOC's role will be diminished. EEOC Vice Chairman Ricky Silberman said that the expansion of remedies to include compensatory and punitive damages is "without a doubt" the act's most important provision and that it will make a "cataclysmic change" in how the law is enforced. Silberman said that EEOC will still handle "more marginal" cases, but that the better cases will bypass the agency—even though caps currently exist on the amount of damages allowed and on attorneys' fees.

Most believe the publicity over Judge Thomas' confirmation to the Supreme Court, plus the subsequent enactment of the 1991 act, will greatly increase lawsuits related to sexual harassment. Even with caps in place, some claim that small firms may find the awards so potentially costly that they may be forced to settle out of court. Only firms with fewer than fifteen employees are exempt. The caps are: $50,000 for firms with up to one hundred employees; $100,000 for businesses with more than one hundred; and $300,000 for companies with more than three hundred employees.

Two bills currently are pending to amend the caps on damages—a proposal by Sen. Edward Kennedy (D-Mass) to lift the caps altogether (S 2062) and a bill introduced by Sen. Orrin Hatch (R-Utah) to eliminate all but a cap of $50,000 against employers with fewer than fifty employees (S 2053). Congress is expected to act quickly on the caps issue, and many predict the caps will be lifted since there is little support in the Senate for treating women differently from other protected groups.

The 1991 Civil Rights Act expanded the remedies available to plaintiffs under U.S. federal civil rights law and allowed for employees to have jury trials, which many believe will tend to increase damage awards. Because of these changes, some plaintiffs' attorneys have tried to have the law applied retroactively to cases that were pending around the time it was enacted, and to conduct that occurred before the law's enactment.

Most courts have ruled that the "substantive" parts of the law—those allowing for punitive damages for pain and suffering—will not be applied to facts which occurred before the law was passed. A few courts have held that the "procedural" parts of the law—jury trials, expert witness fees—can be applied retroactively.

So far, the U.S. Court of Appeals for the Fifth, Sixth, Seventh, Eighth, Eleventh and the District of Columbia circuits have refused to retroactively apply the law. The Ninth Circuit in San Francisco, however, has applied the law retroactively, as well as some courts in New York, Pennsylvania, Puerto Rico, and Virginia. The Supreme Court has refused to rule on the issue twice.

In the Tenth Circuit, which includes Colorado, Kansas, Oklahoma, New Mexico, and Utah, the circuit court has not issued a ruling, but trial courts in Kansas and Colorado have said that the act should not be applied retroactively.

Since each appeals court that has ruled on retroactivity has only ruled on a portion of the Civil Rights Act, some district courts have continued to interpret portions as allowing for some retroactivity. Thus some plaintiffs' attorneys have continued to argue for retroactivity for their clients' cases. In one case, a judge in the U.S. District Court for the Western District of Missouri ruled that in some cases plaintiffs would be entitled to jury trials on particular issues; all the trial judges in that district ruled that plaintiffs are not entitled to the expanded damages section of the act.

The U.S. Supreme Court has said it will resolve the conflict, but most estimate it will be close to a year before a ruling is forthcoming.

Several courts have ruled that the act is not retroactive in its coverage. The U. S. Court of Appeals at New Orleans joined three other federal appeals courts and the EEOC in ruling that the act cannot be applied retroactively to cases pending when the law was signed. The case involved a class action suit alleging on-the-job race bias (brought under Section 1981 of the Reconstruction-era Civil Rights Act) that had been in the courts for eighteen years and had been dismissed (*Johnson v. Uncle Ben's*).

In an earlier case, *Patterson v. McLean Credit Union*, the Supreme Court ruled in 1989 that Section 1981 does not extend to an employer's post-hiring conduct. The 1991 Civil Rights Act, however, overturned the *Patterson* decision, saying Section 1981 covers all aspects of the contractual employment relationship. As a result, employees in *Uncle Ben's* said the 1991 act should be applied.

The appeals court said that the new law is "deliberately ambiguous" and that the holdings of the Sixth, Seventh, and Eighth Circuits are persuasive. The court said that even though *Patterson* was not in effect at the time of the alleged bias, it—and not the 1991 act—should be applied.

Court Rules Students Can Sue Schools

On February 26, 1992, the U.S. Supreme Court, in only its second ruling on sexual harassment, said sexually harassed students may sue schools and school officials for damages and monetary compensation. (In the first Supreme Court ruling on sexual harassment, the 1986 case *Meritor Savings Bank v. Vinson*, the court validated the concept of *hostile work environment* sexual harassment.)

The Supreme Court said Congress intended to let students

try for monetary damages and compensation when it passed Title IX of the Education Amendments of 1972. Title IX bars sexual bias in educational programs that receive federal funding, thus affecting nearly all educational institutions. Lower courts had ruled that Title IX did not allow alleged victims of intentional sex discrimination and/or harassment to sue for monetary damages, but only allowed for seeking "injunctive relief" or halting an illegal practice.

Justice Byron White, in writing for the court, said the earlier rulings, by a federal judge and the 11th U.S. Circuit Court of Appeals, were wrong, and he rejected the Bush administration's contention that Title IX remedies should be limited to back pay and injunctive help. Justice White said: "The equitable remedies suggested by ... the federal government are clearly inadequate ... A damages remedy is available to an action brought to enforce Title IX."

This ruling does not affect sexual harassment lawsuits by teachers, since they are employees. Congress gave employees who allege sexual harassment in the workplace the right to sue for monetary damages under the Civil Rights Act of 1991.

Marcia Greenberger, president of the National Women's Law Center, said the ruling is "a major victory for women" that would "heighten the sensitivity of school officials to what's going on ... We're relieved, especially since the Bush administration had taken the view that no damages were available. This is a major rebuke of the administration's contention. This decision is going to make a big difference."

The court's decision was a victory for Christine Franklin, a former Gwinnett County, Ga., high school student who sued over her alleged sexual encounters with a teacher who, she said, pursued her ardently. The lower courts had thrown out her federal lawsuit, but now must consider the case again.

Franklin's 1988 lawsuit alleged that Andrew Hill, her ninth-grade economics teacher at North Gwinnett High School, began harassing her by initiating sexually suggestive conversations. During her sophomore year, Franklin and Hill allegedly had sexual intercourse on three occasions. At the end of that school year, Hill resigned his teaching position.

Hill is not named in the federal suit, but is the subject of an $11 million civil action filed by Franklin's mother. That suit is pending in Gwinnett County Superior Court. Franklin graduated in 1989 and is now married and living in the Atlanta area.

The Supreme Court's hearing of this case attracted attention because it was the first involving alleged sexual harassment to reach the court since Clarence Thomas became a justice. His confirmation hearings included allegations by Professor Anita Hill that Thomas sexually harassed her while she worked for him at the Education Department and the Equal Employment Opportunity Commission.

Chief Justice William Rehnquist and Justices Antonin Scalia and Thomas did not sign Justice White's opinion. However, in a separate opinion by Scalia, the three said it is "too late in the day to address whether a judicially implied exclusion of damages under Title IX is appropriate" because of laws Congress passed after the 1972 law.

Supreme Court Defines Sexual Harassment

In a swift and unanimous ruling on November 9, 1993, the U.S. Supreme Court issued a broad definition of sexual harassment in the workplace that will enable employees to win suits without having to prove that the harassment caused psychological harm or left them unable to do their jobs.

In the opinion, issued by Justice Sandra Day O'Connor, the court rejected a standard adopted by several lower federal courts that required plaintiffs to show that sexual harassment made their workplace environment so hostile as to cause them "severe psychological injury."

Psychological harm is one factor among many that courts may consider in sexual harassment cases, O'Connor said. But the protection of federal law "comes into play before the harassing conduct leads to a nervous breakdown," she said.

The decision reaffirmed and broadened the court's 1986 ruling in the *Meritor Savings* case. Citing the "broad rule of workplace equality" inherent in the federal Title VII law against job discrimination, O'Connor said the law as applied to sexual harassment was violated when, for any of a variety of reasons, "the environment would be reasonably perceived, and is perceived, as hostile or abusive ... no single factor is required."

The court issued the ruling only twenty-seven days after the case was argued before the justices. *USA Today* reported that the "remarkably quick decision was devoid of rancor, footnotes and excess verbiage. The ruling ran a mere six print-ed pages. The court hasn't routinely written a decision that short for sixty years."

Patricia Ireland, president of the National Organization for Women, said: "That they were so quick and so decisive all across the spectrum sends a very strong message."

The case, *Harris v. Forklift Systems Inc.*, involved sexual harassment allegations made by a manager at a forklift sales firm in Nashville, Tenn., against the firm's owner. The case raised the question of whether repeated sexist comments and vulgar jokes constitute sexual harassment, or whether a per-son must suffer "severe psychological injury" in order to win a suit.

The manager, Teresa Harris, alleged she was harassed by owner Charles Hardy almost from the day she started in 1985. Harris alleged that Hardy repeatedly made dirty jokes and comments such as: "You're a woman. What do you know?" ... "We need a man as rental manager" ... [and] "Let's go to the Holiday Inn to negotiate your raise."

Harris also said Hardy would drop objects and ask her and other women to pick them up, commenting on their cleav-age. Hardy also asked Harris to retrieve coins from his front pants pocket.

After two years of working for Hardy, Harris said she was depressed and drinking as a result of the sexual abuse. She quit in 1987 and filed the suit.

Stanley Chernau, the attorney representing Forklift, said the remarks should be taken in context: "This is not a flower shop. They bought and sold forklifts. Other women at the office testified that they knew the owner was joking, that they weren't offended, and that the woman did not appear offended either."

Forklift said a business dispute between Hardy and Harris's husband was the motivation behind the suit. Testimony showed that Harris often drank beer and swapped dirty jokes and off-color language with male coworkers after work.

Two federal courts sided with the company, ruling that Hardy's conduct was not "so severe as to be expected to seriously affect" Harris's psychological well being.

Women's rights groups responded that it should be enough that a reasonable person is offended. Others oppose such claims, saying companies shouldn't be sued every time a hypersensitive employee hears a tasteless comment. Attorney Barbara Berish Brown said: "It'd be ridiculous to have all types of personal conflict and taste aired in the courtroom."

The Supreme Court said it was wrong for lower courts to focus on Harris's psychological well being. In her opinion, Justice O'Connor used the phrase "reasonable person"and listed factors that constitute illegal harassment. Among them: the frequency of the conduct, its severity, whether the conduct is physically threatening or humiliating, and whether it "unreasonably interferes with an employee's work performance."

Behavior not covered, O'Connor wrote, includes "conduct that is not severe or pervasive enough to create an objectively hostile or abusive work environment—an environment that a reasonable person would find hostile or abusive." O'Connor acknowledged that the definition of sexual harassment "by its nature cannot be a mathematically precise test." Courts should consider all factors in determining whether a work environment is hostile.

In response to the ruling, Harris, now a nurse in Nashville, said she is glad the "focus now is on the harasser rather than the victim." A lower court must examine the ruling and decide how much back pay, if any, Harris is entitled to.

Same-Sex Sexual Harassment

A San Mateo, California, man who said he suffered unwanted sexual advances from his male supervisor filed a $1 million sexual harassment suit in March 1992. His attorney, Paul Wotman, said, "Same-sex harassment is prohibited by law just like opposite-sex sexual harassment." The male employee filed suit against his employer, Social Vocational Services, and his former supervisor.

The male employee claimed that starting in August 1991 his supervisor began making sexual comments to him, and on one occasion invited him and two other workers to his house for drinks. During this invitation the supervisor "added that the male employee would have to lay by the pool naked," the suit stated.

In September, the supervisor allegedly asked the subordinate to go with him for a drive, then grabbed him and tried to kiss him. After the encounter, the man complained to the Social Vocational Services director, who also was the supervisor's roommate. According to the suit, the supervisor received two weeks paid vacation as a result and the male victim got an undesirable transfer.

Sexual Harassment by a Subordinate

A federal district court ruled in March 1993 that sexual harassment of a female manager by her subordinate can violate Title VII of the Civil Rights Act of 1964. The alleged harassment

included the subordinate employee's "threatening and belli-
cose conduct related to" gender that was "derogatory and
insulting to women generally" and "overtly demeaning" to her
personally, the court said.

The case involved a female cashier who was promoted to
manager of a convenience store a few days after being hired.
Afterwards, the male assistant manager continually interfered
with her job, abused her verbally, and made sexual advances.
He often called her a "dumb, stupid old woman."

The manager fired the man after he attempted to physically assault her in the parking lot. However, the general manager of the store overruled the manager and transferred the
assistant to another store instead.

After three weeks, the female manager was told that the
assistant would be returning to her store. She quit and filed
suit, alleging constructive discharge—that she was forced to
quit because of a sexually hostile work environment. The
employer claimed that Title VII does not apply to sexual
harassment by a subordinate.

In its ruling, the court explained that unlike *quid pro quo*
harassment, where the harassment is directly linked to job-
related opportunities, hostile work environment harassment
"concerns conduct that creates a hostile, offensive, abusive
work environment," and such conduct "can be the product of
a supervisor harassing a subordinate, a subordinate harassing
a supervisor, or of harassment between two equal co-employ-
ees." While the job status of the subordinate employee is relevant, the court said it "does not preclude the court from finding that the manager was a victim of sexual harassment."

Male Victims of Harassment

The Federal District Court in Rhode Island upheld charges of
sexual harassment brought by two men in late 1991. The male
employees claimed that their plant manager forced them to

engage in sexual acts with his secretary by threatening them with job loss if they refused.

The men said they were threatened with loss of their jobs, loss of their medical benefits, and with blackballing by the jewelry industry in which they worked if they did not participate in and watch sexual activity between the plant manager and his secretary. The sexual acts occurred during working hours and on overtime during the course of several months before the two men, one on physical disability, left their jobs.

The men said they did not complain to management because the company had no procedure for handling complaints of sexual harassment. Both men filed suit, charging sex bias under Title VII.

The district court stated that "this is the quintessential *quid pro quo* case" of sexual harassment (where sexual favors or activity is required in return for job benefits) and ruled that it was a violation of the prohibitions against sex bias under Title VII. Further, the court said that the law "protects both males and females from sexual harassment" and that the harassment in this case "drastically altered" the terms or conditions of employment and "created a hostile and abusive work environment."

The plant manager and the plant's parent company were ordered to pay back wages plus eight percent interest to the two men. The company also was ordered to designate an officer to handle complaints of sexual harassment and to include a description of the complaint procedure in the company's employee handbook.

Man Wins $1 Million

In June 1993 a Los Angeles County Superior Court jury awarded $1 million to a man who said he was sexually harassed daily by his supervisor, the female chief financial officer of Cal-Spas. The jury ordered Cal-Spas to pay the man $375,000 for his emotional distress, $82,000 for economic losses, and $550,000 in punitive damages. The alleged harasser, his female supervisor, was ordered to pay $10,000 in damages.

The male employee said the harassment began shortly after he started working at the company in 1986 and continued until 1988 when he had sex with his female supervisor at his home. He said he submitted to her sexual request out of fear for his job. He also said that his supervisor would kiss him on the lips, fondle his genitals, demand sex, and subject him daily to unwanted sexual attention. The man said his boss became angry when he announced his engagement to another woman, and from then on his job became intolerable.

His supervisor threatened to get revenge for his becoming engaged, the man said. She had his office torn down and stripped him of his managerial duties.

At the trial, the man's lawyer, Gloria Allred of Los Angeles, produced witnesses who corroborated details of his story. The ten-woman, two-man jury apparently found him more believable than his supervisor and awarded damages. Allred said, "The message is that this country is not about justice for some, but about justice for all ... and that includes men."

Whistle-Blower Awarded $1.3 Million

A former manager for Sentry Insurance Co. was awarded $1.34 million by the California Supreme Court in mid-1992 for being ridiculed, harassed, and finally fired for backing up a coworker's sexual harassment claim. The decision should help managers and other workers who are fired in retaliation for supporting their coworkers in complaints of sexual harassment or discrimination.

The Wisconsin-based Sentry Insurance Company had tried to overturn the jury award, claiming that the manager could only file a worker's compensation claim, which offers very limited damages. The court, in a unanimous decision, said that the manager could sue Sentry for monetary damages because his firing violated public policy. The court also said that Sentry officials had wrongfully pressured the man to not cooperate with the state Department of Fair Employment and Housing's investigation into the sexual harassment complaint.

The case began in 1980 when a Sentry employee who was a liaison officer between the Walnut Creek and the Sacramento offices complained to the manager that a sales manager in Walnut Creek was touching her and taunting her by putting his hands down his pants. The manager reported the complaint to his supervisor, but nothing was done. The sexual harassment continued for a year until the alleged harasser was demoted to sales representative.

At a meeting soon after the man's demotion, the manager's supervisor ridiculed him for supporting the female employee and ordered that the woman be fired. A month later, the manager's supervisor resigned, also after an investigation into sexual harassment claims against him.

Meanwhile, Sentry supervisors threatened to fire the manager, his coworkers accused him of disloyalty, and the in-house attorney pressured him not to cooperate with state investigators looking into the woman's claim. In March 1983, one day after the manager was presented with a life insurance sales award, he was demoted from office manager to sales representative. He left Sentry for another job one month later.

In 1986 a jury awarded the manager $1.34 million for Sentry's wrongful firing and a state Court of Appeals upheld the verdict. Sentry appealed, and subsequently the Supreme Court upheld the original award.

Harassment for Eight Years

The Michigan appeals court ruled in May 1992 that a woman's discrimination suit is not time barred, because the eight years of religious and sexual harassment she endured constituted an ongoing violation of the law. The woman claimed that she was repeatedly harassed during the years by several different supervisors because she is female and Jewish. The woman claimed that her first supervisor said he did not want a woman working for him and that he gave her a derogatory cartoon that her coworkers had drawn. Her next supervisor told the woman she did not need to make a lot of money because, "like all Jews," she was wealthy. Her third and last supervisor called her a Jewish-American princess, "chubbly" (meaning both chubby and ugly), and told her to put away her purse and wear pants and shoes "like the other guys." She sued her employer and her last supervisor under state civil rights law after she was fired, but the trial court dismissed the suit as untimely.

However, the appeals court said that all of the claimed harassment involved the same subject matters—gender and religion—and occurred with nearly every new supervisor. The court said that it was "reasonable" for the woman to believe "that with each transfer and change in supervision the discriminatory conduct would cease. However, with almost each new supervisor came a new "wave of harassment." The court ruled that the conduct was sufficiently related to constitute a pattern and thus avoid the law's limitations period.

Appeals Court Denies Countersuit

The Arizona Court of Appeals strengthened sanctions against sexual harassment in a December 1992 decision. The court discounted a man's claim that a sexual harassment charge filed against him had damaged his professional reputation and caused him to be demoted and transferred. Judge Maurice Portley wrote for the court that "workers should be free to report alleged sexual harassment without fear of liability ... ."

A female employee of Servicemaster by Rees, a Phoenix-based franchise of the national custodial company, complained of sexual harassment to her supervisor after an employee at a Salt River Project office grabbed her ankle while she was cleaning his office. She said his behavior made her feel "uncomfortable."

After her complaint was forwarded by her supervisor to the alleged harasser's company, an investigation was conducted and the man admitted touching her. However, he said that the touching was "misperceived" and that he grabbed her leg to keep her from tripping over an open file cabinet drawer. He was demoted and transferred shortly after the investigation. After his transfer, the man filed suit in Maricopa County Superior Court, saying that the sexual harassment report was defamatory and that it damaged his relationship with SRP.

The court of appeals upheld the lower court's decision that the man's complaint was without merit and that he did not present evidence that the woman's allegations were untrue. The court said he only tried to show that the admitted behaviors had been "misperceived." Further, the court ruled, he did not show that the woman's report was characterized by malice, reckless disregard of the truth, or excessive reporting (three elements in defamation).

The man's allegation that the complaint damaged his relationship with SRP also was denied. The court held that the evidence did not show the woman's claim was improper or that she was "improperly" motivated to make the complaint.

Cynthia Cheney, the woman's attorney, said the decision reinforces an employee's right to report sexual harassment as well as an employer's responsibility to take appropriate action. "The decision will encourage workers to come forward and it will allow the employer to do the right thing without being handcuffed by collateral litigation," she said.

The female employee had contended that her interpretation of the incident was a "protected opinion" and an absolute defense. Cheney said, "Regardless of how [the man] meant it [the touching], what counts is how [she] perceived it. And she perceived it as fooling with her."

Expert Witness Testimony

The U.S. Court of Appeals in Chicago ruled that an expert's testimony may be key to a Title VII sexual harassment action, even when the witness has no direct knowledge about the parties in the case.

In the case, a female coal miner said she was coerced into having an affair by her supervisor, who threatened to fire her and inform her husband of her two previous affairs with miners. The supervisor admitted to having affairs with this woman and nine other women who worked for him, but claimed the affairs were consensual.

The female employee attempted suicide, then tried to return to work two months later but was unable to do so. On the advice of her doctor, she took indefinite sick leave. When she sued the employer for sexual harassment under Title VII, her employer claimed she was lying because she had not complained before of her supervisor's behavior.

The employee's expert witness testified that the majority of victims of non-consensual relationships do not file charges because they fear reprisal or loss of privacy. The district court found the employer liable and the employer appealed, challenging the use of an expert who had no knowledge of the case and who had not interviewed the parties involved.

The appeals court upheld the expert's testimony, saying: "Experts routinely offer general testimony on their field of expertise without knowledge of the case." Since the expert explicitly stated she had no knowledge of the case, the court added that it was not deceived and that the testimony of the witness was properly used to buttress the employee's claim.

Sexual Orientation Not Protected

According to a March 1992 ruling by the U.S. Court of Appeals in Atlanta, a homosexual who was harassed and assaulted by his coworkers has no remedy under Title VII of the Civil Rights Act of 1964. The man, who previously worked for the U.S. Postal Service, was taunted, ostracized, and physically beaten by coworkers who believed he was homosexual.

The employee worked as a mail handler at a bulk mail center in Detroit. A coworker decided that the man was gay and began to taunt him, resulting in a fight between the two. The taunting coworker was fired as a result of the fight, but then "what had begun as a one-man band expanded into a full orchestral assault of verbal abuse."

After enduring three years of taunts and graffiti, the mail handler sued under Title VII for sexual harassment. He said the postal service allowed a hostile work environment to exist because they knew of the harassment and did nothing to stop it. The district court dismissed the suit, saying sexual orientation discrimination is not protected under Title VII.

The appeals court in Atlanta ruled that "Title VII only punishes those employers who withhold such environments [i.e. those work environments free from denigrating comments, verbal abuse, and other tactics of manipulation] from employees based on certain proscribed criteria: race, color, sex, religion, or national origin." The court acknowledged that the facts were "compelling," but said that nevertheless, "homosexuality is not an impermissible criteria on which to discriminate with regard to terms and conditions of employment."

Former Employees Not Protected

The U.S. Court of Appeals in Richmond ruled that a woman claiming sex bias may not sue her former employer under Title VII for retaliation that occurred after she left her job, saying that the law does not protect former employees from retaliation by their ex-employers.

The woman brought a sex-bias suit against the National Institutes of Health after she left her job. She said that after leaving her job, her employer refused to give her credit for on-the-job training and slandered her professional competence as retaliation for filing the suit. Both claims were time barred because the women did not talk with an EEO counselor within the required thirty-day period.

The Richmond appeals court ruled that while most circuit courts have interpreted "employee" under Title VII to mean current employee, applicant for employment, and former employees, it found the reasoning of other courts to be unpersuasive. The clear language of the law "refers to employees and applicants for employment and does not mention former employees," the appeals court said, adding that the court is bound to follow the clear language of the statute. As a former employee, the woman's claim was rejected.

Franchisor is Not an Employer

The U.S. Court of Appeals in Denver ruled in January 1992 that the relationship of McDonald's Corporation to its franchisees is not sufficient to make it liable as an employer under Title VII. A former McDonald's restaurant manager alleged that she was sexually harassed by another employee and filed a complaint with EEOC. Not long after the filing of the complaint, the restaurant was sold back to the McDonald's Corporation by the franchise holder. McDonald's retained all of the existing employees except the complainant.

The woman then added a claim for retaliatory discharge to her EEOC charge and eventually filed suit under Title VII against the former franchisee, the coworker who allegedly harassed her, and the McDonald's Corporation. The district court dismissed the suit against McDonald's and the coworker, stating that neither was an "employer."

The appeals court upheld the district court ruling, saying that "under no plausible theory" is McDonald's the complainant's employer. "McDonald's may have stringently controlled the manner of its franchisee's operations, conducted frequent inspections, and provided training for franchise employees," the court acknowledged, but it did not have control over the franchisee's labor relations with its employees.

Taxing Back-Pay Awards

The U. S. Supreme Court ruled in May 1992 that back pay awards under Title VII are subject to federal income tax withholding. It is not clear if the ruling will apply to awards made after November 21, 1991.

In the original case, Therese A. Burke and several other women employees of the Tennessee Valley Authority won a pay discrimination award under Title VII from TVA, which withheld income tax on the payments. Last year, the Sixth Circuit Court of Appeals split with other appeals courts on the issue and ordered refunds of the withheld taxes. The circuit court held that the awards, while based on back pay, were nontaxable damages derived from personal injuries, i.e., tort-like damages which are exempted from gross income under the Internal Revenue Code.

The Supreme Court reversed that decision and resolved the conflict in the lower courts by ruling that Congress wrote Title VII to restore fully taxable wages to discrimination victims. The court said that while employment discrimination is "an invidious practice that causes grave harm to its victims," the law's remedies, as originally written, consist of restoring victims to the wage and employment positions they would have occupied had the discrimination not occurred (called "make-whole" remedies) and such wages are fully taxable. Nothing in the original law called for "any of the other traditional harms associated with personal injury, such as pain and suffering, emotional distress ... or other consequential damages," the court said.

In footnotes to its opinion, the court said that the 1991

Civil Rights Act amended Title VII to authorize the recovery of compensatory and punitive damages in certain circumstances. Congress's decision "signals a marked change in its conception of the injury redressable." Therefore, the decision may not apply to awards after November 1991.

Some experts predict that plaintiffs in discrimination cases may now demand bigger payments from employers to offset taxes withheld.

Woman Wins $1 Million

A jury in Calhoun County, Alabama, returned a verdict for a female employee against Big B Drugs, awarding her $1 million for her sexual harassment suit. The woman said a store official threatened to prosecute her for shoplifting unless she performed oral sex on him.

The woman said that in December 1989, the store's assistant manager told her he would charge her with shoplifting that an acquaintance of his had committed unless she agreed to sexual behavior. She said she complied with his demands.

The man was fired later that month after pleading guilty to a sexual misconduct charge. He also had been investigated two months earlier by his employer for a sexual harassment complaint by another employee. The company had said it was not responsible for the man's harassment because he was acting outside his authority as an assistant manager.

Court Upholds $710,000 Verdict

In May 1992, a federal court in Kansas upheld a jury verdict for emotional distress caused by sexual harassment and approved the jury's award of $710,000.

In the case, the supervisor constantly criticized his female subordinate's work performance after she rejected his sexual advances. He ranted, screamed, and cursed, threw pencils, files, his glasses, and the telephone, and touched the woman in sexually offensive ways. The woman suffered numerous physical problems, including hives. The employer argued that the man's behavior was not extreme and outrageous and that the company should not be held liable for his behavior.

The court ruled that the ongoing, daily pattern of abusive behavior surpassed the threshold standards for a claim of outrage, and upheld the damage award. The court also ruled that the employer knew or should have known that the supervisor's behavior would cause severe emotional distress.

$625,000 Damage Award Upheld

In March 1992 the Supreme Court upheld a $625,000 damage settlement in a sexual harassment suit brought by an Oregon woman. The woman, Connie Dias, had been fired from Sky Chefs, Inc., after she complained of sexual harassment by the plant manager. Dias alleged that the manager made frequent comments about female employees' appearances, required that they wear dresses and heels, and urged them to show him "a good time."

Because the jury was composed of six women, the company appealed the damages award, arguing that the plaintiff's lawyers had used challenges to eliminate the only three men who were in the jury pool. The court said that if the company had an objection to the jury, it should have said so when it was chosen, not later in the process.

New Interest in Harassment

According to a report on USC radio's "Market Place," many companies have implemented policies regarding sexual harassment after the public attention generated last year by the Thomas–Hill case. But analysts say those changes were too late to address many cases of sexual harassment incidents that had already occurred. An increasing number of complaints are now being filed with the Equal Employment Opportunity Commission and the courts.

Miley Houlihan, editor of *Treasury Magazine*, a publication distributed to 46,000 senior financial executives, said that some people now believe that American companies could be paying a billion dollars or more in the next five years for sexual harassment suits. Houlihan said the social, legal, and judicial climates have all changed, and "we think there's going to be an explosion in successfully litigated sexual harassment cases."

The social situation changed with the accusations by Anita Hill, and many women now feel empowered to file complaints—EEOC's complaints are up 23 percent since the Hill complaint, Houlihan said. Changes in the 1991 Civil Rights Act, allowing for jury trials and compensatory and punitive damages, and the potential for sexual harassment cases to become class action suits rather than individual actions, also are likely to have an impact.

Bonding Firm Guilty of Harassment

A woman trying to get her husband out of jail in October 1992 said the bondsman began to praise her breasts and describe sex-for-bail deals. "I was just in a trapped position because I felt really dependent on him. He was very vulgar, very graphic, in front of my eleven-year-old daughter," she said.

A panel of circuit court judges believed her story and ordered the Statewide Bonding Company of Bluffdale, Utah, to close for ten days, including the July 4th weekend. The judges also ordered the man, a partner in the bonding business, to arrange sexual harassment sensitivity training for himself, his managers, and his employees.

In their opinion, the judges wrote: "[The woman] was in

an extremely vulnerable and disadvantaged position and should not have been subjected to the conduct of [the man], who was clearly out of line."

The man appealed, saying the sexual harassment charge was a plot to get out of paying fees to his company. He claims he only mentioned to the woman that accused prostitutes sometimes call his company and offer sexual favors to get out of jail. "I wasn't making a sexual comment," he said.

The judges also criticized the company's financial dealings, saying money was improperly taken from a man for a bond that was never posted.

The company kept the woman's truck and new thirty-seven-foot trailer, both of which were left as collateral for bonds posted for the woman and her husband, who had been jailed on theft charges. The judges said the property should be returned immediately.

Male Supremacy Author Sued

A former typist at Andy Kane Realty Corp. filed suit in Webster, New York, against a male supervisor for allegedly engaging in "outrageous and bizarre acts," including unwanted touching of her breasts. In her lawsuit, she said she was given an employee handbook written by the man titled "Mastering the Art of Male Supremacy."

The book offers tips to men on how to keep a wife in line: "I don't condone violence—maybe a rolled up newspaper on the rump once in awhile—but no real violence. Besides violence is not the best way. It only worked for the cavemen because there were no alternate methods back in those days," the book states.

According to the woman, the man also used foul and abusive language in her presence, saying such things as "sexatary" and telling her not to be a crybaby when she complained about his behavior. He also gave her a halter top and told her that if she'd wear it to work he would pay her $1 a day.

He denied the allegations, saying the woman is a disgruntled employee who was fired after eleven weeks on the job. "This broad's a nut," he said. "If someone was being sexually harassed, would they stay eleven weeks on the job?"

The suit asks for $3.5 million—$1.5 million for compensatory damages and $2 million for punitive damages. Also named as a co-defendant in the suit is the office manager at another business owned by the book's author. "[This man] also made numerous advances, conducted himself in such a manner as to intimidate the plaintiff by sexual innuendo, and did certain outrageous acts in a sexual manner, including, but not limited to, entering the ladies room at the place of employment," the claim stated.

Offensive But Not Illegal Behavior

A federal district court in New York ruled in June 1992 that workplace incidents such as engaging strippers at company-sponsored social functions and the appearance of a woman on a motorcycle during a sales meeting were "inappropriate" and contributed "to creating a sexually hostile work environment." However, the court ruled that such inappropriate incidents were not sufficiently severe or pervasive enough to constitute a violation of Title VII of the Civil Rights Act of 1964.

A female employee had been offered another job in her office or a similar job in another state when her company was reorganized. She was not happy with either offer and started looking for another job. After finding another job, she complained in her resignation letter about too much drinking and misbehavior at company business meetings, but she did not claim sexual harassment. Later she filed a hostile environment suit under Title VII, stating a number of incidents, including the presentation of sexually suggestive gifts and the showing of a slide of her backside at a company retreat. She said the slide incident caused her constructive discharge.

The court rejected her claim and ruled that the employee attempted to "link isolated incidents of alleged sexual harassment" that occurred during her seven and a half years of employment to her resignation. While the incidents were "wholly inappropriate," the court said they did not alter the conditions of the woman's employment, nor were they severe enough to constitute a hostile work environment. The court also held that the woman would have resigned regardless of whether or not the incidents had occurred.

Individual States' Actions

In addition to the federal and state court decisions, a number of states have taken action on their own to combat the problem of sexual harassment. Their efforts include information-gathering task forces, public hearings and requirements for employee training—even requirements for sub-contractors or bidders to develop policy statements.

California

As of January 1, 1993, all California employers with one or more employees are required to provide each employee with a sexual harassment information sheet and to post a notice about sexual harassment. The agency responsible for compliance, the California Department of Fair Employment and Housing (DFEH), is required by the new law to provide employers with both the information sheet and the notice for posting. However, employers also have the option of creating their own information sheet.

Therese Shafer, President of Protocol VII, a consulting firm in Costa Mesa, California, said "Assembly Bill 2264 places the burden on employers to distribute the California State regulations regarding fair employment and sexual harassment and information on how to contact the Commission. This rule may appear to encourage employees to go outside the company to file a complaint.

"We encourage employers to ensure that their in-house sexual harassment policies include a firm complaint and grievance procedure, and that all employees know about and are encouraged to use these procedures as their primary and first source for resolution. Company support for the employees will go a long way toward preventing, stopping, and resolving this workplace problem and thus minimizing the company's liability," Shafer said.

Management consultant Marcia Haight of Pacific Palisades, California, tells employers that "compliance requirements seem simple: merely inform your employees of sexual harassment legalities and how they can make complaints. But the law is likely to generate more complaints. So you need to see that those complaints come to your organization first. And you need to prepare yourself to deal with complaints so they don't develop into lawsuits." Haight said suits have resulted in awards of up to several million dollars and that penalties are expected to increase. Penalties include make whole awards for the complainant—including front pay or back pay; reinstatement, hiring, or promotion; unlimited punitive and compensatory damages in California; and legal fees including court costs, costs of jury trials, and expert witness fees.

Both Shafer and Haight recommend that employers develop their own sexual harassment information sheet so they can include their own policy and complaint procedure; that they implement a workable sexual harassment complaint procedure; and that they provide training and education to each and every employee.

Connecticut Requires Sexual Harassment Training

Under a state law which took effect October 1, 1991, employers with fifty or more workers must provide sexual harassment training to supervisors. The law requires a minimum of two hours training on federal and state sexual harassment laws and the remedies available for violations. Current supervisors must complete their training within one year of the law's effective date; new supervisors must be trained within six months of being hired. Employers with three or more workers must post information about the illegality of sexual harassment in accessible and conspicuous locations.

Illinois Requires Bidders to Have Harassment Policies

The Illinois Human Rights Act was amended in April 1993 to require bidders and public contractors to have or develop written sexual harassment policies.

The new provision took effect July 1, 1993, and requires bidders or contractors to have a written policy stating (1) the illegality of sexual harassment; (2) a definition of sexual harassment under Illinois law; (3) a description of sexual harassment utilizing examples; (4) the vendor's internal complaint procedure including penalties for harassers; (5) the legal procedures, including those of the investigation and complaint process, provided by the Illinois Department of Human Rights and the Illinois Human Rights Commission; (6) instructions on how to contact the department and the commission; and (7) specific mention against retaliation for those complaining. Upon request, the policy must be provided to the Department of Human Rights.

According to attorney Michael R. Lied of Peoria, while many employers have written policies, very few have policies with the detail required by the amended act. He recommends that vendors wishing to do business with the state should act immediately and revise their policies.

New Jersey

In early 1993, New Jersey developed a Review Committee on

Sexual Harassment to hold public hearings and gather information and testimony from public employees who have experience with the state's current complaint process. The panel is looking at state government procedures on sexual harassment and asking for input from employees of state agencies, colleges, and authorities.

Eileen Shea Pazder, committee chairwoman said, "In order for the review committee to accomplish the objective of thoroughly evaluating the current sexual harassment complaint process, we're asking employees for input. We'd like employees of state agencies, authorities, and colleges to testify."

The panel was created by then-Governor Jim Florio through an executive order to establish a uniform, government-wide policy. A final report to the governor was due in mid-1993.

New York

Governor Mario Cuomo established the Governor's Task Force on Sexual Harassment in mid-1992, the first of its kind in the United States, to assess the extent to which this form of "unlawful discrimination continues to exist in both the public and private sectors of the state." The goals of the task force were to make policy recommendations designed to ensure effective resolution for victims, increase public understanding of sexual harassment and to find ways to eliminate it from the workplace. The task force was authorized to hold public forums for individuals to share their experiences and expertise on the issue and to educate the public.

In addition, a law and regulations subcommittee of the task force was designated to study devising standards for evaluating whether a hostile work environment exists; the effect of temporary restraining orders in sexual harassment cases; the problem of employer liability for defamation actions brought by employees fired for sexual harassment; and limits on discovery proceedings in sexual harassment cases similar to those in rape and sexual assault cases.

A training subcommittee was ordered to prepare information and materials to provide to small businesses, local governments, and other small organizations that lack the resources to develop their own programs. The task force also began working with the Office of Motion Picture and Television Production to organize industry professionals who would volunteer to create a video for school-age children on gender respect and sexual harassment.

In December 1992, Governor Cuomo released a preliminary report from the task force. The report listed critical issues identified by the employees, employers, advocacy groups, unions, lawyers, therapists and victims that spoke to the committee.

The report contains thirty-four recommendations on how to better prevent and stop sexual harassment in the state. According to Judith I. Avner, director of the State of New York Division for Women and a task force member, the public hearings and meetings held so far have demonstrated that sexual harassment is a serious problem in New York workplaces, and it has significant economic and personal costs to both individuals and employers.

Recommendations included in the report:

- The state, in partnership with the private sector, should conduct a public education campaign that enhances public understanding of the conduct that constitutes sexual harassment and provides information about how to prevent it.
- State law should be amended to require that all employers have a policy prohibiting sexual harassment, a process for resolving complaints, and an ongoing education and training program.
- State agencies should be required to adopt a uniform policy and complaint-resolution procedure.
- The State Legislature should have strong policies against

sexual harassment, effective complaint procedures and training programs for all members and employees.

- State law should be amended to grant attorney's fees to a prevailing plaintiff in a sexual harassment case.
- State law should be amended to prohibit discovery into and testimony about the plaintiff's prior sexual history.

In June 1993, Cuomo proposed a bill that would revamp the state's human rights law, adding a section called the "Sexual Harassment Prevention Act of 1993." The provision would declare sexual harassment an unlawful discriminatory practice and would give employers a role in combating and eliminating it. The bill requires legislative action, but is still worrisome to some in the business community who say it is just another government mandate.

However, Governor Cuomo, in conjunction with his task force, sees businesses as needing a push on the issue of sexual harassment. A memo accompanying the proposed bill said, "Because prevention is the best approach to sexual harassment in the workplace, and employers have not voluntarily addressed this need, legislation is necessary to require prevention efforts."

That viewpoint resulted from the more than thirty public hearings, regional meetings, and private interviews held around the state in 1992. According to the task force report, the sessions brought out "graphic and disturbing descriptions of the economic, physical and emotional impact of this illegal behavior on (victims), their families, their coworkers and their workplaces."

Since the report states, and the Governor believes, that prevention is a prime element in the elimination of sexual harassment, Cuomo's proposal outlines three specific steps employers should undertake:

1. Policy statements: the bill would require that businesses adopt a policy statement "to ensure a work environment

which is free from sexual harassment," with specific behaviors deemed unacceptable to be listed with a range of disciplinary actions that might be taken by the employer and/or by law.

2. Complaint processes: employers would be required to approve and maintain an internal complaint process that complies with due process to investigate and resolve claims of sexual harassment.

3. Dissemination: companies would be required to post their policies prominently at the workplace and to give a copy of the policy to each employee on an annual basis. Employees also would receive an outline of the complaint process and other avenues of complaint, such as New York's Human Rights Commission and the federal Equal Employment Opportunity Commission.

Wallace Altes, president of the Albany-Colonie Regional Chamber of Commerce, who also was a member of the task force, said, "Some of the stories (the task force heard) would make you sick." However, he predicted that many businesses, particularly small businesses, would come out against the bill, because of the growing resistance against any government mandate.

Marlene Kennedy, editor of the *Capital District Business Review* in Albany, said in the *Rochester Business Journal* that "although its specificity may seem burdensome to business, the Cuomo bill affords employers some protection, too: from allegations of spotty compliance by victims and claims of defamation by perpetrators. And given the time and money that could be spent defending against those charges, the bill might not be so onerous after all."

7

SEXUAL HARASSMENT IN U.S. INDUSTRIES

"I had sexual harassment on the job when I was 17, and when you ain't got no money, you'd be surprised what you put up with."

Cyndi Lauper,
*rock star and
recording artist*

I was sitting by myself, relaxing in the spa next to the hotel's outdoor pool, when two male fire fighters walked by. They stopped to talk for a minute and soon our discussion turned to the point of my being in California—that I was there to conduct sexual harassment training for the very fire department they worked for. One man asked serious questions about the program and the subject, while the second firefighter started to flirt with me. He made various comments about how I looked in my swimsuit, looked me over, and generally acted as if he were trying to pick me up at a bar.

I knew he would be in one of my training sessions, and I didn't want to alienate him before we even met in a session by confronting him about his behavior. So I tried the old method of turning the discussion back to business and totally ignoring his flirting comments—thinking all the while that I just couldn't believe he could be this dumb. I'm not saying that this was necessarily sexual harassment—but it was risky behavior that was out-of-line and inappropriate. The man's behavior was not OK with me or with the other firefighter.

Most of all I felt sorry for the other firefighter—he was

obviously very embarrassed and at a loss over what to do or say to his coworker. At one point his mouth actually fell open and he stared wide-eyed at his colleague. I hoped that afterwards he might have mentioned, when it was just the two of them together, his opinion that such comments were inappropriate, but it probably would have been to no avail. It's amazing how, where, and when incidents such as this occur, and I'm still, after all these years, surprised when they do.

All studies and surveys of sexual harassment during the last fifteen to twenty years have shown, though, that sexual harassment occurs in all age groups, salary ranges, job categories, and racial groups. In short, no one is immune from being a victim, or for that matter, from being a harasser. The evidence also shows that no area of business or industry, public or private, is immune either.

HARASSMENT IN HOLLYWOOD

At a symposium in the summer of 1992, Hollywood focused attention on one of its most difficult problems: the casting couch. The meeting was sponsored by the women's committees of the Screen Actors Guild and the Directors Guild of America, and was organized by actress Lisa Pelikan of "Return to the Blue Lagoon." Pelikan said many celebrities who were invited declined to attend the symposium because they did not want to be identified. "They all wanted to talk about it in private ... they were too scared to do it publicly," she said.

Among the stories told at the symposium was the experience of director Martha Coolidge from "Rambling Rose." Coolidge said when she was trying to break into Hollywood, a studio head ended a meeting in his office by grabbing her, mauling her and sticking his tongue down her throat. Gregory Harrison, the actor from "Trapper John, MD," said a casting director tried to get him to pick up scripts at her home, where she wanted him to join her in the jacuzzi. Actress Christine Lahti from "Leaving Normal" said that when beginning her career, a casting director urged her to sleep with some of his director friends to get roles in their television commercials.

Lahti said she made her story public because she wants to "encourage women and men who are sexually harassed to speak up and not accept it as a part of life. Although I don't get harassed much anymore, it does break my heart to see my fellow actresses on the set putting up with it, bearing that humiliation because they just don't feel they have the power to stop it."

Neither Coolidge, Harrison nor Lahti ever filed formal complaints. Symposium panelist Dr. Linda Durre, a clinical psychotherapist specializing in sexual harassment, said most victims of harassment don't. "You're afraid of either not being believed or accused of not being able to handle it, not being able to take a joke or accused of starting it," she said.

Rodney Mitchell, the affirmative action officer for the Screen Actors Guild, said people in show business also are "afraid they won't work again in this town and that they'll be placed on some list. Some of this (fear) is clearly real." Harrison said that when he rebuffed the advances of the casting director she blackballed him from seven series at the network where she worked, even though show producers wanted him on the series.

Those in show business can take their complaints to their talent or trade guilds or to the California Department of Fair Employment and Housing. The Screen Actors Guild has received many complaints, but most victims do not want their names used, which can prevent the Guild from taking action, Mitchell said. In such incidences, he said, "We just maintain a file on the alleged harasser."

Pelikan said that until now, sexual harassment in the entertainment industry has "been a dark secret." Many at the symposium felt that the meeting was an important first step in addressing this industry-wide problem.

THE RECORDING INDUSTRY

In 1992, Geffen Records agreed to pay a former secretary an estimated $500,000 in an out-of-court settlement of a sexual harassment case in West Hollywood. The settlement closed a legal action that had the entire record industry debating sexual harassment. The case involved alleged harassment by a Geffen executive.

Later, a second female employee told the *Los Angeles Times* that she plans to name other high-ranking officials at the record company in another suit, this one for $5 million, which will be filed later in Los Angeles Superior Court. The woman said the same man also harassed her verbally and physically during her employment from 1984 to 1990, and that on one occasion he allegedly unzipped his trousers and showed his penis.

She claimed that three top Geffen executives were told of the harassment, but they did nothing to stop it. "I personally told three top executives under David Geffen of the abuse and nothing was done about it. Obviously they did not take my complaints seriously. In order to maintain my self-esteem as a professional, I was forced to quit."

In the first suit, the woman alleged that the general manager of Geffen Records' DGC label had repeatedly harassed her, going so far as to masturbate at her desk and physically block her escape. She also claimed that Geffen officials had tolerated a long history of complaints by women about the man's "outrageously sexually deviant behavior," including the second woman who complained.

Geffen officials, who had initially issued a statement saying the man had resigned to spend more time with his family, later acknowledged that he was terminated as a result of an investigation into the allegations. They said at that time that they had no prior knowledge of the kinds of behaviors he allegedly engaged in with the woman.

Rock star Cyndi Lauper addressed a range of topics on her album released in 1993, "Hat Full of Stars," including incest, wife abuse, abortion, and racism. Lauper said she was troubled by the Republicans' emphasis on family values in the 1992 presidential election and that she sympathized with Anita Hill. "I've had sexual harassment on the job when I was 17, and when you ain't got no money, you'd be surprised what you put up with."

HARASSMENT ON CAPITOL HILL

According to a March 1993 survey by the *Washington Post*, women working on Capitol Hill say they routinely lose out on pay raises and promotions to male colleagues, and a third of the women questioned said they had been sexually harassed by coworkers, lobbyists, congressmen or senators.

Of those who said they had experienced harassment, one-third said the harassment was from a congressman or senator. Fifty-nine percent of all respondents said they or an aide they personally knew had been the victim of sexual harassment on the job. Six out of ten said not being taken as seriously as men was a problem. Nearly two out of three said unequal pay for equal work was a problem.

The survey was of 603 women and 200 men who worked for House and Senate members.

In the two years following the Thomas–Hill controversy, at least two major sexual harassment scandals involving U.S. Senators erupted. The first surrounded Brock Adams, a Democratic Senator from Washington state, and included allegations from at least eight women who chose to remain anonymous and one woman who went public with her claims. Of those allegations, perhaps the most serious were made by Kari Tupper, a young woman who said that as early as 1988 Adams had made improper sexual advances toward her after drugging her at his home.

To make the case even stranger, Senator Adams was long known as a leading advocate for women and feminist causes, including securing more money for breast cancer research, and pushing legislation that would tighten standards for mammography equipment and screening, help with infertility prevention, and increase the participation of women in clinical research trials.

Adams chose in 1992 to terminate his re-election campaign, saying he wanted to protect supporters and his family from further damage.

In 1992, the second major scandal, involving Bob Packwood, the Republican Senator from Oregon, came to light. Accusations were made by more than twenty women who alleged that Packwood made inappropriate sexual advances to them over a number of years, from 1969–1980, and then threatened several of them after they complained publicly in an effort to silence them.

Some people demanded that Packwood be removed from office for lying about his sexual conduct during the 1992 elections. The Senate Rules Committee rejected this effort. However, the Senate Ethics Committee is investigating the charges. Packwood, like Adams, also has been a leading proponent of women's issues.

One Man's Thoughts

In a January 1993 article in the *Detroit Free Press* titled "Washington is Crawling with Packwoods," journalist Joseph Sobran had some interesting thoughts on Washington's ongoing sexual scandals. Sobran said we need a Kinsey Report on Capitol Hill—a sort of statistical profile of sexual conduct among the "ruling class." But, he continued, part of the problem is that those on "the Hill" are less likely than the rest of us to tell the truth, so such a survey would be useless.

However, Sobran's most scathing remarks were about power and politics: "Let's face it: The system produces predators. These are men who survive the grueling Darwinian struggle to get into office in the first place, a struggle that weeds out most of the normal people, leaving the spoils to the truly power-hungry. The victors arrive with a strong sense of entitlement, which gets stronger in proportion as they feel immune from being ousted. They spend other people's money with abandon, handing out favors, running up multi-trillion-dollar debts, passing the burden along to taxpayers, and pausing only to dine with lobbyists and grab waitresses."

A Letter to Senator Packwood

Following is a letter by Ellen Bravo, National Director of 9 to 5, the National Association of Working Women. It originally appeared in the *Chicago Tribune* in March 1993.

Dear Sen. Bob Packwood (R-Ore.):

I was sorry to learn of allegations of sexual harassment against you. You've been a strong public supporter of women's rights.

And yet your conduct with women, as you now admit, conflicted greatly with this public image.

The 10 women who described your behavior did not easily speak up nor did they "come forward." Like Anita Hill, they were contacted for an investigation. Six others have joined them.

As someone who has spoken with hundreds of women (and some men) who have been sexually harassed, I was deeply disappointed in your response to the allegations.

First you said it didn't happen. "It's not in my nature," you claimed.

Then you said if anything did happen, it was the

fault of the women; they were after you, sexually delinquent, or simply liars. Your staff prepared memos designed to discredit several of them.

Apparently your advisers told you there were too many specifics for you to make a believable denial. So you offered an apology—except you didn't acknowledge doing anything wrong. You spoke of your intentions, not the content—or impact—of your behavior.

Your fourth attempt put the blame on alcohol. Only on the fifth try, after the Senate Ethics Committee investigation looked like a go, did you say the obvious: "What I did was wrong."

Thankfully, you realize trust is something which must be earned and, once broken, earned again.

And at least you haven't taken the tack of some commentators, who claim your behavior wasn't so bad. After all, they say, it wasn't rape. One even compared groping and forced kissing with "bad etiquette, like belching at the table or picking your nose."

Still, you've missed some important points. The alleged incidents weren't just wrong, they were violations of Title VII of the Civil Rights Act of 1964, which bars discrimination on the basis of sex. Members of the Senate are exempt from that law, however, surely the voters are right to hold you to its standard.

People's lives were changed by your misconduct. Women who otherwise would have stayed, left for other jobs. Their careers—in some cases their marriages—were disrupted.

Many must deal with the emotional consequences of your actions. You were, after all, a trusted and admired boss, they said.

You say that you "didn't get it" and now do.

You even say you'll get counseling on the issue of sexual harassment, if needed. Can you blame those who think you raised not your consciousness but your level of political manipulation by telling the public what you thought it wanted to hear. Can you re-earn public trust while on public pay?

We're glad you'll cooperate with the Ethics Committee's investigation, which should examine your response to the allegations as well as the incidents themselves. We hope you'll also accept that there should be consequences for your behavior.

Here are some things you can do immediately to begin to make amends:

- *Apologize to the women you tried to discredit.*
- *Apologize to voters for misleading them about newspaper inquiries on this topic prior to your re-election.*
- *Invite the women you harassed to meet with you. Let each speak as long as she needs to about the injury she sustained. Simply listen.*
- *Become a leader in the effort to remove congressional exemption from anti-discrimination laws.*
- *Advocate for sexual harassment awareness training for all senators and their staffs.*

Had you been honest about the allegations when they first surfaced, Sen. Packwood, and had taken the steps listed above, the voters of Oregon might have re-elected you anyway. Recent political history has taught us this—cover-up is almost as reprehensible as the original transgression.

Sincerely, Ellen Bravo.

Final Words on Packwood

In mid-1993, buttons went on sale in Oregon that were intended to be worn on a woman's lapel and had printed in very small type: "If you can read this, then you must be Bob Packwood." As the senator has continued to fight the allegations and subsequent Senate investigations, many people feel he should simply quit the fight, since he has lost effectiveness. But Packwood has not yielded.

In December 1993, twenty-four years' worth of Sen. Packwood's personal diaries were seized by Federal District Court Judge Thomas P. Jackson in Washington, D.C., after the judge was presented evidence that the senator had altered some of the entries in September and October, knowing at the time that Congress planned to subpoena the diaries. The Senate ethics committee had indeed issued a subpoena for the diaries on October 20 as part of its yearlong investigation, but Packwood had not turned over the material by the time Judge Jackson issued his order in December.

The ethics committee is investigating whether the tampering was an attempt by Sen. Packwood to obstruct its inquiry. Impeding a congressional investigation can be a federal felony punishable by up to five years in jail.

FIRE FIGHTERS AND POLICE

In December 1992, the San Francisco Fire Commission suspended a firefighter for sexual and racial harassment, an action taken for the first time in the commission's one hundred twenty-four-year history. A captain was found guilty of five charges of un-officelike conduct, and was suspended sixty days without pay—a penalty worth about ten thousand dollars. The captain, a twenty-two-year veteran of the department, also was ordered to attend sensitivity training before returning to work.

The commission made its decision after hearing three months of testimony. There was no corroboration of the allegations made by a black, female rookie firefighter.

The charges stemmed from the way she says she was treated when sent to a station in the Richmond SF district for a twenty-four-hour shift. She was the only woman and the only minority at the station during that shift.

The woman said the captain's behavior toward her was so offensive that she went to the station's basement to avoid him. He allegedly commented on her physique, made lewd gestures with his tongue, grabbed his crotch in front of her and said, "You don't have any balls, do you?"

The captain also allegedly made racist remarks about a black character from the television comedy show "In Living Color" and suggested that the mayor would be receptive to a letter from her about dental benefits because she was black.

The captain's attorney, Alan Davis, said the complainant committed perjury and that another female firefighter had testified strongly for the captain's character.

The commission president, James Jefferson, said fire commissioners believed that the fire fighters who testified on behalf of the captain were doing so to protect him. Jefferson was one of the two commissioners who believed that the captain should be fired for his behavior. "He set the standard for everyone out there," Jefferson said. "For him to be the one who is victimizing a new recruit coming in for a day was an offense of a very serious nature, and he should not be an officer in the San Francisco Fire Department."

Concerns of Policewomen

In May 1993, the City Council's Public Safety Committee in Seattle, Washington, released a study designed to determine why so many female police officers leave the department. The study was launched to find out why the percentage of female officers has fallen in recent years from 12 percent in 1987 to 10 percent in 1993, despite Seattle's efforts at increased recruiting and retention.

While the study showed that the majority of women were satisfied or somewhat satisfied working for the police department, a number of problems were identified, including sexual harassment. The women said that, for the most part, they liked the work and the camaraderie, but they also cited sexual harassment, scheduling, and the city's discouragement of leaves as problems.

"Twenty-four percent said sexual harassment is a big problem while 38 percent said it is a somewhat big problem," said Phyllis Lamphere, the assistant police chief who oversaw the study. Eighty percent of the respondents said they had experienced sexual harassment; 76 percent said they had never complained about it. Some of the women said they did not complain because of peer pressure, a feeling that nothing could be done, lack of a support system for handling complaints, or because they handled the problems themselves.

The most prevalent forms of sexual harassment revealed by the study were those that made the work environment "slightly hostile" to "occasionally hostile." Most harassment consisted of forms of joking that put women down, some comments or jokes were of a sexual nature, and some referred to women as stupid or incompetent in certain jobs. The report said: "Some of the activity consisted of writing sexual messages or descriptions of women on the (mobile computer terminals) in the patrol vehicles. Some of the insensitive joking was about gays and lesbians."

Lamphere said that the information presented needs to be offered in a way that does not complicate the issues further for women. "Almost every woman who responded to the survey and interview requests stressed the importance of not allowing this process to further divide male and female officers in the department."

Policewoman Awarded $75,000

In late July 1991, the Portland, Oregon, City Council agreed without discussion to settle the claim of a female officer who said she was subjected to "continual, frequent and oppressive" harassment and discrimination during the three and a half years she was employed. According to her lawsuit, the woman has been on disability leave since June 1990 because of illness caused by stress.

The suit alleged that a Portland Police Bureau sergeant harassed the female officer a number of times, including an incident where she was held upside down. She claimed the sergeant held her upside down to expose her breasts. The complaint also said the sergeant called the female officer demeaning names, placed his hands on her body, and questioned her about her sex life.

HARASSMENT IN HOUSING

Fair housing experts believe that sexual harassment in housing is widespread and mostly affects low-income and minority women. While the civil rights law in this area is relatively new, some experts say harassment in housing is more insidious than harassment in the workplace.

According to a 1987 article in the *Wisconsin Law Review*, "When sexual harassment occurs at work ... the woman may remove herself from the offensive work environment. When the harassment occurs in a woman's home, it is a complete invasion of her life."

Housing experts categorize the abuse into five areas: abusive remarks, unsolicited sexual behavior, asking for sex in return for something such as rent, coercion of sexual activity by threat or punishment, and punishment upon rejection of sexual overtures.

Shellhammer v. Lewallen is the watershed case in the field of harassment in housing. The case involved a Toledo, Ohio, landlord who evicted a married couple after the wife refused to have sex with him or pose for nude photographs. In that 1983 federal case, the court affirmed that sexual harassment in housing violates the federal Fair Housing Act.

Shanna Smith, who is the director of programs for the National Fair Housing Alliance in Washington, D.C., was a "tester" in the *Shellhammer* case. She acted as a prospective renter and was told by the landlord, Nor Lewallen, that she would not have to pay rent if she would have sex with him whenever he wanted. Smith also said Lewallen would not accept her rent payment.

"When he refused to accept my money, and said I could live there for free if I slept with him, he was conditioning the rental of the unit on having sex," Smith said.

Women often do not report harassment because they are afraid they well be evicted, and often their complaints are not taken seriously. Smith recommends that women who are being sexually harassed at home take the following actions:

- Get legal counsel right away.
- Contact a fair housing group. "My first choice would be a private fair housing center," Smith said, "since they can begin an investigation without notifying the person they are investigating. HUD must notify them."
- Call the police. "If you are in immediate danger of him entering your unit or of him assaulting you, call the police and make a report," Smith said.
- Take notes. "Make notes of times, dates and what he says. If there are witnesses, get their names."

SEXUAL HARASSMENT
OF JOURNALISTS

Katherine McAdams, an assistant professor of journalism at the University of Maryland, surveyed women reporters and editors in Washington, D.C., and released the results in August 1992. Eighty percent of the 102 journalists who responded said sexual harassment on the job is a problem; sixty percent of those said they had been subjected to it personally, in incidences involving coworkers, sources, or both. About fifty percent said their companies' have written policies concerning sexual harassment.

"Harassers use their tactics ... as power plays to keep women journalists 'in their place,' " McAdams said. "It makes it more difficult for them, than for men, to get news and to move ahead in the field." Stories from the survey included one journalist covering Capitol Hill who said a news source grabbed her leg under the table as she tried to interview his boss, and another reporter who told of how one source continually discussed his sexual exploits.

Anna Padilla, human rights director for the Newspaper Guild in New York, a union representing journalists, said, "We find this all over the country, in all departments, from the newsroom to the mail room."

Expectations High Despite Discrimination

In June 1992 the Advertising Women of New York released a survey of two thousand industry members, which showed that women in communications still feel subtle gender discrimination, including sexual harassment. Sixty-five percent of the women said that the "old boys" network and a sexist culture in their organizations hinder their success, especially in advertising.

However, 75 percent of the women said they feel their

chances for success are better in the business than they were ten years ago, and many said they expect better prospects within the next five to seven years.

Specifics of the survey were: 45 percent of women in broadcasting and 44 percent of the men said they expect a happier future; 40 percent of women in publishing expect things to be better; but only 35 percent of women and 38 percent of men in ad agencies expect things to improve.

On the Negative Side

Many people in the print and media business feel that the positive role of women in the business is greatly overestimated and that those few women in the field are placed in high-visibility positions, i.e. anchoring or co-anchoring a news program—but that the status of women throughout all levels of the industry has not really changed much.

As an example, Linda Ellerbee, a columnist with King Features Syndicate, recently reported on an incident at a prestigious awards ceremony, where a man, who is the head of a television network, reached over and grabbed the thigh of the woman sitting next to him. The woman was also head of a television network. The two of them had never met before this particular evening. The woman told Ellerbee that she was, of course, outraged by the incident, but was not surprised, since she'd just read the new AAUW report that said four out of five teenage girls are sexually harassed in junior high school and, she added, "Network television is a lot like junior high."

HARASSMENT IN THE JUDICIAL AND LEGAL SYSTEM

According to a study by the Ninth U.S. Circuit Court of Appeals in San Francisco, more than half of the women lawyers practicing in federal courts in California and eight other Western states have been sexually harassed. The two year gender-bias study found that 60 percent of female attorneys in the Ninth Circuit said they had been sexually harassed by men in the court system, having been "the target of unwanted sexual advances or other forms of sexual harassment" by lawyers, clients, judges, or other court personnel. One-third said a male colleague had harassed them in the past five years, with forty percent saying a client did the harassing.

The report was released August 5, 1992, and is the first study of gender bias by a federal appeals court. More than three thousand lawyers and two hundred thirty judges were surveyed across California, Alaska, Arizona, Guam, Hawaii, Idaho, Montana, Nevada, Oregon, and Washington—the area covered by the Ninth Circuit. Most respondents said they feel they are treated fairly by judges in the courtroom, but female lawyers said the gender bias problems occur "off the record" in judges' chambers or in courthouse and law firm corridors.

The study showed that gender bias also affects women who file suit or who are defendants in federal courts. "Women's testimony may simply be disbelieved or discounted as complaints about life rather than treated as evidence of legal claims," the study said.

Opinions over whether or not gender bias exists differ between men and women. For example, in district attorneys' offices, 57 percent of the women said men have a better chance at getting important cases, but only 8 percent of the men thought the same. In addition, 29 percent of female lawyers said they had seen male attorneys single out female non-lawyers for demeaning treatment, but only 8 percent of male attorneys said they had. More than a third of the women said they had seen judges cut off female but not male attorneys; only 6 percent of the men reported seeing this.

U.S. District Court Judge John C. Coughenour, who directed the study, said, "I don't think I appreciated how different the perceptions of men and women were. A significant percentage of women in the profession think this problem exists, and if they think so, then it is a problem." He added that the women in the study did say that the federal courts are less biased than state courts and law firms.

The report said that some gender bias is subtle. Slightly more than 30 percent of the women attorneys said that judges are more strict with women lawyers than with men. Women said they are sometimes addressed by their first names or as "dear" or "honey," while men are called "Mr." and "counselor." One woman reported being called "little girl," and many women reported inappropriate comments about their attire.

More than half the women attorneys reported hearing colleagues question women judges' competence, and 38 percent said they've heard disparaging remarks about the presumed sexual orientation of female judges.

Many specific examples of bias and harassment were given in the study. One female lawyer said that during a settlement conference she was asked to leave the room so the federal magistrate could tell a dirty joke. One female prosecutor said that during an in-chambers conference, the male judge and attorneys discussed the *Sports Illustrated* swimsuit issue; another time a judge called her "menopausal" when she objected to a ruling. One female attorney said a colleague's client tackled her to the ground in the office and that when she asked her colleague to take control of his client, he refused, and both men said that she must be frigid.

The study's findings contradict the belief that differences in male and female perceptions also are generational. "The differences between men and women in perceptions and attitudes characterize younger, as well as older, practitioners." The eight-member group that conducted the study asked that lawyers and judges develop programs to combat gender bias.

Other task forces across the United States also are studying sexual bias in the courts. The studies, sponsored by courts and bar associations in twenty-three states and the District of Columbia, have reported widespread bias in state judicial systems. Similar studies are under way in fourteen other states.

One Judge's Opinion

Maryanne Trump Barry, sister of real estate tycoon Donald Trump, was appointed Federal District Judge in Newark, New Jersey, in 1983 by Ronald Reagan. In a November 20, 1992, speech to more than nine hundred federal law enforcement agents and officials, she clearly expressed her views on women and sexual harassment.

Judge Barry told of being criticized herself some nine years ago by feminists because of the language that she used. She said she still feels stung by the tongue-lashing she was given by one female attorney for calling a young woman "girl."

Judge Barry said she now asks prospective clerks how they would react if she made a similar slip. Some, she said, "visibly coil up like cobras, narrow their eyes and their mouths, and spit out some answer which usually includes the word 'shocked.' " The smarter ones, who apparently understand the judge's sense of humor, laugh it off, and they are the ones who get the clerkships she said. "Needless to say, I don't want a woman working for me who's waiting for me to shoot myself in the foot," she said.

Undue sensitivity and an excessively confrontational attitude of some women in the workplace poisons relationships between men and women, Judge Barry said, adding that because of a few "professional hypochondriacs," well-meaning men are afraid to be themselves. She said these attitudes of some women prevent the more serious problems women face from being addressed. Making a major issue out of minor infractions not only angers men needlessly but trivializes the serious problems women face in advancing in the predominantly male world of law enforcement, she said.

"It has also made work less fun. Frivolous accusations reduce, if not eliminate, not only communication between men and women, but any kind of playfulness and banter," she said. "Where has all the laughter gone?

"I stand second to none in condemning the sexual harassment of women, but what is happening is that every sexy joke of long ago, every flirtation, is being recalled by some women and revised and re-evaluated as sexual harassment. Many of these accusations are, in anybody's book, frivolous." Judge Barry's comments were made to the Interagency Committee on Women in Law Enforcement meeting in Washington, D.C.

Lawyers In the United States

The American Bar Association went on record in February 1992 as opposing sexual harassment of any kind in the workplace and recognized that in law firms the problem is particularly serious. In a voice vote of its five hundred eighteen-member House of Delegates on the resolution, the ABA stated that sexual harassment is a "discriminatory and unprofessional practice that must not be tolerated in any work environment."

The chairman of the ABA's Commission of Women in the Profession, Cory Amron, stated that the "Thomas hearings have catapulted the issue into the public consciousness, from blue-collar workers to professionals." Amron added that "this issue is now truly a matter of national concern."

Amron also pointed to a 1990 survey by the ABA Young Lawyers Division to support her statement that there is ample evidence of sexual harassment in the legal profession. "It revealed 85 percent of female lawyers had experienced or observed at least one form of sexual harassment during the previous two years." The study also showed that 46 percent of the women lawyers "experienced or observed several different forms of sexual harassment" during the two-year period.

"In fact, the survey found that 78 percent of all male lawyers observed at least one form of sexual harassment during the time frame, and 68 percent of male lawyers observed more than one form during that period," Amron added. She urged the ABA to educate lawyers and serve as a role model to help eliminate sexual harassment, saying the Thomas hearing showed there is "a disturbing lack of understanding."

The Commission on Women's Issues report stated that the Thomas hearings "sparked an unprecedented public debate and educational process about the widespread, pernicious, but often hidden problem of sexual harassment." The report added: "Given the prevalence of sexual harassment in all sectors of the working world, it is regrettable but not surprising that sexual harassment occurs within the legal profession."

Judges Believed Hill's Testimony

According to a study published October 21, 1991, in the *National Law Journal*, state and federal judges believed Anita Hill's allegation that she was sexually harassed by Clarence Thomas by a 2–1 margin.

The survey of one hundred judges showed that 41 percent of those responding found Hill's testimony to be more credible than Thomas's. Twenty-two percent of the respondents believed Thomas; 37 percent were unsure.

The *National Law Journal* survey was conducted the day after the Senate voted to confirm Thomas. The findings contrast sharply with public opinion polls that showed the majority of the general population believed Thomas's testimony.

Dean James Simon of New York Law School was quoted as saying that Thomas's peers in the legal community are "going to approach him with a good deal of skepticism, if not cynicism, in the short term."

Additional survey findings: 72 percent of the judges said that Thomas's credibility was damaged in the course of the confirmation hearings; about half said he should not step down from a sexual harassment case scheduled to come before the Supreme Court; and 30 percent said he should.

About half of the judges said the credibility of the Supreme Court was not hurt by the hearings, while 85 percent said they believe the credibility of Congress was damaged.

Harassment in Connecticut

A Connecticut task force study published in September 1991 showed sex bias pervades that state's legal system, including judges who whistle at female lawyers, make offensive suggestive remarks, and make sexual advances toward those lawyers.

The task force was commissioned by Chief Justice Ellen A. Peters of the Connecticut Supreme Court in 1987. The task force published a two hundred-page report after three years of study. The study concluded that "women are treated differently from men in the justice system and, because of it, many suffer from unfairness, embarrassment, emotional pain, professional deprivation and economic hardship." The task force also said that women lawyers are less likely to get lucrative case referrals or judicial appointments than men.

The report included many examples of insulting remarks made to and reported by female members of the Connecticut bar. One judge publicly complained about the "feminization of the public defenders' office" and said that women cannot handle criminal clients roughly—for example, pushing the clients up against the wall. The judge said that as a result, these cases are not handled properly. Other incidents included in the report were:

- a judge "wolf-whistling" at a passing female lawyer during a lunch break;

- a prosecuting attorney who said to a female defense attorney "Do you want to try them on?" when she asked to examine a rape victim's clothing;
- a judge using crude language and stating to a female attorney, in the courthouse hallway in front of several male colleagues, that she would be as busy on a certain case as a bride "on her wedding night;" and
- numerous sexual advances toward female attorneys by judges, other lawyers, and court personnel.

Judge Francis X. Hennessy, task force co-chairman, said: "Treating a woman in this manner undermines her ability to function properly in the system because the woman loses credibility in the eyes of her client and even in the eyes of the court. Gender bias breeds unfair treatment and unfair results."

Justice Peters said that some of the incidents of offensive remarks came from ignorance and insensitivity rather than maliciousness. "This problem is pervasive throughout our society," she said, adding that the conclusion of the task force that sex bias pervades the legal system came as "no surprise."

The study also said that sex bias in the judicial system is not limited to the courtroom. A lawyer in New Haven said the Judicial Selection Commission regularly asks female candidates such questions as "How does your husband feel about you seeking a judgeship?" and "How will you handle your children or having a baby if a judgeship is given to you?"

Lawyers and judges surveyed confirmed a tendency shown in other studies to give women lighter sentences than men. The exception was among female juvenile delinquents who spend more time in detention than boys because judges believe the girls need more protection.

Task force recommendations included: changing the language in judicial rule books and codes of conduct to make them gender-neutral; providing courses on sex bias for judges, lawyers, and other participants in the legal system; and condemning and punishing sexist behavior by judges, lawyers, and other officials and court personnel.

The instances reported in the study did not result in disciplinary action because the task force did not ask for names. Judge Hennessy said the task force felt attorneys would be reluctant to come forward if they were asked to give names, but in the future such complaints could result in punishment.

Similar Findings in Georgia

In August 1992 the Georgia Commission on Gender Bias in the Judicial System released its report, totaling some four hundred eighteen pages, stating that male attorneys are given more respect in Georgia courts than their female counterparts and that sexist remarks and jokes are frequently heard in open court. The report was presented to the all-male Georgia State Supreme Court and concluded that women should be encouraged to seek judgeships and prosecutorial positions.

A member of the commission, Appeals Judge Dorothy Beasley, said the recent appointment of a woman to the position of Rockdale County district attorney proved that times are changing. Ms. Cheryl Fisher Custer was appointed as the first female district attorney in Georgia's history.

According to Judge Beasley, "Women are better educated, and women are being brought up to take their equal place in decision-making positions."

Sexual Harassment In Law Firms

The following section was written for inclusion in Shockwaves by attorney Carolyn Cairns of Stokes, Eitelbach & Lawrence, P.S., Seattle, Washington:

Sexual harassment is no stranger to law firms. Law offices are probably no worse than other workplaces with respect to sexual harassment, but they are no better.

Although studies indicate that sexual harassment is just as prevalent in law firms as it is in other workplaces (a 1990 American Bar Association survey found that 85 percent of women attorneys and 78 percent of male attorneys have experienced or observed at least one form of sexual harassment during the prior two years), it is less likely to be reported, even internally, let alone in a public forum. A 1989 National Law Journal survey found that 60 percent of women partners and associates in the nation's two hundred fifty largest firms reported experiencing sexual harassment at some point in their careers.

The legal community has an effective grapevine and the consequences to one's career can be great. This is particularly true if the victim is an associate but also is true for paralegals and legal secretaries.

If one begins with an understanding that sexual harassment is primarily an issue of power and its abuses, it is easy to understand how sexual harassment could occur and go unreported or unaddressed in law firms. Big egos are not uncommon in the legal profession. In many ways these big egos are a plus—no one wants to be represented by a shrinking violet with a self-esteem problem. Unchecked, however, a small number of lawyers may come to believe that they are entitled to get what they want and get it with impunity. This is not a large group—most lawyers, egos and all, have a clear sense of appropriate conduct.

The training that is given young associates in many law firms, particularly large firms, may sometimes create an environment in which a problem partner can abuse his or her power. Young associates often seek out or are assigned a "mentor," an experienced partner, usually in the practice area that interests the associate. The mentor trains the associate in the law, teaches them the ropes, gives them tips in "firm politics," guides their career and sometimes protects them. These mentoring relationships are often informal, and rarely in writing, but in many firms are considered crucial to one's success in the firm and advancement to partnership. These relationships are usually positive and productive relationships for the associate, partner and firm. It is not difficult to see, however, how a partner could abuse the mentoring role by sexually harassing the associate. When a partner crosses the line, the associate, like most victims, may not be certain of what is happening, may choose to ignore what in retrospect will be obvious indications of a problem. The associate needs the support of that partner and may make every effort to preserve that relationship. Once the partner's intent becomes obvious, it may be difficult for the associate to handle—a few words from the partner to his colleagues will doom the associate's career.

The management structure of law firms aggravates a problem of sexual harassment. Most corporate structures are pyramids, with ever-diminishing layers of increasing authority—there is a chain of command. If one does not obtain redress from one's immediate supervisor, then, at least in theory, one can go to the supervisor's boss and on up the hierarchy. Law firm management is horizontal. Partners are just that—partners to each other, not bosses. Each partner is, in effect, a CEO. To be sure, law firms have managing partners and sometimes executive committees, but neither of these play a traditional supervisory role. Managing partners and executive committee members are peers to the offending partner.

Most partnership agreements make it difficult to oust an offending partner, a two-thirds vote of all partners being a typical requirement. A partner in a law firm is "employed at will" only in the strictest sense of the term.

It is a small wonder then that sexual harassment victims at law firms often do not make internal complaints. They have a reasonable fear that the partners will "circle the wagons" and that they will be without power, allies and recourse. Historically, these victims usually quit before their careers are irretrievably lost.

Now, increasingly, these victims are hiring attorneys to

represent them. Although sexual harassment in law firms is not uncommon, lawsuits against law firms and partners are quite rare. The reason, of course, is that these cases nearly always settle prior to a complaint being filed. A sexual harassment suit against a law firm, especially one of medium to large size, is nearly certain to attract media attention. This is not publicity that any law firm wants. Clients do not like their law firms becoming renowned for sexual harassment. Clients do not want to hire attorneys whose judgment, not to mention ethics, is so poor that they engage in sexual harassment.

The person accused of sexual harassment is almost invariably a partner and nearly as often will be married. The fact that the accused is a partner will probably impose liability on the law firm as well. The partner's marital status has little legal significance but clearly affects the partner's desire to settle.

Other factors which cause these cases to settle in high numbers are the costs of litigation, the unlikelihood of insurance coverage, damage to careers on both sides and the reality that lawyers as a group are not popular with the public and that a jury may take a very dim view of a partner who engages in sexual harassment. The displeasure of juries tends to translate into large damage awards. Punitive damages also are a very real possibility.

Sexual harassment cases can settle in many ways. Often the victim is paid to leave, thereby reinforcing the reluctance of victims to come forward. If there is a problem, who is the firm going to keep—the secretary or associate? Or the partner who bills a half-million dollars a year and keeps four lawyers busy? Ten, and even five years ago, this was a rhetorical question. Recently, however, there have been cases where the partner was actually pushed out. As one might expect, these ousted partners often have other problems and an accusation of sexual harassment may be the last straw. The fact remains, however, that law firms are increasingly unwilling to protect offending partners beyond what is necessary to protect the firm, and they are sick and tired of paying sexual harassment claims because of an out-of-control colleague.

Prevention of sexual harassment at law firms involves many of the same procedures and safe guards used by other employers—a strongly worded written policy which describes a variety of harassing behaviors, a complaint procedure which is genuinely calculated to encourage victims to come forward, training, thorough investigations and appropriate remedies. It may, however, be difficult to have partners face up to the fact that something beyond nicely phrased policies is required—they must be willing to impartially evaluate claims and actually take action against an offending partner. They also must convince their employees that they are committed to doing so or the employees will not feel safe in blowing the whistle. The policy and complaints procedure, for example, should encourage employees to bring their complaints to people within the firm who are perceived by the employees themselves to be powerful. It is a mistake at most firms, for example, to require all complaints to go to an office manager or personnel director, since these people, however competent, are not usually considered powerful enough to challenge a partner. Office managers or personnel directors should be options; so should the managing partner, the partner assigned to personnel issues and an influential woman partner (if there are none of the latter, that in itself is a problem which will not escape the staff's notice). Many policies identify several individuals the complaining employee may go to, but also advise the employee that she or he may go to any partner the employee chooses. The partners must understand that any knowledge or suspicion by any partner will almost certainly constitute knowledge of the firm and such information must be reported immediately.

An objective and thorough investigation must be conducted. If there is any question as to the firm's ability to do this (and there often will be), an investigator should be brought in from the outside.

Finally, the firm must be receptive to the findings. Partners are owners and it is difficult for co-owners to discipline each other; however, law firms, like any other employer, must take appropriate action to ensure that the harassment stops. Depending on the findings, the firm could issue a written reprimand of sorts and/or the partner could be counseled or sent to psychological counseling. The partner may be asked to pay any damages. Where the harassment is serious or repeated, the firm should consider more drastic measures, such as asking the partner to leave.

Some firms have amended their partnership agreements to address such issues as who will pay these claims—the alleged harasser or "the firm," that is, the other partners. Whether offended by the financial loss, the risk to the firm, the poor exercise of judgment or the breach of ethics—many law firms will hold the offender accountable. In some cases and with some work, it is then possible for the victim to stay and have a productive career. Law firms that have taken this tact have been rewarded in many ways, not the least being the knowledge by the firm's employees that it is possible to speak out against a powerful partner—and survive.

A WARNING TO SKI RESORTS

The U. S. Forest Service has said that posters of scantily clad women which appear in maintenance sheds and lift shacks are examples of sexual harassment and must be removed. The Utah resort operators where the posters were found said that this type of problem is no more common in ski areas than in other industries, but that the difference is that some resorts are on public lands and their corporate activities are more regulated. District Forest Ranger Michael Sieg said, "We wanted to give a wake-up call to the ski areas that 'Your permit is dependent on this.' Everybody needs to know how seriously we're taking it."

Ski area managers at Alto, Snowbird, Brighton and Solitude were asked to remove questionable posters and to ensure that employees and managers receive training on sexual harassment. The Forest Service also asked for reports from the resorts on how they plan to deal with complaints of harassment ranging from sexual stereotyping in job assignments to actual assaults on women. Sieg said, "I've been told the ski patrol is the last bastion of sexual harassment. What brings it home to me is the saying, 'What you permit, you promote.' "

According to Gloria Williams, an instructor at Alta, women used to be relegated to teaching children and new skiers, but that practice is changing. "If I prove I can teach higher levels, I am given that opportunity. We're professionals. We're in the teaching business."

Others say that swapping off-color jokes also is a problem, particularly because of the relaxed environment of the ski resort. Christine Katzenberger, an instructor at Snowbird, said, "We've definitely had to watch out for that, but we've started to learn our lessons. Instructors are more professional now, and we're more interested in retirement plans, sexual harassment training ... the ski industry is about six years behind other industries."

John Loomis, a vice president at Snowbird said, "I don't have a problem with Forest Service monitoring at all. We have what they need if we're not already a step ahead of them." Snowbird, Alto, and Solitude resorts said they have sexual harassment policies already in place.

Five female employees sued Alto over sexual harassment, accusing a male supervisor of assaulting them. The suit said that when the women complained, the company did nothing. The man no longer works at the resort and four of the five women received out-of-court financial settlements. The fifth woman is still pursuing her suit in U.S. District Court. One of the four women who settled her suit said, "It was a one-shot, individual problem. People are learning from it. The environment is 90 percent positive, and I love my job."

MEDICINE, HEALTH, AND SCIENCES

According to a survey by the American Medical Women's Association released in February 1992, at least one in four women doctors is sexually harassed on the job. The association set up a hotline for harassment complaints and is conducting a broader study of the problem.

The survey of two hundred doctors from the association's Massachusetts chapter showed that more than half of those responding said they had received unwanted sexual attention. Twenty-seven percent had been sexually harassed during the one-year period ending in 1990.

Dr. Sharyn A. Lanhart, professor of psychiatry at Harvard Medical School and chair of the association's subcommittee on gender equity, said "only 18 percent of all physicians are women. These types of incidences are more common when women are a minority in a work force."

The survey found that two-thirds of the respondents said they had received offensive comments about their gender. Half of the general surgeons and 37 percent of the internists responding reported sexual harassment.

According to another study published by the California Medical Association in 1991, more than half of the senior students surveyed at ten U.S. medical schools reported experiences with sexual harassment. The study was part of a larger survey of student opinions of how they are treated during their medical training.

About 97 percent of the students who responded said they were mistreated or harassed at some point in medical school. Fifty-five percent, including a fourth of the male students, said they were subject to some type of sexual harassment.

Of the women who responded, almost half said they experienced some type of sexual harassment from classmates and pre-clinical faculty. Nearly two-thirds said they had at least one experience of harassment from clinical faculty or residents. Of the five hundred eighty-one students who responded, one

man and three women said they had been directly propositioned for sexual favors.

The study was conducted by three Chicago researchers
and was published in the *Western Journal of Medicine*. The
survey began in 1988, three years before sexual harassment in
medicine received national attention with the resignation of
Dr. Frances Conley, a neurosurgeon at Stanford Medical
School. Conley resigned her position in 1991, complaining
that she and female students were subjected to years of sexual harassment.

Dr. Frances Conley, 50, quit her twenty-five-year teaching
post at Stanford University, claiming male surgeons caressed
her legs under the operating table, called her "honey," and
blamed her debating style on pre-menstrual syndrome. One of
the country's premier female neurosurgeons, Dr. Conley said
she put up with snide comments and unwelcome touching
because she feared that speaking up would cost her her job.
When she learned that students were complaining of the
same harassment, she said she could no longer keep quiet.

"I felt terribly guilty because for the past twenty-five years
I was a facilitator (of this behavior) by not promoting the environment to change," she said. "I might not have resigned
except that women medical students came to me with repeated complaints. They said, 'We are being fondled, very bad
comments are made about us, such as the shape of our bodies.'" Conley said "the straw that broke the camel's back" was
the neurosurgery division's failure to hire a new chairman
from outside of Stanford, which she said might have cleared
the air.

At a news conference following Conley's announcement,
the dean of Stanford's Medical School, David Korn, urged
Conley to return, saying he regretted her decision and that he
planned to meet with her. "I would love to have Dr. Conley
stay," he said. Korn said he was unaware of any specific
instances of sexual harassment such as those that Conley outlined in letters to the media, and that he doesn't believe "that

she has been the target of abuse of any kind." Korn did not deny that there is some sexism at Stanford, but said he would debate whether it should be termed excessive. "Yes it's here, but I think it's no worse or better here than anywhere else."

Korn questioned Conley's allegations, saying she never formally filed any sexual harassment complaints. He said there were only two such complaints made during the past seven years. He went on to say that "there is excessive male dominance and insensitivity in medicine, and it is probably more acute in surgery than elsewhere ... but as to specific instances, I'm not aware of that.

"Stanford has had for a number of years a clear policy about sexual harassment," Korn said. "I wish to state clearly for the record that the School of Medicine does not and will not tolerate inappropriate sexual behaviors or actions, for they degrade the learning and working environment of this institution."

Dr. Conley joined Stanford as an intern and was chairwoman of the faculty senate at the time of her resignation. Her resignation, effective September 1, 1990, cited a pattern of sexist behavior and an environment in which women are continually demeaned. She said she had been repeatedly fondled and propositioned by male doctors who apparently thought it was all in good fun. "In medicine," she said, "men are dominant and women are subservient ... (That's) the time-honored tradition."

In the fall of 1991, Dr. Conley withdrew her resignation and said she would work within the system to change male doctors' attitudes about women. She also said her actions depended on the resolution of her complaint against Dr. Silverberg and his appointment as department chairman. Dr. Conley said she would not return as long as Dr. Silverberg was chairman.

In April 1992, Dr. Silverberg, acting chairman of Stanford's neurosurgery department, was demoted and agreed to undergo gender sensitivity training, according to school officials.

Silverberg had demonstrated a "troubling insensitivity" in his working relations with women students and doctors, Korn, the medical school's dean, reported. Silverberg said in a statement that "it was never my intention to demean or insult any woman, but it is now clear to me that some things I said or did in jest or from affection were taken as signs of disrespect." Regarding the university's confidential report on his behavior, Silverberg said, "I don't believe I've done anything wrong or different than any other chairman at the medical school."

According to *The New York Times*, Silverberg considered himself a victim of a tidal wave of public opinion on the matter of sexism in the workplace. "Dr. Conley whipped up a sense of hysteria and the university responded to that call to arms, so to speak," he said.

On hearing of the report and the university's action, Conley said, "If indeed what we're hearing from Dr. Silverberg is true [regarding his demotion], the university can congratulate itself. They took on this issue, handled it very seriously and the decision they made is a brave one. With a lot of academic institutions fighting this tooth and nail, this puts Stanford in a leadership position."

Silverberg is to take a gender sensitivity course and undergo counseling, and his progress will be monitored. Donald Gibbons, spokesman for the Stanford Medical Center news service, said, "He won't be able to just go to some seminar and sit in the back of the room and snooze."

At the National Institutes of Health

According to a report commissioned by the National Institutes of Health, the division of NIH in Bethesda, Maryland, has operated for years as an "old boy-younger women network" in which some female employees were promised promotions and raises if they had sex with their male managers. The report was written by an outside consultant after four months of study. It said that in the agency's main supply division, the network of sexual favoritism "thrived boldly and obviously for several years, and went unchallenged until recently."

The director of NIH said she believes there is evidence of an ongoing pattern of discrimination and harassment on the basis of race and sex at what is known as the governments' foremost medical research facility. Diane Armstrong, director the agency's Office of Equal Employment, said the study raises very serious concerns and that they "see a lot of issues around favoritism."

John Mahoney, the deputy director of management, said the report's results were a surprise to him, but that the report prompted him to issue a "firm and aggressive" directive to managers about sex discrimination and sexual harassment. "I have made it clear to managers that they are accountable within their authority," he said.

The report did not conclude that there had been sex between employees, but that some supervisors consorted with younger, often single and attractive women whom they supervised. Male supervisors and female employees often met at the Bethesda Naval Officer's Club.

The report said: "One objective for some males was sex" in exchange for "high performance ratings and/or promotions" and that employees stated that "if one gave sex and received an outstanding or excellent rating, a sizable sum of money would come to the person, and money would also come to the person if promoted." It also said that five women in the NIH division said they had been propositioned for sex by male managers. One secretary said sexual harassment prevented her from accomplishing her work. Although many people knew of the network, no one reported it because, the report stated, the supervisors who would have been told of the practice also were key members of the network.

As a result, the agency plans to conduct two inquiries: one study by another outside consultant to determine whether

NIH can reprimand supervisors identified in the report, and secondly, the appointment of a task force to investigate discrimination complaints and set up a disciplinary system.

In the World of Astronomy

According to a recent article by Diana Steel in *New Scientist*, the most talked about workshop at a recent conference of scientists at John Hopkins University was the one concerning the status of women in astronomy. The scientists in the workshop developed a document with the aim of breaking down barriers to women's full participation in science. Many at the conference believe the document will affect research areas far beyond astronomy.

Astronomer Meg Urry said, "Not dos and don'ts, exactly, but something more like the Magna Carta or the Declaration of Independence. The charter recommends education about sexual harassment on such issues as pornography on display in laboratories and inappropriate advances from supervisors and colleagues."

Laura Danly, a postdoctoral fellow at the university, recalled a "horribly depressing" experience she had while giving a talk. She found out later that men in the audience had spent the time during her talk rating her appearance.

MILITARY SERVICES

The Department of Veterans Affairs is offering group therapy to female veterans for the first time—a response to the pervasiveness of sexual harassment in the military. Dr. Susan H. Mather, the VA's assistant chief medical director for public health, said the number of women seeking help for sexual harassment has been on the rise since the Tailhook scandal

last year. In addition, the Navy has announced the establishment of a toll-free hot line for sexual harassment complaints.
The hot line is to be installed by the end of the year. It will
give advice and counseling and track complaints to gauge the
effectiveness of programs to eliminate harassment.

'No Women Policy' in Fighters or Tanks is Changed

In early November of 1992, a presidential commission voted
"yes" on allowing women on aircraft carriers, but "no" to
women in fighter planes. This left the decision to the incom-
ing Congress and the White House to act on the commission's
recommendations in 1993.

The commission spent $4 million and seven months to
research the issue, with the final vote of the fifteen commissioners coming down to a one-vote margin. The prevailing
view was that the risk of women being taken prisoner was too
great to justify female pilots flying combat missions. The commission also went on record against allowing women to face
direct land combat.

Retired Army General Maxwell Thurman said, "The idea
that we would position women so that they could be subjected to depravity, violence [and] death as prisoners is one that I
will not sign up with."

Lt. Paula Coughlin, the Navy's outspoken pilot who went
public with the Tailhook allegations, said, "This is just as damaging for the morale of women in the military as what happened to me and others in the hallway in Las Vegas last year."

Sarah F. White, a master sergeant in the Air Force reserves,
spoke for the commission's conservative bloc, attacking her
"radical" opponents: "I call into question the nature of the
women who would want to kill others or be killed themselves
in order to achieve equal opportunity. This is degrading to
women and society at large."

Retired Army Col. W. Darryl Henderson argued that female pilots cannot withstand a fighter plane's high G-forces during their monthly menstrual periods. He also said that female pilots would interfere with the "male bonding" that builds morale in elite units.

Commission Chairman Robert Herres, a retired Air Force four-star general, said the Air Force would be stronger if it were allowed to choose qualified women as combat pilots. The senior sailor on the commission, retired four-star admiral James R. Hogg, also favored allowing women to compete for combat pilot jobs. He said "the quality of the talent pool" would increase if women were eligible to fly in combat.

The no-women policy was changed April 28, 1993, when then-Defense Secretary Les Aspin announced that qualified female flight officers in all services could enter combat units. Because the Pentagon had foreseen the eventual end of the combat exclusion for female pilots and flight officers, the Navy was ready to begin immediate selection and assignments, a Navy spokeswoman said.

"We anticipate that approximately twenty to twenty-five (women) will be in combat squadrons by March of next year," she said, and that another twenty to twenty-five will join carrier-based units by the middle of 1994.

Army Takes Action on Sexual Harassment

According to a senior U.S. Army official, the Army started an extensive investigation in 1992 into sexual harassment at two large installations in St. Louis after complaints from many women about the problem. Consultants who had been sent by the Army previously to see whether sexual harassment was taking place on the bases brought the women's complaints to the Army's attention.

The Army sent consultants to seven installations around the country in an effort to avoid a scandal like the Tailhook incident. In the Army complaints, however, only civilian employees and supervisors have been involved.

The Army said that investigators are examining as many as one hundred accusations of verbal harassment and unwanted sexual advances by senior and mid-level supervisors against female subordinate employees at the Army Aviation and Troop Command and the Army Reserve Personnel Center. The two commands employ sixty-four hundred uniformed and civilian workers in the St Louis area.

Michael P.W. Stone, secretary of the Army, ordered this investigation after the consultants reported problems at the two commands. According to Robert Silberman, the assistant secretary of the Army for manpower and reserve affairs, the Army is "alarmed by the reports, but I'm reluctant to discuss any details until we have done a more in-depth review."

The Army plans to institute a training program for all personnel—from privates to generals—and implement an improved system for reporting sexual harassment complaints. "Some soldiers are not clear on what precisely sexual harassment is and what they should do about it," he said.

Navy Pilots and the Tailhook Scandal

In June 1992, an initial Navy investigation into sexual abuse and harassment at the Tailhook convention in Las Vegas in September 1991 found that dozens of women, rather than the five or so who initially filed complaints, were assaulted there. The investigators were able to identify only two suspects despite evidence that dozens of officers took part. Investigators said that many pilots, some with senior rank, refused to cooperate with them.

Rear Admiral Brent Baker, the chief Navy spokesman, said that field commanders would soon begin a process that is the military equivalent to grand jury proceedings for the two suspects, as well as for nine other officers under suspicion, including a captain. The proceedings are to consider evidence for possible court martial or administrative punishment for the officers. Navy officers said they are deeply troubled by the pilots lack of cooperation with investigators.

In July 1992, Navy Lt. Paula Coughlin, one of the twenty-six women who were sexually harassed and assaulted at the Tailhook convention, reported that the civilian investigator assigned to her case had pressured her for dates and for a romantic involvement. Her specific allegations were that Naval Investigative Service Agent Laney S. Spigener pressured her to date him and called her "Sweet Cakes" while she was reviewing photographs of Navy and Marine aviators to identify those who had assaulted her. Spigener had been assigned to investigate charges from women who said they had been fondled and disrobed while being pushed down a gauntlet of drunken aviators at the Tailhook convention.

Navy spokesman Cmdr. Mark Van Dyke said the Naval Investigative Service removed Spigener from the case and reassigned him to other duties after Lt. Coughlin filed her complaint about his behavior. Spigener was then suspended without pay for three days.

Van Dyke also said the agent made "no apparent attempt to demean, threaten or harass Lt. Coughlin. His conduct was considered to be a matter of poor judgment in that the agent attempted to establish a relationship deemed to be improper with a victim."

Further reports indicated Spigener had been suspended for seven days without pay a year earlier for "unauthorized use of the authority of his position" when he verbally confronted a woman who was attempting to publicize his relationship with a woman who was not his wife. The woman he was involved with allegedly was an enlisted Marine's wife.

Following this revelation, the *San Francisco Examiner* said in an editorial that the old military acronym SNAFU (situation normal all fouled up) needs a contemporary reinforcement in light of the Navy's response to the Tailhook incident.

"If there is no Navy regulation against unmitigated stupidity," the *Examiner* suggested, "perhaps acting Secretary Sean O'Keefe can see that one is instituted pronto for use in just such situations as these. In the meantime, we suggest the Navy adopt a new acronym that accurately describes its current institutional approach: UOTC—Unclear On The Concept."

As of October 1992, a year after twenty-six women were assaulted by drunken naval aviators at the Tailhook convention in Las Vegas, no officers had been charged. However, major changes have taken place at the top of the Navy chain of command and a report issued at the beginning of October brought about additional changes.

The report, issued by the Navy's inspector-general, showed that the Navy's handling of the complaint was insufficient. Among the findings:

- The admiral who was leading the investigation, Naval Investigative Service Chief Duvall Williams, believed "men simply do not want women in the military." He got into a "screaming match" with Assistant Navy Secretary Barbara Pope after calling female navy pilots "go-go dancers, topless dancers, or hookers." He said that one of the Tailhook victims, Lt. Paula Coughlin, was the kind of woman who "would welcome this type of activity" because she used profanity in her statement to NIS.

- Navy investigators shielded the top officers. Few of the twenty-one hundred witnesses who were questioned were asked if they had seen admirals near the gauntlet of pilots where the women were assaulted.

- Navy Under Secretary J. Daniel Howard, overseer of the Tailhook inquiry, claimed that the admirals "hamstrung" him and hampered his investigation. The report said directly that he failed to ensure that the Navy "conducted a comprehensive investigation."

- H. Lawrence Garrett III, the Navy secretary who resigned

after the scandal broke, observed women's legs being shaved in a hospitality suite during the 1990 Tailhook convention and visited four hospitality suites near the gauntlet in 1991, according to a retired Navy captain who was with Garrett and who passed a lie detector test. Garrett denies these allegations but refused to take a test.

Following the report, Acting Navy Secretary Sean O'Keefe relieved Williams and two other admirals involved in the investigation. Secretary O'Keefe stated that the Navy finally realized that the "demeaning behavior and attitudes toward women has gone on too long ... we get it."

Some people still didn't get it. In December 1992, it was reported that Admiral Robert Kelley, the Navy's Pacific Fleet commander, was reprimanded for telling a sexually explicit joke during a staff meeting—a violation of Navy policy. Several staff members, including three women, reported Kelley making a joke about male genitals. The Admiral himself has ordered harsh punishment for officers found guilty of engaging in sexual harassment.

The Answer to Tailhook?

An editorial in the August 16, 1992, *Los Angeles Times* by Mary Edward Wertsch addressed a problem that many experts have seen when working in the area of sexual harassment— alcohol and alcoholism. Often, people accused of sexual harassment were drunk at the time of their offense or have alcohol abuse problems.

Wertsch's article, titled "The Pathology Is Alcohol," begins: "The Tailhook scandal, in which hundreds of Navy and Marine officers engaged in licentious, offensive, even criminal behavior against women at a convention in Las Vegas, has spawned four separate investigations and brought down the secretary of the Navy. But when it comes to remedial action to change this offensive behavior in the military, the only thing discussed is sensitivity training ... ."

Wertsch said this approach is "laughable" to people who have served in the military or who were raised in it (which she was; Wertsch is the author of *Military Brats: Legacies of Childhood Inside the Fortress*, published by Fawcett/ Columbine in 1992). Not that sensitivity training isn't needed, but to focus on what she called Neanderthal sexual attitudes ignores a much more pervasive problem: alcohol abuse.

Her research showed that the alcohol bill for the three-day convention in Las Vegas ran about $7,000 per hospitality suite. That amount is shocking, but not particularly surprising, she said, because "drunkenness has long been accepted in military life as a way to encourage bonding and let off steam for men drawn taut by the stress of putting their lives on the line. The military's own studies reveal a problem of such dimension that it should long ago have been raised as a national security issue."

Wertsch said a twenty-year-old Navy study found the proportion of problem drinkers in the Navy to be as high as 38 percent. Three years ago, in a study released by the Defense Department comparing military and civilian drinking habits, the rate of very heavy drinking in the military was shown to be nearly twice that of the civilian population. Despite the problems, Wertsch said, the military continues to sell cheap, untaxed liquor at base stores and to permit happy hours at base clubs where drinks can be bought for as little as 25 cents.

"The revelation of Tailhook is that the military is sadly out of sync with the values of the civilian community that supports it. Even more telling, however, is the fact that the military is even out of sync with its own reality: the assumption that alcohol fosters cohesion conducive to high performance on the battlefield certainly was proved wrong by the totally dry Gulf War, in which the military seemed to have performed to its own great satisfaction without benefit of booze," Wertsch wrote.

Wertsch believes that mandatory sensitivity training will

help pacify current critics of military behavior but accomplish little else. The total organizational solution, she said, should include prohibitions against offensive behavior and required stress-management training at all levels—because it is simply not realistic to train men to kill, give them no training in how to manage stress, then essentially hand them a bottle of liquor and expect them to conduct themselves in a civilized manner.

"Tailhook should be the watershed event that finally forces the Defense Department to dissolve its longstanding, pathological partnership with alcohol," Wertsch said.

Final Report on Tailhook is Worse than Expected

On April 23, 1993, the Pentagon's inspector general released the long-awaited report on the Navy's 1991 Tailhook scandal. According to the report, more than eighty-three women and seven men were assaulted during three days of parties where vast amounts of alcohol were consumed. The report said: "The assaults varied from victims being grabbed on the buttocks to being groped, pinched and fondled on their breasts, buttocks, and genitals ... Some victims were bitten by their assailants, others were knocked to the ground and some had their clothing ripped or removed." The report said abuses at the 1991 convention were not significantly different from those at previous conventions and that the behavior was widely condoned by the Navy's civilian and military leaders.

"What happened at Tailhook '91 is the culmination of a long-term failure of leadership in naval aviation," the report stated. "What happened at Tailhook '91 was destined to happen sooner or later in the 'can you top this' atmosphere that appeared to increase with each succeeding convention."

The report detailed what occurred during the convention, held September 4–7, 1991, at the Las Vegas Hilton and attended by some four thousand people. The report was based on interviews with more than twenty-nine hundred people.

Chapter headings used graphic phrases to describe the

sexual behavior, including "streaking," "ballwalking," "moon-ing," "leg shaving," "belly/naval shots," "chicken fights," "butt biting" and "zapping."

Excerpts from the Final Tailhook Report

Following are excerpts from the final report on the Tailhook scandal that shook, and is still shaking, the entire Navy. The headings are titles of the report's main sections.

Executive Summary

Many attendees viewed the annual conference as a type of "free-fire zone" wherein they could act indiscriminately and without fear of censure or retribution in matters of sexual conduct and drunkenness. Some of the Navy's most senior officers were knowledgeable as to the excesses practiced at Tailhook '91 and, by their inaction, those officers served to condone and even encourage the type of behavior that occurred there.

Our investigation disclosed that 83 women and 7 men were assaulted during the three days of the convention. In total, 117 officers were implicated in one or more incidents of indecent assault, indecent exposure, conduct unbecoming an officer or failure to act in a proper leadership capacity while at Tailhook '91. Further, 51 individuals were found to have made false statements to us during our investigation. It should also be noted that the number of individuals involved in all types of misconduct or other inappropriate behavior was more widespread than these figures would suggest. Furthermore, several hundred other officers were aware of the misconduct and chose to ignore it.

Witnesses and Navy Cooperation

Most of the officers interviewed responded in a serious and cooperative fashion. Other officers were far less cooperative and attempted to limit their responses so as to reveal only minimal information.

The evidence revealed that other officers deliberately provided false information to us. Some squadron members appeared to maintain unified responses that were often contradicted by the testimony of witnesses not assigned to those squadrons. Similarly, individual officers specifically lied to us about their activities unless directly confronted with conflicting evidence.

Indecent Assaults

By most accounts, there were few women in attendance at earlier conventions. According to most descriptions, Tailhook conventions in earlier years were largely "stag" affairs. Reportedly, "unwritten" rules prohibited officers from bringing spouses or cameras to Tailhook. There are also reports that during earlier years, a large proportion of the women attending Tailhook conventions could be described as "prostitutes" or "groupies."

The nature of the gauntlet activities apparently changed some time in the mid- to late-1980s when the gauntlet started to involve males touching women who walked through the hallway. Some witnesses suggested this was a progression from the cheering, catcalls and ratings of women typical of earlier Tailhook conventions, to more physical contact in which officers would pinch and grab women's breasts, buttocks and crotch areas as the women attempted to traverse the hallway.

A male Navy lieutenant described one unsuspecting woman's passage through the gauntlet. He stated that on Friday night at approximately 11 p.m., while standing in the third floor hallway in the area of the elevators, he heard people chanting and pounding on something in a rhythmic drumming manner. He observed approximately 200 men lined along the hallway walls.

He compared the activity to a high school football practice type of gauntlet. He saw a woman enter and it seemed to him that "she did not understand it was a gauntlet." As she attempted to walk through, he observed her being "groped and molested." She was obviously "not enjoying it" and "was pushing hands away from places she did not want them." As she approached the gauntlet, he "saw a look of fear in her eyes. She fought her way through the gauntlet and busted out the side through a suite." He said the look of fear in the woman's eyes caused him to realize the gauntlet was not just a playful situation and he became concerned for other women in the hallway and the vicinity of the gauntlet.

Another female civilian victim told us that, as she walked up the hallway, at least seven men suddenly attacked her. They pulled down her "tube top" and grabbed at her exposed breasts while she attempted to cover herself with her arms. She fell to the floor and the assault continued. She bit several of her attackers in an attempt to stop their assault. After a few moments, they stopped their attack and she was allowed to get up from the floor. She turned and ... observed another woman screaming and fighting her way down the hallway as she too was attacked.

Indecent Exposure

One form of indecent exposure that occurred at Tailhook '91 involved "streaking," a term used ... to describe the actions of males who removed their clothing and walked or ran nude past on-lookers.

Another form of indecent exposure, referred to as "mooning," involved individuals baring their buttocks within view of other attendees.

The third form of indecent exposure engaged in by naval aviators at Tailhook '91 involved publicly exposing their testicles, commonly referred to in the naval aviation community as "ballwalking." Eighty individuals reported to us that they witnessed ballwalking at Tailhook '91. We identified 14 military officers who ballwalked during the convention.

The terms "belly shots" and "naval shots" describe the practice of drinking alcohol (typically tequila) out of people's navels.

Witnesses and participants reported that three male officers drank belly shots from the navel of a female officer. This occurred in the VAW-110 suite on the same night the female officer had her legs shaved by two of the male officers. The female officer reported that a few of the women who participated in belly shots wore short dresses and no undergarments and exposed themselves while doing belly shots.

Another type of assaultive behavior that occurred on the third floor of the Hilton Hotel during Tailhook '91 involved individuals biting attendees on the buttocks. That activity was commonly referred to by witnesses as "butt biting" or "sharking." The origin of butt biting at Tailhook is unknown, but one Marine major reported that, in his squadron, "sharking" was a common activity between males and females dating back about 20 years.

Other Improper Activity

Over 200 witnesses told us they observed leg shaving at the 1991 symposium. This activity occurred on the third floor during Tailhook '91 and involving the shaving of women's legs and pubic areas by male aviators. Our investigation disclosed that leg shaving has been an element of unit parties in the Navy for years.

Officer Attitudes and Leadership Issues

Tailhook '91 is the culmination of a long-term failure of

leadership in naval aviation. What happened at Tailhook '91 was destined to happen sooner or later in the "can you top this" atmosphere that appeared to increase with each succeeding convention. Senior aviation leadership seemed to ignore the deteriorating standards of behavior and failed to deal with the increasing disorderly, improper and promiscuous behavior.

Navy Problems Persist

After the scandal of the Tailhook Convention in 1991 involving Navy pilots, many people felt that Navy personnel were at least somewhat more aware of the costs and consequences of sexual harassment. Nevertheless, several of the most serious incidents of sexual harassment occurred only a few weeks or months after the final Tailhook report was released.

In May 1993 in Keyport, Washington, two Navy sailors were demoted and sentenced to thirty days' hard labor after admitting they had sexually harassed a female crew member aboard their torpedo boat. The 19-year-old female crew member, a recent boot camp graduate, alleged she was subjected to abuse in December 1992.

The men's actions consisted of grabbing her and throwing her over the side of the ship while it was at a torpedo test range in Nanaima, British Colombia. They also were accused of holding her down while they simulated sex acts.

The abuse by the male sailors took place after the men had attended a daylong training session on combating sexual harassment in the Navy. The training was ordered Navy-wide after the attention of the Tailhook convention.

In July 1993, aviators from several reserve squadrons in the San Diego area distributed T-shirts with lewd statements about Rep. Patricia Schroeder of Colorado. The T-shirts featured a mock front page of a fictitious newspaper called "The Investigation Daily." The front page had a large headline that made crude remarks of a sexual nature about Rep. Schroeder, a senior Democrat on the House Armed Services Committee. Other offensive remarks appeared elsewhere on the page.

Rep. Schroeder was one of the most outspoken critics of the military's sexual harassment problems and specifically criticized the lack of effective leadership during the Tailhook scandal. In 1992, she was the target of a lewd banner hung at the officers club of the Miramar Naval Air Station near San Diego. During that episode, the Navy relieved five officers of their commands and reprimanded sixteen others for their involvement with the sign and for sexually suggestive skits that were performed at the air station during a social event.

Comdr. Craig Quigley, a Navy spokesman, said the Navy was investigating the squadrons involved in the T-shirt episode and he denounced the messages printed on them. "The tone and the conduct of the mock newspaper on the shirt is totally unacceptable, and we regret any offense taken by individuals subject to those comments. We've told the squadrons involved not to sell, distribute, wear or display these shirts, on duty or off duty."

Rep. Schroeder said through a spokesman, "It makes you wonder whether the training is ever going to get through to some people in the Navy." She was speaking of efforts by the Navy and other services since the Tailhook scandal to undertake a program to combat sexual harassment in which sailors and other officers must attend sensitivity training and which stiffens penalties for offenders.

As of late 1993, the Navy was still in the process of disciplining those involved in the Tailhook scandal. Vice Admiral J. Paul Reason was reviewing one hundred twenty cases of alleged misconduct; the cases were referred to the Navy by the Pentagon's inspector general. Seven senior officers have been disciplined, including the resignation of Navy Secretary H. Lawrence Garrett 3d, who attended the 1991 convention. Thirty-nine other officers have been disciplined, with twenty-nine of those receiving immunity to testify against others.

Vice Admiral Reason asked to use a rare legal procedure to

punish officers without letting them defend themselves by issuing letters of censure in approximately a half dozen cases. The *San Diego Union-Tribune* said that in these particular cases the government was unlikely to win court-martial decisions. The admiral's staff made the request after one of the officers accused of wrongdoing at the Tailhook convention asked for a court-martial instead of an administrative hearing, believing that the Navy did not have enough evidence to win a court-martial conviction. Subsequently six other officers refused to accept non-judicial punishment prescribed for them and demanded courts-martial as well.

An attorney for the officers said Vice Admiral Reason has the authority to unilaterally reject the officers' request for courts-martial and recommend them for administrative action anyway. The officers cannot appeal his decision.

While a letter of censure, like a court-martial conviction, would ruin an officer's military career, the two are very different. Once a letter of censure is issued, the recipient has no right to appeal, as is possible in a court-martial, but can only make a written rebuttal.

The Tailhook group resumed its conventions in the fall of 1993 in San Diego, even though the Navy and most of the corporate sponsors have withdrawn their support. W.D. Knutson, the group's chairman, said that members of the group consider the convention, which they call a symposium, to be "an important function of our organization. They want to show unity and support, and to press on with shaping the future of the organization."

Navy Tries Green/Yellow/Red Light System to Stop Harassment

In mid-1993 the Navy sent a one-page bulletin to all commanding officers in a quarterly information packet called the "Captain's Call Kit" to attempt to define sexual harassment.

The one-page bulletin was to accompany a longer brochure called "Resolving Conflict: Following the Light of Personal Behavior" that was distributed to Navy and Marine officers. Both documents boil down a more in-depth training program on sexual harassment developed after the Tailhook scandal by the Standing Committee on Women in the Navy Service.

The one-page flyer, designed to be displayed on bulletin boards, uses simple, clear language and traffic light colors to group acceptable and unacceptable behaviors between men and women. The green zone (Go) includes neutral, non-gender, non-sexual social behaviors such as "placing a hand on someone's elbow," or asking "How was your weekend?" The yellow zone (Slow down to Stop) includes whistling, unwanted poems, violating personal space and questions about personal life. The red zone (Stop) includes sexual favors in return for employment rewards and sexual assault and rape.

While many Navy officials are pleased with what Rear Adm. Kendell Pease, the Chief of Navy Information, calls the "sound bite, bumper sticker" approach, others say the approach simplifies and discounts the seriousness of the problem. Some say that a complex, subjective issue with so many nuances cannot be reduced to a few color-coded dos and don'ts. Even those who doubt the program believe that the Navy's intentions are positive, but believe that sexual harassment is not a problem that can be codified and regimented.

According to Maureen Dowd, writing in *The New York Times*, "It is a difficult period for the American military culture, which has always operated by the book, grounded in certitudes on everything from the exact angle of a salute, to the exact way to fold the corners of a bed sheet, to the exact day to switch from winter to summer uniforms. Now the military finds itself awash in gray areas as it tries to define proper sexual behavior … "

Barbara Pope, the former assistant Secretary of the Navy who investigated Tailhook and who helped develop the traffic-light training system, believes the list is a good idea because it helps provoke thought and discussion. However, she also said that personal training sessions sometimes underscore how such sound bite phrases can be interpreted differently by different people. Admiral Pease said the "red light-green light" list was a good way of getting the attention of rank and file military and should be used as a supplement to the Navy's training sessions.

Pease also stated that the Navy's toll-free hot-line for Sexual Harassment Advice and Counseling (800-253-0931 in the United States and 703-614-2735 overseas) has received more than five hundred calls in the last three months and that approximately 50 percent of the calls seeking advice have been from men. "This is a young, mobile Navy that uses switchers, green is on and red is off, and understands that environment," he said. "We have a lot of young kids who understand automobiles and traffic signals and this gives them something they can understand and put in their own terms. You don't realize how low we have to get. You do have to be simple. This is not being taught in the home."

The text of the one-page bulletin, "What Is Sexual Harassment?" follows.

Everyone knows that sexual harassment will not be tolerated in the Navy—but what constitutes sexual harassment still seems to be confusing for some sailors and Navy employees. That's because sexual harassment includes a wide range of behaviors. Some of these are obvious and easy to recognize, while others fall into gray areas and may be perceived as sexual harassment even if the behavior was not intended that way.

Adding to the confusion is the fact that a person's intention is not the only deciding factor in these cases. The way the action or "joke" is perceived by the recipient and others in the workplace, and its impact, also determines if it is sexual harassment.

To make it easier to understand, think of behavior in terms of a traffic light with green, yellow and red zones.

GREEN—Go
These actions do not constitute sexual harassment. They are typical interactions and common courtesies that happen regularly in an office environment. Some examples:
- *Performance counseling*
- *Touching which could not be perceived in a sexual way, such as placing a hand on a person's elbow*
- *Counseling on military appearance*
- *Everyday social interaction such as saying, "Hello, how are you?" or "Did you have a good weekend?"*
- *Expressing concern or encouragement*
- *A polite compliment or friendly conversation*

YELLOW—Slow down to stop
Many of these behaviors fall into the gray areas but others are obvious examples of sexual harassment. Examples:
- *Violating "personal space"*
- *Whistling*
- *Questions about personal life*
- *Lewd or off-color jokes*
- *Leering or staring*
- *Repeated requests for a date after being told no*
- *Suggestive posters or calendars*
- *Foul language*
- *Unwanted letters or presents*
- *Sexually suggestive touching*
- *Sitting or gesturing sexually*

RED—Stop
These behaviors are always considered to be sexu-
al harassment and if they continue, punitive actions
will be taken. Examples are:
  • *Sexual favors in return for employment rewards*
    and threats if sexual favors are not provided
  • *Sexually explicit pictures, including calendars or*
    posters
  • *Sexually explicit remarks*
  • *Using office status to request a date*
  • *Obscene letters or comments*
  • *Grabbing, forced kissing, fondling*
  • *Sexual assault or rape*

Ellen Bravo, national director of 9 to 5, said such lists can be confusing. She said several examples of the green light area, such as "counseling on military appearance" or "touching which would not be perceived in a sexual way" are so vague that they might be yellow light or even red light, depending on the manner in which they were done.

"The reason why personal training is so important is that things that seem to be OK, like compliments, may not be OK depending on how they are delivered. The phrase, 'Gee, your hair looks terrific, Miss Jones,' might be innocent enough, until the tone of voice is intimate and the guy leans in very close and breaths heavily in your hair as he says it."

A *New York Times* editorial said: "Still, the Navy deserves some credit for an earnest if awkward attempt to clarify the dos and don'ts of sexual behavior for people who never seemed to have learned them ... [These people] reflect the American culture out of which they come—a culture in which sexual harassment is common and sexual braggarts like California's Spur Posse (a group of young men awarding each other points for sexual conquests) become the guest-most-wanted by the nation's talk shows.

"It may be hard to believe that servicemen must be told

that asking 'Did you have a nice weekend?' is OK, and 'grabbing, forced kissing, fondling' is not. But experience suggests that a clear code of conduct is needed. The Navy's guide may be simplistic, but like a reading primer, it's a start."

More Positive Efforts by the Navy

On June 25, 1993, the Navy appointed Rear Admiral Marsha J. Evans as Commander, Navy Recruiting Command—the first woman in Naval history to be responsible for worldwide recruitment of men and women for Navy officer and enlisted programs. In an interview, Evans said the Navy is in the process of reviewing their entire recruiting strategy for a diverse Navy. Just as any large corporation would, she said, the Navy is targeting the market to find out where minorities and women are and how to go about recruiting them to the service through a detailed, strategic program. Evans noted that diversity, which has been a focus of the Navy for some time, is of particular interest now, since as of April 29, 1993, all Naval officer aviation programs—all pilot and naval flight officer assignments and recruitment—are genderless.

As for the Navy's "green/yellow/red light program," Evans said, "I think the program is terrific, it's a significant first step. It's an opening, a start to get people to focus on the problem and to exercise caution." After completing a worldwide trip to examine recruitment processes and diversity programs, Evans said, "I don't think there's anyone in the world in the Navy who doesn't know that we take sexual harassment very seriously. We've discharged over forty people in the last year, some with as many as eighteen years of service, for serious charges of sexual harassment.

"The Navy's overall program to address the problem of sexual harassment is made up of three parts: education and training, leadership and command emphasis, and a get-tough aspect—if you engage in this type of behavior, as far as the

Navy goes, you're out of here," Evans said.

The Navy's Record of Progress

In April 1993, Rear Admiral Evans addressed members of Congress and their key staffers regarding the positive progress of the Navy with regard to women in the service. Following are the key points of Admiral Evans' briefing:

> *The Navy has a solid record of progress in integrating women and fully utilizing their talents. Navy women now serve in every career field and in every type of unit that is open to them, constrained only by law (Title 10 Section 6015). Specifically women can now be assigned to any unit or vessel in the Navy except those which have primary objectives to seek out, reconnoiter, and engage an enemy. Women officer aviators may be permanently assigned without restriction to all aviation squadrons regardless of type mission.*
>
> *Women are recognized and respected as contributing members of the Navy-Marine Corps team. Officer and enlisted women are serving in key leadership roles ashore and afloat, including top level command and flag (admiral) rank. In general, promotion rates have been equal to or better than their male counterparts. Examples include: 4 women commanding Navy ships (AOs, 2 diving & salvage), 6 flag/flag selects, and 15 command master chiefs—9 are of afloat commands.*
>
> *The number and percentage of women serving in non-traditional roles has steadily increased. Over one-third of Navy women are trained in non-traditional occupational specialties such as engineering, ordinance, and construction. One-quarter of Navy women are currently serving aboard ship or in avia-*

tion squadrons.

Tailhook has overshadowed the steady, significant progress in expanding professional opportunities and achieving fair compensation for women that has occurred over the past two decades.

A (very) few individuals who were involved in Tailhook have tarnished the reputation of an entire organization. The vast majority of Navy men and women were outraged by what occurred at the convention and are committed to doing whatever is necessary to ensure it never occurs in the future.

Tailhook was a transforming event. It has resulted in fundamental change in how the Navy views the societal and institutional problem of sexual harassment and gender discrimination. The Navy now recognizes that its eradication requires strong measures to address root causes in the culture that have prevented full acceptance of women as professional peers. The Navy is committed to achieving lasting changes in attitudes and behavior.

The Navy is well under way on a course of action to eradicate sexual harassment, promote cultural changes and increase equality. The strategy is built around four key components:

1) Top leadership commitment to solve the problem;

2) Revised education and training for every member of the Department, with special emphasis on leader training;

3) Holding offenders accountable; and

4) A systematic approach to combatting sexual harassment.

On October 6, 1992 the Secretary of the Navy directed the implementation of 80 specific initiatives that carry out the strategy.

Highlights of the initiatives include:

- *Establishment of a top-level Standing Committee on Military and Civilian Women on the Department of the Navy to advise the Secretary on all matters related to women;*
- *A toll-free 1-800 sexual harassment counseling and advice line staffed by trained counselors;*
- *A plain-language policy that prohibits sexual harassment and clearly sets out roles and responsibilities to prevent it;*
- *Improved education and training at all levels to emphasize the core values of honor, courage and commitment, standards of conduct and appropriate behaviors, the prevention of sexual harassment and the responsibilities of leaders;*
- *Periodic culture and climate assessments and a Department-wide reporting and tracking system with an integrated data base to track formal sexual harassment complaints and reported incidents of sexual assault and rape to provide an accurate yardstick of progress in changing attitudes and behaviors;*
- *Design of an informal complaint resolution system to provide members with behavioral competencies to resolve the complaints in the work center;*
- *Gender-integrated recruit training to lay the foundation of team work and mutual respect from the start of one's Navy career; and*
- *Expansion of opportunities for women to participate in fleet training and joint training exercises to gain valuable experience in naval operations.*

The Navy has been recognized as a leader in devel-

*oping a comprehensive approach to eradicating sexu-
al harassment and gender discrimination. Other federal agencies and private institutions have consulted
with the Navy particularly on our strategies to eliminate the root causes of inappropriate behaviors and
attitudes that reflect lack of respect for and underval-
uation of the contribution of women to the team
effort.*

Veteran's Affairs

According to a report issued by a federal investigative agency
in late January 1993, two of the most powerful men at the
Veterans Affairs Medical Center in Decatur, Georgia, harassed
female employees, and the hospital's director did nothing to
stop the harassment. The report, which was written by the
VA Office of Inspector General (IG), accuses the hospital's former associate director and its chief medical examiner of blatant sexual harassment and indicates that three other high-
ranking personnel were guilty of harassment as well.

The *Atlanta Journal-Constitution* obtained an unedited
version of the IG report anonymously and published the findings. The original report released to the media was edited
with names, job titles, and other identifying information
blacked out.

The report was very critical of the hospital's former director. It said that the IG investigators interviewed twenty-four
VA employees who said they knew of incidents of sexual
harassment involving the associate director, and that even
after employees complained about his behavior to the district
counsel and to the IG hotline, the former director "apparently
found no reason for convening an administrative investigation
into the Associate Director's conduct." The report stated that
"the Associate Director was named in about half of our interviews as sexually harassing women, and the Director was

made aware of some of the behavior of the Associate Director, yet no apparent actions were ever taken." Such behavior "set the tone" at the hospital.

The IG investigators interviewed thirty-seven women who said they had been harassed, with some allegations dating back ten years. Specifics contained in the report:

- *Associate Director; allegations:* Thirteen women testified that he made inappropriate personal remarks and issued invitations tinged with sexual innuendo. According to one woman, the associate director frequently stopped in her office, even though he had no business to conduct. "On one occasion, he grabbed her wrist and began sniffing ... up to the level of her breast, then said, 'I don't know what you're wearing, but it certainly does things for me,' or words to that effect." *Job Status: Retired in August; is collecting regular retirement benefits.*

- *Chief of Medical Staff; allegations:* Seven women testified that during a ten-year period he made inappropriate comments to them or touched them in sexually suggestive ways. In one case he tugged at a woman's undergarments; in other cases he attempted to feel the fabric of clothing they were wearing, the women said. Most of the women said they were in his chain of command and were concerned about their jobs if they complained. Two women said they had told him directly to stop his behavior, but it continued despite their protests. *Job Status: Transferred to an undesignated position in the Atlanta office of the regional director; pay grade unchanged.*

- *Chief of Personnel; allegations:* Six women testified that he harassed them during a six-year period by engaging them in long, unsolicited sexual discussions. Some of the women said he described past and present affairs between men and women at the hospital. Two of the women said they thought his telling them of the affairs was his way of telling them how they could get ahead at the hospital. Another woman said he commented about her "good body" and told her she would advance at the hospital. *Job Status: Transferred to an undesignated position in Atlanta office of regional director; pay grade unchanged.*

- *Equal Employment Opportunity Coordinator; allegations:* Eleven women testified that he asked them to help him masturbate because, as a triple amputee, he could not masturbate and hold the cup for a needed sperm sample at the same time. He told the women he thought he could trust them to keep it a secret, they said. When asked by investigators about the incidents, the hospital's director said he had been told of the problem "nine or ten years ago." *Job Status: Transferred to prosthetics department at his request, shortly after the investigation was started; lower pay grade.*

- *Associate Director, Rehabilitation Research and Development Center; allegations:* Several women said he continually referred to women as members of an "Itty Bitty Titty Club" and one woman said he made crude remarks about her pregnancy. She said she told him to stop but he did not. The women said they feared for their jobs and did not complain. *Job Status: Serving in same position.*

The *Journal-Constitution* story said none of the men named could be reached for comment. However, one of the attorneys involved, Ms. Joyce Kitchens, said, "My clients got caught up in an avalanche of anger and frustration, but they're innocent." This latest scandal came on the heels of numerous reports from Veterans Administration institutions nationwide where women have complained of sexual harassment.

In March 1993 the Veterans Administration announced plans to study combat stress in women, including the problems caused by sexual harassment and assault. The agency will open a special facility at the National Center for Post Traumatic Stress Disorder in Boston. Dr. Jessica Wolfe, director, said the research project will be the first to examine the stressful effects of war on women.

In April 1993, the U.S. House of Representatives passed a bill that includes a provision to crack down on sexual harassment at Veterans Administration facilities. Rep. Christopher Smith, a member of the House Veterans' Affairs Committee, said, "The legislation was the result of an extensive examination by our committee of sexual harassment and employment discrimination in the VA—an examination that made it painfully clear that the VA's settlement procedures are inadequate and in need of a decisive legislative fix." He went on to say that the language in the provision "enhances the confidence of those VA employees who may someday need the services provided by the legislation—it's a bold step toward rooting out sexual harassment in the federal government."

The law would create an Office of Employment Discrimination and Complaints Resolution, including trained counselors and investigators working inside the VA to resolve cases of sexual harassment. It also would require the appointment of administrative law judges to conduct hearings and make judgments on complaints. Cases would be reviewed by the EEOC or federal courts.

"Testimony from witnesses has clearly shown that the VA's system for resolving sexual harassment complaints has failed miserably,"Rep. Smith said.

A number of women testified before the House committee in September 1992 with complaints of sexual harassment. Among them was a nursing supervisor who said she was harassed routinely by the former chief of the Federal Service Department at one VA facility in New Jersey. She said that after she reported the harassment, the man began denying her leave requests, changed her job title and position, reduced her duties, excluded her from meetings, restricted how she performed her duties, and moved her office into a basement with only a desk, a phone, and a broken chair. The man later admitted the charges, pled guilty to one count of "abusive sexual contact" and was given two years probation, fined $3,000, and ordered to perform three hundred hours of community service at a women's facility.

RELIGION

A former priest and theologian who had been forced into retirement by the University of Notre Dame admitted in March 1992 to sexually harassing his students, saying his actions were "a default in my responsibilities as a priest." He said he resigned for "other unrelated reasons of my own," even though the university asked him to leave. He wrote in a statement to the *National Catholic Reporter,* "I have been making amends by offering apology to people I had offended and receiving their forgiveness, and I have been trying to submit to whatever transformation the Lord affords me."

The priest said he "saw what I had done as a default in my responsibilities as a priest, a member of a religious brotherhood and a mentor."

One Notre Dame graduate student said the priest propositioned him as an undergraduate in 1987, three years after the two men first met. "I called him for help, and I got the distinct impression that to get his help I would have to be physically intimate with him," he said.

The man said he decided to identify himself in an effort to pressure Notre Dame to admit the incident and take steps to protect students from recurrences. He is co-chairman of Gays and Lesbians of Notre Dame and St. Mary's College.

Notre Dame conducted an investigation into allegations by students against the priest and then asked for his resignation in 1990. He was placed on a one-year sabbatical with his tenure to expire at the close of the 1991–92 academic year. He was a former chairman of the Notre Dame theology department and a provost.

Sexual Harassment By Clergy

The Minnesota Court of Appeals ruled in late 1991 that the First Amendment does not bar an associate pastor from suing her former church for sexual harassment by her supervising pastor.

A former associate pastor filed charges with the state human rights department, alleging that her supervising pastor made unwelcome sexual advances toward her, touched her in a sexual way, and, against her objections, insisted she accompany him outside the workplace. She says she complained to the church authorities and they did nothing. She was discharged three months later for failure "to conduct the pastoral office efficiently." She sued the church, the synod, and the pastor for sexual harassment, retaliation, breach of contract, defamation, and wrongful termination. The church argued that the suit violated the First Amendment's separation of church and state, and the trial court dismissed the case.

The appeals court ruled that the sexual harassment claim "is related to pastoral qualifications or issues of church doctrine," and reinstated the suit. The court held that the harassment claim posed no danger of excessive state involvement with religion, since the claim was based on pre-discharge conduct. However, the claims relating to the woman's firing must be dismissed, because inquiring into the reasons for the employee's discharge could involve the state in matters of church doctrine.

HARASSMENT IN SPORTS

According to Reuters, former *Boston Herald* sportswriter Lisa Olsen received a reported $500,000 out-of-court settlement in early 1992 for dropping her sexual harassment charges against the New England Patriots, players Zeke Mowatt, Michael Timpson, and Robert Perryman, and team-owner Victor Kiam.

Olsen said, "One of the reasons I filed this suit was to force them to take it seriously … Now it is time to move on with the rest of my life." The trial was scheduled to start March 1992, but Olsen told *The Herald* one reason she settled was that her father has cancer and a trial would have put additional strain on her family.

Olsen alleged she was sexually harassed in the locker room at Foxboro Stadium on Sept. 17, 1990, by three players while she was trying to interview another player.

Olsen filed suit in April 1991 against the New England Patriots, charging sexual harassment and civil rights violations. She had been covering the Boston Bruins for the *Boston Herald*, and had worked for the paper for four years.

Her attorney said, "She has to leave the state, at least for now," and did not say when she would return. However, the paper's editor, Robert Sales, said Olsen's departure would not be permanent. "Sometime in the near future she's going away for awhile, and at the appropriate time she will return. She will still be an employee at the paper and one hopes she will continue to be the effective employee that she is when she returns."

Olsen's suit was filed in Suffolk Superior Court against the NFL team, owner Victor Kiam, former general manager Patrick Sullivan, former media services director James Oldham, and three players—Zeke Mowatt, Michael Timpson, and Robert Perryman. The suit alleged intentional infliction of emotional distress and intentional damage to her professional reputation. It asked for unspecified monetary damages.

Olsen alleged that in September 1990 she was sexually

harassed while trying to conduct an interview in the locker room. According to court documents, Olsen was interviewing Maurice Hurst, a Patriots player, when Mowatt, who was naked, displayed his genitals and made sexual remarks while egged on by Timpson and Perryman. The suit states she was harassed again, two days later, when she returned to interview players. The suit alleged that general manager Sullivan called her around September 23rd and "threatened her with remarks which included a warning about skeletons that might be in the closet."

Olsen's attorneys said that since that time she has endured abuse from some of the fans at sporting events. "A great number of times she is yelled at, screamed at, sees negative graffiti about her ... her car was vandalized. She's frightened all the time," one attorney said.

Olsen also has received hate mail and harassing phone calls. "Nobody should have to go through this just for trying to do their job," Olsen said. "If anything, this suit will make it easier for others so that something like this won't happen to other female journalists."

Olsen said she intended to drop the issue after the NFL fined the team and the players. But she decided to sue after Victor Kiam, the team's owner, joked about the incident while speaking at a banquet, and because Mowatt and Perryman did not pay the fines.

"What Kiam did was treat Lisa Olsen like the butt of a joke instead of a person," said one of her attorneys. Another attorney said, "He (Kiam) apologizes and does it again, which shows he had no sincerity. Kiam is older and in a higher position and should have known better than the young players."

Kiam's office said he would not be available for comment; the Patriots team also declined to comment.

"The harassment has continued," one of Olsen's attorneys said, "and she has to get some justice from the courts. She's frightened all the time."

Inflatable Dolls Banned in Boston

Management of the Boston Red Sox baseball team issued a statement condemning the practice of fans bringing inflatable dolls to games after a fan complained to a newspaper about other fans fondling the dolls and making obscene gestures. The statement said, "Such conduct is reprehensible and the club has made special efforts and will continue to make special efforts to prevent such occurrences in the future."

The team said only two such incidents have occurred this season, but stepped up security on these recent complaints. One fan said, "I don't think that's right when there are little boys and girls around."

Richard Levin, a spokesman for Commissioner Fay Vincent, said he has never heard of similar incidents in other ballparks around the country. "We certainly don't condone the behavior, but we understand the Red Sox have it under control." However, fans who attended a game following the complaints, said that when the dolls were passed around at that game, security was slow to respond.

Ellen Zucker, president of the National Organization for Women's Boston chapter, welcomed the Red Sox statement, but said that more should have been done sooner. "I think when we get reports that they were quicker to remove beach balls than sexual dolls that were used for lewd sexual acts, there is reason to be concerned. That they are moving quicker on it now is a good sign."

Zucker called the inflatable doll behavior a "rapelike" act and said this incident and the Lisa Olsen incident raises disturbing questions. "The lessons we as women have been taught is that we are not welcome at sporting events. We are not welcome in locker rooms and we are not even welcome as spectators," she said.

Fans who sit in the bleachers at Fenway Park (where the doll incident occurred) have a reputation for fun-loving rowdiness, usually demonstrated by doing the wave and tossing beach balls. However, security reports that beer drinking sometimes gets out of hand and ten to twenty fans may be ejected during a game.

Naked inflatable dolls have appeared at other sporting events in Massachusetts as well. At Foxboro stadium, vendors sold naked "Lisa Dolls" following the complaint by Olsen against the Patriots.

HARASSMENT AT AIRLINES

A United Airlines female co-pilot filed a lawsuit in California state court against the UAL Corporation, alleging numerous incidents of sexual harassment by male pilots and other employees. Kathy Gillies charged that she was "tackled" in an assault by a pilot who wanted to have sex with her, that she was asked by an instructor if she wanted to engage in sexual intercourse, and that she was shown pornographic pictures by other crew members.

She also alleged that after she complained to supervisors at United about the assault by the pilot they refused to guarantee that she wouldn't fly with him in the future and that United refused to provide gender-sensitivity classes for pilots.

A United spokesman said the airlines had not seen the complaint and was unaware a suit had been filed. "However, United doesn't condone any form of sexual harassment or discrimination and we treat any such claims with utmost seriousness," he said. United has 8,010 pilots, 398 are women.

Air Canada Drops Name-Tag Plan

Air Canada reversed its requirement that all employees wear name tags after complaints and worries from employees about the growing incidence of violence against women—

especially harassment and stalking. Cheryl Kryzaniwsky, president of the Canadian Auto Workers' Air Canada local union, said, "With a 75 percent female membership, we were concerned about ... violence." In January 1993, when the airline announced that name tags would be mandatory, the union told members that they had the right to refuse unsafe work, including problems the name tags might bring about. Within two weeks of the start of the mandatory name tag program, Air Canada announced that wearing name tags is optional.

8

YOUNG PEOPLE, SCHOOLS, AND EDUCATION

> *It is not uncommon for boys to make lewd comments to girls in school hallways or to pass sexual notes about them in class. The boys also grab girls' breasts, pull down girls' gym shorts, and in some schools the boys have "Friday flip-up day," during which they chase girls and try to lift their skirts. I call this gender terrorism.*
>
> Dr. Nan Stein,
> Director, Sexual
> Harassment in
> Schools Project,
> Wellesley College

I was staying in a Dallas motel room with two of my young nieces, watching TV and reading scary books after a long day of "family-reunioning." One of the girls, who was only ten at the time, was laying beside me on the bed and started to tell me a story. She said there was a boy at school who would come up to her and other girls and ask to see their hair, and when they would point to their heads, he would say, "No, I don't mean that hair," meaning instead their pubic hair. She said he would grab their butts and their breasts and use foul and dirty language with them. She said her girlfriend said it was sexual harassment, and my little niece wanted to know what I thought.

I'm sure you must be thinking that since I'm in the sexual harassment business, and since this was my niece, that I must have overreacted ... but I think you'd be surprised. I just asked her some clarifying questions and then asked who she'd told. It was then I felt as if I were talking to a forty-year-old ten-year-old.

She gave me all the same reasons for not speaking up that I hear from adult women: that the person she would have to tell (her mother, father, counselor, principal, teacher) either wouldn't believe her, would tell her to ignore it, or would blame her, or simply that it was too embarrassing to go to them. I asked if she wanted me to help. She said yes, and the next day I told her father.

Needless to say, he did not think it was funny or to be ignored, and when it was reported to the school, a number of complaints about the same little boy came out. His behavior was stopped by the school officials.

Sexual harassment of students is not new. The story I've just told happened more than eight years ago, and we are just now seeing serious and widespread attention being given to the problem in high schools, junior highs, and even elementary schools. According to numerous stories in the media during the last two years, there is a disturbing trend involving young women and men in the United States. These events, for example, were reported in April 1993:

- A 13-year-old girl in Ft. Worth, Texas, was held down by six boys age 12–14 while another boy sexually assaulted her on a crowded school bus. Reportedly other students witnessing the assault laughed while the girl struggled.
- In Los Angeles, a group of young men who called themselves the "Posse" were accused of raping and molesting girls as part of a group competition to score "points" for sexual conquests. The victims were ages 10, 13, 15, and 16. The boys were awarded their points regardless of the consent or willingness of the girls.
- Approximately twelve teenage boys in Glen Ridge, New Jersey, gathered in a friend's basement to watch sexual acts performed on a mentally retarded girl, age 17, who

lived in their neighborhood. The girl was sexually violated with a baseball bat, a stick, and a broom handle.
• School officials in Dallas, Texas, agree that one of the primary causes of fights between black and Hispanic boys
is the lewd treatment of girls in public, including crude
remarks and forced fondling in hallways.

In a national study released in April 1993, girls age 9 to 19
reported being pinched, grabbed, subjected to obscene
remarks and even raped by male classmates. One young ninth-
grade girl in Dallas said boys constantly demand that girls perform oral sex.

Cheltzie Hentz was a seven year-old girl who said she was
teased and taunted by boys on her bus while riding to school
in the Eden Prairie, Minnesota, school district. In October
1991, her mother, Sue Mutzier, filed a sexual harassment suit
on her daughter's behalf, saying, "When I put my child on the
bus I have a right to know that she will have a safe and relatively happy ride to school without being harassed and forced
to listen to profanities." School officials had no comment. In
April 1993, Cheltzie Hentz, then eight years old, became the
youngest person to ever win such a complaint against a
school district under Title IX of the 1972 Education Act. The
act grants authority to the U.S. Department of Education to
investigate complaints, order remedies and withhold funding
from districts that don't comply.

School counselors say that many girls have problems with
self-esteem because they are pressured to have sex and treated in derogatory fashions. Some say the girls are alternatively
treated as "bitches" or courted as "babes." One counselor said
that then when girls do give in to promiscuity in the hope of
becoming popular, they are treated badly and feel a loss of
self-esteem and self-respect.

Rena Pederson, editorial page editor of the *Dallas
Morning News*, wrote in a column, "I hesitate to bring this up
because it is an uncomfortable subject and there are no easy

solutions to offer. But it is perplexing: Why is it that women have made progress in being respected for their intellectual abilities in many fields, and yet seem to be losing ground when it comes to being treated as disposable sexual objects?"

It seems fair to say that after the Thomas–Hill controversy and the Navy's Tailhook scandal, the focus of sexual harassment has shifted to America's classrooms and schools. Simply trying to apply the same standards in schools that are applied in American businesses may make some sense, but not totally. When the harassment is student to student, the situation is substantially different than when it occurs employer to employee, employee to employee, or even teacher to student.

In student to student harassment, both involved parties are usually children, or at least minors, and often in the midst of puberty with hormones running wild. But when does normal sexuality and experimentation and flirting turn to harassment? Many parents of boys and girls are saying it should be stopped sooner than later, that we've allowed it to go too far for too long, mostly at the expense of girls and young women.

Minnesota and California have passed laws requiring school systems to adopt sexual harassment policies, with the California law allowing for suspension or expulsion of harassers as young as fourth grade. Additionally, a nationwide study, mentioned above, added fuel to the fire over harassment in the schools.

The study, conducted by the joint efforts of three parties— Nan Stein, head of the Center for Research on Women at Wellesley College, the National Organization for Women's Legal Defense Fund, and *Seventeen* magazine, is titled "Secrets in Public," and resulted from a survey *Seventeen* conducted of its readers. Of the forty-two hundred girls responding, 89 percent reported being touched, pinched, or grabbed by other students; and 39 percent said they had been sexually harassed at school on a daily basis during the previous year.

The study said harassment at school peaks during ages 13 to 16, and that many girls suffer poor self-image problems during this time. It also said that by ignoring these behaviors, the schools contribute to the problem. All schools should immediately develop sexual harassment policies and guidelines for handling complaints.

In *Sexual Harassment and Teens: A Program for Positive Change* (Free Spirit Publishing), these types of behaviors are cited as problems:

- Using the computer to leave sexual messages or to play sexually oriented computer games
- Rating an individual based on appearance
- "Snuggies"—pulling underwear up at the waist so it goes in between the buttocks
- Making kissing sounds or smacking sounds; licking the lips suggestively
- "Spiking"—pulling down someone's pants
- Howling, catcalls, whistles
- Inappropriate touching—breasts, buttocks, etc.
- Verbal comments about parts of the body, or about clothing, etc.
- Spreading sexual rumors
- Sexual or dirty jokes
- Massaging the neck and shoulders
- Touching oneself sexually in front of others
- Graffiti

While educators say their increased awareness is in part a result of the Thomas–Hill controversy, many say it was the 1992 Supreme Court ruling that brought about real changes. In that case, involving Christine Franklin, a Georgia teenager, and the Gwinnett County, Georgia, school system, the court ruled that a student may sue the school for damages when the school failed to react appropriately to her complaints.

Franklin said her teacher harassed her and eventually forced her to have sex with him and that the school did not respond when she complained. The Supreme Court's ruling is that a student may sue for and collect damages under Title IX

of the federal Education Act of 1972, which bans sex discrimination in schools and colleges. While the Gwinnett case
involved teacher–student harassment, arguments continue on
how far Title IX will be expanded—to student–student harassment, for example.

The National School Boards Association, for one, has
argued that holding an employer responsible for the conduct
of its employees is quite different than holding it accountable
for student actions. Most report, however, that school boards
are concerned about possible liability, and many experts
believe it to be an inevitability.

The Alpine Utah, school district adopted a policy that
gives students the same protection from sexual harassment
that it provides employees. The policy prohibits sexual harassment of students by employees of the district as well as by
other students. Depending on the severity of the offense, students who harass can be suspended or expelled; employees
can be suspended or terminated.

Nancy Benda, director of the Florida Department of
Education's equal education opportunity program, stated,
"We still have that 'boys will be boys' attitude, but less of it
now since the Gwinnett case … Once you talk about
$300,000-plus in legal fees, that kind of gets someone's atten-
tion." Among the students themselves, most boys and girls say
they are against sexual harassment—the problem is in the lack
of understanding of exactly what it is and the impact it has on
its victims.

Pederson, in the *Dallas Morning News*, said, "Surely we
are all losers when our young men do not know how to treat
young women with respect, as valued partners on earth and
in life. If sex to young people is not only increasingly imper-
sonal, but dehumanizing, then we are not just talking about
youthful indiscretions, but a pattern that does not augur well
for men and women."

A Second Major Study on Harassment in Schools

In June 1993, the results of a second major study on sexual harassment in U.S. school systems was released. The study was commissioned by the American Association of University Women and was titled "Hostile Hallways." It showed that 85 percent of all girls and 76 percent of boys said they have experienced sexual harassment at school. One out of four girls said they had been sexually harassed by a school employee.

This survey, conducted by Lou Harris and Associates, studied more than sixteen hundred eighth- through eleventh-grade students in seventy-nine schools. The survey defined sexual harassment as "unwanted and unwelcome sexual behavior which interferes with your life;" desired kissing, touching, or flirting were not included in the definition. The students were given fourteen descriptions of physical and verbal harassment and asked how often they experienced any of the behaviors at school.

The most common complaint was sexual comments such as jokes, gestures, or looks, reported by 76 percent of the girls and 56 percent of the boys. The second most common complaint was being touched, grabbed, or pinched in a sexual way. In addition, 13 percent of the girls and 9 percent of the boys said they had been "forced to do something sexual other than kissing." Of all students, 18 percent said they had been sexually harassed by a school employee.

The most common years for harassment to occur were the sixth through ninth grades, with the seventh grade being the year of most harassment. The students said the hallways were where most harassment occurs.

One senior at a Washington state high school said, "The administrators will stand there and say 'Knock it off! Knock it off!' But nothing really matters. It's rude and unrelenting."

One-third of the girls and 12 percent of the boys said they did not want to attend school after experiencing harassment.

Nearly the same percentages said they did not want to talk as much in class after being harassed.

Some recent incidents and cases include:

- A 15-year old in Mason City, Iowa, lost weight and dropped in grade points when other students started calling her "a whore and a slut." She has filed a sexual harassment suit with the U.S. Department of Education against her school.
- The mothers of two middle school girls have filed complaints because one of the girls was pinned on the seat by a boy who then kissed her, pulled out his penis, and rubbed it against her leg.
- A 15-year-old girl in Petaluma, California, has filed a federal lawsuit alleging the school didn't protect her rights under Title IX when other students humiliated her by comments such as "Have you had sex with a hot dog?" She settled out of court for $20,000.

While the numbers of girls and boys reporting harassment were similar—85 percent and 76 percent respectively—Anne Bryant, executive director of the AAUW's education foundation, said "the impact on girls is far more devastating." For example, almost five times as many girls as boys (39 percent compared with 8 percent) who have been harassed say they're afraid in school. Furthermore, 43 percent of harassed girls feel less confident about themselves as compared with 14 percent of boys.

Part of AAUW's strategy in releasing the survey results is to make adults and children more aware of the rights and responsibilities with regard to sexual harassment at school. The association is sending seventeen hundred and fifty copies of model sexual harassment policies for schools to all its branches, as well as how-to materials for setting up workshops for parents and educators.

Experts say they are not sure if the increase in sexual harassment in schools is because of an actual increase in such behavior or an increase in complaints, but most agree that the reason students hit and bully and tease each other are the same reasons sexual harassment occurs.

Joan Cole Duffell, director of community education for the Committee for the Children in Seattle, Washington, said in *USA Today*, "We know underlying a lot of this is a basic lack of empathy among children. Many, many children are being raised with a real lack of social skills, and one of the most critical is the ability to empathize. Sexual harassment is just one example of how that's manifested in school."

Advice for Students

Dr. Nan Stein at Wellesley advises students who believe they are experiencing sexual harassment to notify a guidance counselor, a teacher, or the principal. Find a person who believes you and who will do something about it.

"Sexual Harassment at school is very commonplace," she said. "It's part of the daily fabric of school life."

Her other suggestions for handling sexual harassment:

- Don't ignore it because sexual harassment does not go away when ignored. If it makes you feel uncomfortable, scared, or intimidated, do something.
- Keep a journal, a written record of each and every incident, including names of people who may have seen the harassment; save any other written materials such as notes or pictures.
- Try to tell the harasser to stop, although this can be difficult; or with an adult's help, write a letter to the harasser, keep a copy, and have the adult deliver the letter.
- Stop blaming yourself for causing the harassment; many victims of harassment, including students, feel confused, embarrassed, scared or trapped; remember—the school should handle the situation and stop the harassment.

• If the school is unable or unwilling to handle the situation, students can file a complaint with the U.S. Department of Education.

Training for Teachers

In late April 1993, a bill was introduced in Congress to fight the problem of girls being treated differently, and more negatively, in schools than boys. The proposed legislation is in response to the findings of a 1992 study by the American Association of University Women. The study showed that discrimination against girls exists in schools, including teachers giving more attention to boys. The new bill would require funds to be set aside for training teachers in gender-fair practices, as well as other actions.

Gangs Result from Sexism

Child development experts report that to most people gang development is disturbing, but to girls in neighborhoods where gangs exist, seeking a gang's protection makes perfect sense. Therapists describe communities where the impact of racism and sexism are magnified by sexual victimization.

Dr. Liz Sparks, clinical director at Roxbury Comprehensive Community Health Center, said, "They go through a degree of sexual harassment you and I would not believe. You don't hear much about that piece of the violence against women—but the teen-age girls in this community are really inundated with it."

The center's program director, Barbara Bullette, said the girls "talk about being grabbed on the breasts or buttocks in public, not even on the sly. They said the boys just seem to feel they own the other person's body. They wanted to know if it happens to adults too."

Other experts said that probably 50 percent of the girls have been sexually molested by age 5 or 6. Many have been raped and some are victims of incest. For many, the man is still in the home, and the girls are not believed when they tell their mother. The primary issue driving girls into gang membership is a response to sexism.

James Garbarino, author of "Children in Danger: Coping With the Consequences of Community Violence," said, "We have a lot of girls out there who are mad as hell about the way they've been treated. Their reaction is to say that the best way to be safe is to be powerful and strong." But such an approach often fails, he said. "We have young men in their 20s, even early 30s, coercing sex out of these young girls," creating an average ten-year age gap between the age of the mother and the age of the father.

College Level Sexual Harassment

Almost one out of five students at the University of Tennessee at Chattanooga have been sexually harassed by a professor or staff member while at school. The survey, a random sampling of five hundred sixty-eight students during the 1991 spring semester, found that 19 percent had experienced some form of sexual harassment.

Of the students reporting sexual harassment, 15 percent said it was in the form of unwanted sexual statements; 6 percent cited unwanted personal attention; 5 percent cited physical or sexual advances; and slightly more than 1 percent cited unwanted sexual propositions—all from professors or staff members.

According to C. Ann Taylor, a psychotherapist in private practice in Atlanta, parents should talk to their children about how to deal with sexual harassment—before they're confronted with it. "You can't wait to get in a situation and decide what to do," she said. "You've got to have some idea of what to do whether it's sexual harassment or rape." Waiting until it happens and hoping it will work out is "fairy-tale, Cinderella stuff; everybody will not live happily ever after," she said.

Joanna White, an instructor of child and family counseling at Georgia State University, said a parent's discussion about sexual harassment should be appropriate to the child's development level. "With a sixteen-year old you might be more clear with suggestions on how to deal with it," she said, but with a six-year old, the discussion should be more general. With younger children the issues should be about self-esteem, feeling good about themselves, and teaching them to have a positive sexual identity. With older children, parents should try to first instill in them that they are in control of their bodies and that if anything feels uncomfortable—words, innuendoes—they should tell the offending person.

Taylor also said it is important to educate girls and boys about sexual harassment and to teach young boys about respect of other people in general, and of girls in particular. "We need to work on … not having the conquest of females as a rite of passage," she said. "We need to give young men another way to say 'I'm a man' that's equally as powerful and certainly as valid."

As for what's happening in the school settings, several higher learning institutions in Florida provide education on sexual harassment for student enrollment. At the University of Miami, an entire course on sexual harassment will be offered for the first time next spring. At Miami–Dade Community College, the subject of harassment, which already is discussed in human resources and managerial psychology classes, will be more prominent in business and accounting courses. A spokeswoman for MDCC said that sexual harassment is discussed in a wide variety of courses, from business and English to women's studies and black studies. Florida Memorial College scheduled a special sexual harassment seminar for students shortly after the Thomas–Hill issue.

Little information is available about what is being done in

primary and secondary level education. Some effort has been directed by schools or school districts at training for teachers and staff, but much needs to be done to educate students.

Wellesley College appointed educator Nan Stein to conduct a three-year study of sexual harassment and abuse in the schools. The study is being done through the college's Center for Research on Women and will identify case studies, outline strategies to prevent and eliminate the problem, develop training for school personnel, and discuss the creation of public policy regulation.

Rape and Harassment Alleged at Higher Education Levels

A school-appointed fact-finding panel at Texas A&M University investigated allegations of rape, sexual harassment, and gender discrimination in early 1992. The investigation was in response to a five-page letter sent to the university's president, William H. Mobley, by four female students. The women said that female Corps of Cadets members had been subjected to discrimination and blatant verbal and physical abuse. The letter included allegations that:

- a female cadet was raped by a male cadet on campus while his roommate watched; when she reported it to a senior cadet she was told to not even seek counseling because it would give the corps a bad name;
- upperclassmen often will not acknowledge a traditional handshake known as "whipping out;" when one female corps member tried to give the handshake she was punched in the eye by a male cadet;
- male cadets who befriend or support the women are punished and threatened by upperclassmen;
- a male cadet attending a "Midnight Yell Practice" pep rally wore headgear on which he had written slurs

against women; and
- of eight qualified women who applied to the Ross Volunteer, a special cadet unit, none was selected.

The woman who wrote the letter on behalf of the four female cadets said the women want to remain anonymous because they fear retaliation. The letter was written shortly after another female cadet reported that she was physically and verbally accosted at knife point by three male cadets in daylight in a campus parking lot. The male cadets were upset that she had been accepted into their elite cavalry unit.

John Koldus, vice-president for student services, confirmed that twenty male cadets faced administrative charges on this incident, and if found guilty, their punishment could range from a written reprimand to expulsion. Their special unit, Parson's Mounted Cavalry, was temporarily disbanded.

In the rape incident, the male cadet was given a semester of university conduct probation after corps authorities conducted an inquiry. He then left the corps on his own.

President Mobley met with the women and formed an eight-member inquiry panel, consisting of students, faculty, administrators, and a non-university affiliated psychologist. The panel is to assess the validity of the women's accusations; recommend ways to eliminate harassment and discrimination in the corps; and recommend ways to ensure that proper disciplinary and/or criminal penalties are applied, if necessary.

A female cadet said, "Women have been in the corps since 1974. Every year the attitude gets better and better, weeding out those who don't approve of women in the corps. A new attitude of welcoming women is becoming the standard."

Texas A&M is the nation's seventh-largest university, with forty-one thousand students, including eighteen hundred eighty cadets, seventy-six of whom are women. The corps is a four-year federal and state supported military education program and is supervised by the military and retired military officers from Army, Navy, and Air Force ROTC programs.

$347,500 Settlement at the University of Washington

The University of Washington agreed to pay $125,000 to a former student to settle a civil suit in August 1991. The student claimed that a forestry professor sexually harassed her and that the university did not handle the case appropriately. The university also agreed to pay up to $222,500 in fees and expenses to the woman's attorneys.

The university admitted no guilt and the student did not give up her claim that the suit had merit. The settlement includes a list of changes that the university administration will seek in how it handles sexual harassment cases. In many cases the faculty must agree to changes in procedure which the administration wants to make. The woman's attorneys, Marilyn Endriss and Kenneth Shear of Seattle, said they hope the changes will protect the rights and privacy of students and make the process of deciding guilt more fair.

In the suit, the student, Teri Ard, now 25, alleged that Professor Graham Allan touched her sexually and made inappropriate sexual remarks from September 1987 to February 1989 while she was an undergraduate in forestry. Allan was fired in June 1989 after the university's Human Rights Office conducted an investigation, but he was reinstated when a faculty appeals panel reconsidered his case.

The faculty panel ruled that the Forestry Dean who investigated the allegations had not proved that sexual harassment occurred. The student's attorney's alleged that the panel put the woman on trial, bringing in humiliating and irrelevant evidence and not allowing her attorneys to represent her.

At the time of the settlement, Allan still maintain his innocence, saying, "Whatever reason she's getting funds from the university, it's not anything I did. I can tell you most definitely I never harassed her." He said he planned to resume teaching, but the Forestry Dean appealed the decision to reinstate Allan to the university's president, William Gerberding.

The university's executive vice president, Tallman Trask, said the university settled the case because it had become "exceedingly complex and expensive." He also said the university did not want to risk losing a major issue concerning liability for harassment. The question is at what point the university has a responsibility to know a professor is sexually harassing students, even when there has been no formal complaint. In this case, the female student said that a student advisor and several administrators knew that the professor might well be sexually harassing students, yet the university took no action until she made a formal complaint.

Other problems the vice president noted concerned the faculty panel's cloudy conclusion, which stated that the committee did not know whether the professor sexually harassed the student or not. The Dean of Forestry, however, said "there was no doubt in his mind" that Allan harassed the woman. Furthermore, the university's assistant vice provost for human rights and affirmative action, who initially conducted the investigation, concluded that the professor did harass the student and should be fired.

Of the $125,000 that is to go the woman, $71,500 is for general damages and $53,500 is to compensate her for medical, therapy, travel, and other expenses. The student moved to Georgia after filing her complaint, saying she could not emotionally handle being on the university campus, particularly because of the retaliation by the alleged harasser and his family. She said the man, his wife, and his children ran an advertisement attacking her in the university's student newspaper, and leafleted her at a conference at which she was a speaker. She also said they called her mother late at night and followed her around.

Vice President Trask said that not all of the settlement was for harassment, but that most of the amount paid had to do with how the university handled the complaint. He cited the $71,500 that was designated for damages.

After the student filed her suit, the university filed suit

against the alleged harasser and his wife to force them to pay their share of the damages. Trask said court rulings have somewhat limited these claims, but that they are "still valid."

Finally, as part of the settlement, the university agreed to seek changes that would allow it to have an administrative law judge to decide faculty appeals of decisions in sexual harassment cases, rather than the current practice of faculty appeals panels for disciplined faculty members.

The university also will allow students the right to have an advocate of their choosing present if students are called to testify at hearings. It will consider retaliation by a professor as additional grounds for discipline of the professor. It will guarantee privacy for students filing sexual harassment complaints as long as it does not interfere with the rights of the accused.

The university also agreed to require administrators to inform a student that official action can be taken only by the Human Rights Office, the ombudsman or a dean, and to direct the student accordingly. The woman's attorney said this is to discourage faculty and administrators from dissuading students from pursuing complaints, or giving informal advice.

The female student who brought the claim earned her undergraduate degree from the University of Washington in early June 1991, although her last sixty credits were earned at a school in Georgia. "I'm very pleased with the results," she said of the settlement. "I hope this sends a message to the faculty that they can no longer consider sexual harassment victims, whether they be graduates or undergraduates, as insignificant." Her attorney said, "All goals accomplished."

Sexual Harassment Guidance for Educational Institutions

When the Equal Employment Opportunity Commission's Guidelines on Sexual Harassment went into effect in November 1980, the agency said that the guidelines reaffirmed their position that sexual harassment is a form of sex discrimination and is therefore an "unlawful employment practice" under Title VII of the Civil Rights Act of 1964. Title VII and the guidelines are relevant to sexual harassment on campus because they apply to all employees, including student workers.

Students at academic institutions are protected from sexual harassment by Title IX of the 1972 Education Amendments. Title IX is administered by the Office for Civil Rights, which defines sexual harassment as "verbal or physical conduct of a sexual nature, imposed on the basis of sex, by an employee or agent of a recipient (an institution receiving federal funds) that denies, limits, provides different, or conditions the provision of aid, benefits, services, or treatment protected under Title IX."

The parallels between Title VII and Title IX indicate that the interpretations of both are similar and that sexual harassment is sex discrimination under both.

The first case directly addressing student sexual harassment was *Alexander v. Yale University,* filed in 1977 by an undergraduate woman charging that she received a lower grade on a paper in the course when she refused the professor's sexual overtures. The District Court maintained that sexual harassment may constitute sex discrimination under Title IX. Its ruling stated, "It is perfectly reasonable to maintain that academic advancement conditioned upon submission to sexual demands constitutes sex discrimination in education, just as questions of job retention or promotion tied to sexual demands from supervisors have become increasingly recognized as potential violations of Title VII's ban against sex discrimination in employment."

In 1980 the Court of Appeals dismissed Alexander's original complaint, stating that she failed to prove her case and that Yale had addressed her main concern by establishing a grievance procedure.

The National Advisory Council on Women's Education

Programs has developed perhaps the most widely publicized and used definition of sexual harassment in educational environments:

" ... *objectionable emphasis on the sexuality of sexual identity of a student by (or with the acquiescence of) an agent of an educational institution when: (1) the objectionable acts are directed toward students of only one gender; and (2) the intent or effect of the objectionable acts is to limit or deny full and equal participation in education services, opportunities, or benefits on the basis of sex; or (3) the intent or effect of the objectionable acts is to create an intimidating, hostile, or offensive academic environment for the members of one sex ...*

"Academic sexual harassment is the use of authority to emphasize the sexuality or sexual identity of a student in a manner which prevents or impairs that student's full enjoyment of educational benefits, climate, or opportunities ...

"[It may be described as:] (1) generalized sexist remarks or behavior; (2) inappropriate and offensive, but essentially sanction-free sexual advances; (3) solicitation of sexual activity or other sex-linked behavior by promise of rewards; (4) coercion of sexual activity by threat of punishment; (5) assaults."

Gender harassment is another form of sexual harassment or sex discrimination and is defined by the Modern Language Association's Commission on the Status of Women in the Profession as "... considerably less dramatic in its manifestations than sexual harassment, but because it is more widespread, it seems more pernicious. It consists of discriminatory behavior directed against individuals who belong to a gender group that the aggressor considers inferior ... The forms are often verbal—statements and jokes that reveal stereotypical discriminatory attitudes."

Sexual Harassment Policies on Campus

The University of Virginia faculty adopted a ban in May 1993
on sexual relations with the students they teach or supervise.
This ban was a compromise of an original proposal to forbid
all contact of a romantic or sexual nature between all teachers and all students. The original proposal was challenged as
unconstitutional, with the American Civil Liberties Union saying banning sex between consenting adults violates constitutional rights of privacy and free association. The ban is part of
a plan to eliminate sexual harassment and intimidation of students by teachers. Other universities and colleges have followed suit.

PART FOUR:
LOOKING AHEAD

9

WHAT CAN BE DONE?

*Do relations have to continue to be so poi-
sonously adversarial? Or is it possible that
women have achieved enough power and
prominence—enough voice in the society,
that we can broaden and deepen a dialog
about sexual harassment to give shades
and shadows to crime and punishment,
and perhaps look for a cure.*

Judy Mann, *The
Washington Post*,
March 3, 1993

The human resources director of an international insurance
company called a few months ago to ask if I would conduct a
one-on-one counseling session with a harasser. I told her I did
not usually do such sessions, and that if the man had attended
a good training program and still didn't understand what he
could and couldn't do, that maybe it was a problem of poor
supervision rather than education.

In other words, I have often found that it is not the case in
which a person, most often a man, can't understand the information about sexual harassment, it is that he won't understand—he refuses because he doesn't want to "get it," because
"getting it" would mean he would have to change. In such
cases it is up to the person's supervisor to say "get it" and
change, or else get out—it becomes a disciplinary and leadership issue.

The human resources director explained that the harasser
had been involved in two cases, the first being when he stuck
his hands down a female employee's slacks at an after-work

reception, and a second instance that involved a less serious infraction. After being disciplined for the second incident, he came to the director's office in anger over being disciplined for the first instance. "You mean he does not understand that putting his hands in a woman's slacks is inappropriate?" I asked. The director said she wasn't sure, and that's why she wanted me to talk to him.

Needless to say, I declined. There are some cases that seem hopeless from the beginning.

A report on sexual harassment issued by the U.S. House Armed Services Committee in early 1993 said that sexual harassment of women in the military will end only if the services' top leaders lead a determined fight, as they did against racial bias and drug abuse. Former Defense Secretary and House Rep. Les Aspin, D-Wisconsin, who at the time was chairman of the committee, said, "The services have the programmatic and administrative tools they need to combat sexual harassment. Whether they work depends on the degree of commitment of the senior leadership of the Defense Department and the services."

According to the committee's analysis, the military was able to make profound internal changes in order to overcome deep-rooted racial discrimination after World War II and widespread drug abuse in the 1960s and '70s because of three main stages in each case:

1) Recognition of the problem followed by unsuccessful attempts to solve it;
2) A "watershed event" (such as Tailhook) that cast doubt on the military's ability to carry out its missions and exposed it to public embarrassment; and
3) A wholehearted commitment by the uniformed top leadership to change behavior in the lower ranks.

These three stages apply to any organization, group, or even countries dealing with sexual harassment.

THE BASIC STEPS
IN ORGANIZATIONS AND GROUPS

Those who have worked in the field of sexual harassment for good lengths of time and have solid backgrounds and experience in dealing with the problem will always give the same or similar answers when asked what to do about sexual harassment. There are a few basic and fairly simple steps that do not change. It is not that the steps are easy to undertake or accomplish—each step takes commitment, time, and great energy and persistence—but they are not difficult to understand. They are those steps that would be used anytime to accomplish an overall, long-lasting change in an organization or group of people:

1) If necessary, and only if truly necessary, conduct an anonymous survey to determine the extent of the problem. Do not ask open questions such as "Have you ever been sexually harassed?" Ask if the person has ever been subjected to particular offensive behaviors, and provide a list. Ask who did the harassing, a manager, supervisor, coworker, or customer, and what the recipient did about it. If they chose not to use company complaint procedures, ask why. It is possible to assume that the problem in the organization is the same or approximately the same as other surveys have indicated, and skip this step.

2) Make sure that commitment and support from those at the top is in place. Whether this is the top management of the organization, or the top leaders in a group, community, or country, no program will be as effective as it could or should be if those at the top are not supportive.

According to Ellen Bravo, when Richard Teerlink, chief executive officer at Harley-Davidson Inc., gave a "sharply worded talk to one hundred fifty key managers after the Clarence Thomas–Anita Hill hearings, 'word was out in the hallway,' right away, as one manager put it. Teerlink make it clear that managers would be held accountable for the environment their workers have to live in ... People saw Teerlink's remarks as a very strong message that Harley-Davidson will not take harassment lightly."

3) Develop and post a written policy statement that specifically addresses sexual harassment. The policy should spell out clearly the complaint procedures, how and where to report problems, how investigations are conducted, and provide a variety of options for the complainant to follow in making a complaint. Do not go overboard and ban any and all sexual or romantic behavior. The goal of a policy statement is not to neutralize the work environment, but to spell out appropriate and inappropriate behaviors—unwelcome, offensive and unwelcome behavior. The policy must be clear, easy to read and easy to understand.

In mid-1992 a metropolitan government in Arizona published and reaffirmed its policy regarding sexual harassment in the workplace. Originally developed in the mid-1980s, the policy is well-written, comprehensive, and practical. The policy's straightforward and descriptive language should be particularly helpful to employees in understanding the problem and the city's stance against harassment of any kind:

> *"The City is an equal employment opportunity employer. There shall be no discrimination or harassment against any employee with respect to race, color, national origin, sex, religion, age or handicap. This policy applies to all of the Town's activities, wages, reviews, leaves, training, benefits and all other conditions and terms of employment.*
>
> *Harassment of any employee by any other employee or supervisor on the basis of race, color, national origin, religion, age or handicap is a violation of State and Federal Employment Discrimination laws. The City will not tolerate harassment of its employees or guests by anyone. Harassment is an insidious practice; it demeans and offends individuals who are*

subject to such conduct. It creates unacceptable stress for the entire organization. Significant costs are involved, morale is adversely affected and work effectiveness declines.

One of the most common forms of harassment is sexual harassment which is defined as:

1. *Unwelcomed or unwanted sexual advances. This includes petting, pinching, brushing up against, hugging, cornering, kissing, fondling or any physical contact considered unacceptable by another individual.*

2. *Requests or demands for sexual favors, including: subtle or blatant expectations, pressures, or requests for any type of sexual favor accompanied by an implied or negative consequence concerning one's employment status.*

3. *Verbal abuse or kidding that is sex-oriented and considered unacceptable by another individual. This includes innuendoes, jokes, sexually-oriented comments or any other tasteless actions that offend others. The use of obscenities or vulgar expressions is one of the most common forms of verbal abuse.*

4. *Displaying an intimidating, hostile or offensive attitude because of rejected sexually-oriented demands, requests, physical contacts or attentions.*

5. *Interfering with a coworker's performance by exchanging unwanted sexual attentions or sexually-oriented conduct that reduces personal productivity or safety on working time.*

6. *Condoning a working environment that is not free of sexually-oriented innuendoes, or any other tasteless actions that could offend others.*

Both males and females can be victims of sexual harassment; both males and females can be guilty of

> *sexual harassment.*
>
> *Like sexual harassment, harassment on the basis of race, color, national origin, religion, age or handicap is unlawful and creates an intimidating, denigrating, hostile and offensive working environment. Harassment of any kind will not be tolerated by the City.*
>
> *Personal harassing or condoning harassment of others will be dealt with swiftly and vigorously by disciplinary action up to and including termination. Each employee has an affirmative duty to maintain a work place free of harassment and intimidation. If you feel you have been discriminated against, or harassed, please report it to your supervisor or the City Manager. If this does not bring result, speak with the City Attorney. The City will see that the problem is resolved. You may at any time contact the Equal Employment Opportunity Commission or the Arizona Attorney General's Civil Rights Division concerning employment discrimination or harassment."*

4) Some organizations have begun using ombudsmen to help in the complaint process. Ombudsmen, or informal problem solvers, are being hired in increasing numbers to reduce tensions and deter litigation about workplace problems. According to the *Wall Street Journal* in May 1992, more than five hundred companies with more than five hundred employees each now have ombudsmen on staff, with medium-sized and large companies having more than doubled use of the problem solvers in the last five years. Many believe the increase is because of the rise in lawsuits by employees for discrimination, wrongful discharge, and sexual harassment.

Ombudsmen may be especially helpful in the area of sexual harassment, where investigations are particularly delicate. The usual procedure is for an ombudsman to listen to the complaint and to try to solve the problem before it becomes a major and damaging issue to either the employee or the company. An ombudsman is different from other human resources personnel because they are neutral, and take no stance on behalf of management.

5) Be prompt, fair, thorough, and complete in investigating and resolving complaints of sexual harassment. If the complaint is substantiated, make sure the punishment fits the crime—neither too light nor too severe for the infraction committed. Being too lenient or too strict can damage the effort to eliminate the problem.

In determining whether or not to hold an employer liable for sexual harassment occurring in its workplace, U.S. courts have weighed heavily the employer's response to the employee's complaint of sexual harassment. Failure to investigate the employee's claim has been viewed very unfavorably both by the courts and by the EEOC (*Katz, Rogers, Woerner*). Failure to investigate may be excusable if it is based on the advice of counsel and the employer turns the complaint over to an agency that conducts its own investigation (*Huebschen*).

If an employer acts promptly and appropriately to investigate and correct any alleged sexual harassment, the employer may be able to later raise this corrective action as a successful defense against liability. In one of its administrative decisions, EEOC said that in the case of harassment by a coworker, prompt and appropriate disciplinary action by the employer is adequate to relieve the employer of responsibility (*CCH EEOC Decisions 1983 6834*).

Federal District Judge Alfred M. Wolin ruled in March 1992 that the City of Hillside, New Jersey, was not responsible for a police sergeant's alleged sexual harassment of a civilian dispatcher. The ruling in the city's favor was partly because of the way the city handled the complaint: hiring an independent investigator to look into the charges and beginning its own internal investigation the day the charges were filed.

No support for the dispatcher's claims was found by either investigation. The judge ruled that the results of the "exhaustive investigations," combined with the sergeant's denial of the allegations, enabled the city to avoid liability and dismissed the claims.

However, Judge Wolin would not say that hiring an independent investigator and following that investigator's recommendations would always be enough to relieve the employer of liability. His ruling suggested that the intensity or thoroughness of the investigation also is important.

The city's attorney said the decision should comfort employers. In such cases where the employer is cleared by an investigation, the employer "can be spared the effort of having to litigate these allegations in federal court," he said.

This ruling is the first by a court in the federal circuit that includes Delaware, New Jersey, and Pennsylvania to deal with the kinds of actions an employer should take to avoid or limit liability when a harassment charge is investigated and found to be groundless.

In addition to hiring an outside investigator, the city also told the sergeant to stay away from the dispatcher and he transferred to another department a month later. The city also wrote a sexual harassment policy nine months after the complaint was filed.

6) Make sure that no retaliation toward the complaining party is being taken by the accused, others involved, or coworkers or friends who have taken sides. A ruling by the Oregon Bureau of Labor and Industries in early 1992 stated that retaliation against those who complain of sexual harassment must be eliminated, noting that "the public interest is furthered by having employees come forward with complaints without fear of retribution." Oregon's labor commissioner, Mary Wendy Roberts, said women who file sexual harassment claims against their bosses often become targets for retaliation. Retaliation can range from direct threats of job loss to more subtle tactics such as shunning the woman or treating her more strictly than other employees.

Elden Rosenthal, a Portland attorney who handles sexual

harassment suits, said, "In every sexual harassment case I've
ever been involved with, retaliation was always there in one
form or another. That to me is just another part of what makes
sexual harassment from a male superior to a female employee
so ugly." Paulo Barran, another Portland attorney specializing
in employment issues, said most sexual harassment cases that
end up going to a jury trial include a claim of retaliation. Juries
will add to the damages awarded if retaliation can be proved.

A recent case involving a former female manager for
Portland-based Fred Meyer Stores included charges of retaliation. The woman filed a $1.1 million suit against the retail
chain and her former supervisor. She claimed that the work
environment became intolerable after she filed a sexual
harassment complaint.

The woman was second-in-command at the Chico,
California, Fred Meyer Store, and said she was sexually
harassed by her supervisor, the store's manager. She said her
supervisor stalked her by lurking around her home, repeatedly telephoning her, and making lewd remarks. She also alleged
that he would rub her shoulders and "press himself against
me." Her suit stated that when she asked for a raise, her supervisor conditioned that raise on sexual favors.

Fred Meyer dismissed the supervisor from his $80,000-a-
year job after conducting an investigation. However, the
woman claimed she was then retaliated against by being
assigned a heavy workload, criticized for her performance,
and threatened with loss of her job. As a result, she said she
developed a host of illnesses that prevent her from working.

Her former supervisor filed for personal bankruptcy.
Therefore the woman cannot collect damages from him if she
wins her lawsuit. A spokeswoman for the state Labor Bureau
said it is not uncommon for individuals and small businesses
that are defendants in such cases to wind up in bankruptcy.

7) Provide training for each and every employee. As Bravo
said, "Training should be ongoing and on paid time. The program should make sure those experiencing harassment know

their rights and what to do, help those who are uninformed understand what harassment is and is not, and inform any hard-core harassers that they won't get away with it." Managers and supervisors should be trained in how to handle complaints and incidents.

Glen H. Mertens, a trial attorney with Ford & Harrison of Los Angeles, wrote in April 1993 that sexual harassment training is not only a good preventative measure, but a "compelling defense at trial." Mertens said:

Sexual harassment training programs are generally viewed as a form of "preventative maintenance" by employers. While it is true that a well thought-out program of training should help to minimize the number of harassment-related lawsuits, the significance of a good training program may be understated if the employer focuses only on that prophylactic benefit. A good training program may also provide the employer with a viable defense should a sexual harassment dispute escalate to litigation.

In 1990, an ambulance company in Seattle provided sexual harassment training to its employees after one of its female dispatchers complained about alleged harassment. The training program took place during several days and was directed at the company's entire work force.

Nevertheless, the female dispatcher and a female supervisor initiated legal proceedings against the company, alleging that they had been sexually harassed. It was clear from the depositions of the two plaintiffs, however, that the alleged sexual harassment had ceased after the training program had been presented.

At the trial in Seattle, the training program became an important issue. The jury returned a defense verdict in favor of the ambulance company. As counsel representing the ambulance company at the trial, I spoke with several of the jurors after the trial was over, and the jurors indicated that they had been impressed by the fact that the company had made a good faith and highly visible response to the female dispatcher's original complaint.

The jurors seemed to be very impressed with the fact that the harassment that the two women had complained about completely stopped after the training program was presented. The jury found that the ambulance company had done everything it could to address the complaints of harassment and had been successful in its efforts. If the company had not put on such a strong training program when it did, the jury might well have returned an entirely different verdict.

Cases such as this one underscore the importance of a well thought-out sexual harassment training program. Indeed, the need to focus on such programs is perhaps more important now than it was back in 1990. Recent judicial decisions and, in states such as California, legislative developments are forcing employers to develop and implement plans to eliminate sexual harassment in the workplace.

These plans and programs should no longer be viewed merely as preventative maintenance "luxuries" that are not truly essential to the running of a business. Any attorney in a trial involving a sexual harassment complaint who has a choice between telling the jury that the client had a training program in place or did not have one knows what the choice would be. In this day and age, any business person who believes that human resources can be effectively managed without a program designed to specifically address sexual harassment may not be in business much longer.

8) Make sure that the effort to stop and prevent sexual harassment includes follow-up and follow-through. Follow-up on complaints and situations to make sure they stay resolved satisfactorily. Follow-through on training and education by conducting annual or bi-annual refresher workshops; require new supervisors to go through a second training; make sure that new employee orientations include information on sexual harassment.

9) Include employee unions as part of the solution of sexual harassment issues. According to Sally Barker, a St. Louis

attorney, there is an increased awareness of sexual harassment by unions, and she advises certain educational steps to help unions handle the anticipated increase in complaints. Barker said these steps also are to aid in the representation of competing interests between bargaining unit employees:

- Provide information about the problem of sexual harassment, including hostile work environment harassment and *quid pro quo* harassment, to shop stewards and other union representatives.
- Inform those responsible for responding to complaints that both the complaining employee and the alleged or actual harasser are entitled to representation and access to the grievance procedure.
- Educate all union members about their right to be free from harassment and emphasize the possible differences in perception from person to person, i.e. what one sees as horseplay, another sees as harassment.

The union should respond to an employees' complaint of sexual harassment by advising that employee to notify management, Barker said. Then, if management does not respond, the employee should discuss filing a grievance with the union. When such a grievance is filed, the union should:

- notify any bargaining unit employee who has been accused of harassment;
- investigate both the claims of accused and accuser fairly before deciding whether or not to arbitrate the grievance; and
- notify all employees who are affected of the decision and the arbitration.

The union should contact its attorney when facing a particularly difficult case of competing claims to determine how to proceed. The union also should consider adopting a neutral approach to the presentation of competing claims in arbitration. Barker also suggests that the union not discipline members who bring sexual harassment complaints and that investigations be handled confidentially whenever possible.

The 1988 survey by *Working Woman* magazine on sexual harassment indicated that in Fortune 500 firms where sexual harassment policies have been in place for some time, the majority of women working in those firms still do not believe that the complaint procedures will bring about results. The study showed that:

- only 21 percent believed complaints were dealt with justly;
- more than 60 percent believed charges are completely ignored or the harassers receive only a token reprimand;
- many times the women who complained were told to take a workshop "dealing with difficult people" or they later received poor performance reviews;
- behavior such as that at Tailhook is not limited to such times and places. One female marketing executive at a Fortune 500 firm said she had been "patted, poked and squeezed to death at industry meetings;" and
- sexual harassment takes an extraordinary toll on its victims. The *Working Woman* survey showed that 25 percent of those experiencing harassment said they were later fired or forced to quit; 27 percent said their self-confidence was greatly undermined; 12 percent cited ill-health as a result. These issues are of serious concern and pose substantial costs to the businesses and organizations where these women work.

According to Ellen Bravo, national director of 9 to 5, the National Association of Working Women, "If this situation exists at the Fortune 500 companies, one can assume an even greater problem among medium-size and small firms. At the same time, many men today feel confused and under siege, wary that they'll be hauled into court or summarily dismissed for an innocent compliment."

Judy Mann wrote in the March 3, 1993, edition of *The*

Washington Post, "Feminist argue that sexual harassment is a power play. Beneath it is an animosity and lack of respect between the sexes that is damaging the women who are the targets and the men who are getting caught. 'Off with their heads' may have been a fine reproach for the Queen of Hearts, but we seem to be stuck there. We need to move on and start talking about changing their heads too."

GLOBAL ACTIONS

Although it is sometimes discouraging to see the amount of work that needs to be done to make any significant impact in combating sexual harassment, many, many countries have made efforts in positive directions. Many have initiated public awareness campaigns, through use of the media, brochures or other means. Some direct their efforts at employers, while others focus on the general public, and still others target young people. The subject matter runs the gamut from sexual jokes, comments and demeaning remarks, to actual physical violence against women—based on the belief that all these behaviors lie on the same continuum. A variety of sectors are involved in the effort, from federal, state and local governments, to business and industry, unions, associations, and volunteer and civic groups.

This section cites some of the more innovative and unusual approaches being tried in a number of countries. This list is by no means inclusive of all the new ideas and programs being implemented. It is merely a sampling.

Australia

The Australian Human Rights and Equal Opportunity Commission initiated a national media campaign in 1989-90 to increase public awareness about sexual harassment. The campaign was especially directed toward young women and used the slogan SHOUT (Sexual Harassment is OUT). The stated objectives of the campaign were to raise young women's awareness by using simple and effective messages; to put forth the message that sexual harassment is wrong and that something can be done about it; to assist young women in developing skills to deal with harassment; and to increase awareness of employers and the general public about harassment, emphasizing its impact on young women.

A follow up telephone survey was done and a hot-line established after the media campaign, both of which showed that sexual harassment is one of the most important problems for young Australian women. Other results were that women and girls were more aware of sexual harassment and what it is after the campaign; more than one-third of the young women surveyed said they had experienced sexual harassment; most believe the employer should be responsible for monitoring the workplace and keeping it free from harassment; and that most women and girls were encouraged by the campaign to report and not tolerate sexual harassment. The campaign's slogan was one of the most frequently remembered messages from the campaign.

Belgium

In 1986, the Secretary of State for Social Emancipation initiated a public awareness campaign in cooperation with the Ministry of Employment and Labour. The program included sending posters, stickers, pamphlets, and information kits to employers and employees in the public and private sectors, trade unions, and women's organizations.

Canada

The Gender Equality in Decision Making program was first conceived in 1989 by judges involved with the Western Judicial Education Centre based in Vancouver, Canada. During the gender-sensitivity program, judges meet for three days with victims of sexual assault, attend seminars by people who counsel assault victims, and watch a five-hour video on incidents of sexual bias in the courtroom.

Calgary Judge Gary Cioni, program chairman, said, "We're trying to illustrate to the judges that gender bias is not an abstract issue. We're trying to show them that it has very real and devastating effects." The program, cited as the best in North America, was created in reaction to a number of media articles about gender bias in the courts. While judges are not required to attend, an element many women would like to see changed, estimates are that more than 80 percent of provincial court judges in Western Canada have participated.

Norma Wikler, a sociologist at the University of California who created the first gender-equality program for U.S. judges in 1980, said 90 percent of the judges who attend the program said they were more aware of gender bias in the courtroom afterwards; two-thirds said they expect to be more sensitive to women in their courts.

Judge Cioni said: "It's not an easy thing to go through because it causes men to take a hard look at themselves. But dealing with a biased judge is not easy either. If you don't have fairness in your court, you have nothing."

The Netherlands

The Netherlands is one country where the government has chosen to direct its awareness campaign at violence toward women in general. The program was initiated in 1991 with plans to continue for a number of years. The campaign is primarily directed at the attitudes of men and boys towards sexual violence and shows examples of sexual violence at work by use of television spots and folders and brochures available at local post offices. In addition, a number of government ministries jointly published in 1991 a brochure providing information about what sexual harassment is and what can be done about it.

Japan

The increasing number of sexual harassment cases in Japan has brought about an increase in the number of public and private events and initiatives organized to combat sexual harassment in the workplace. For example:

- A February 1993 symposium on sexual harassment was held in Tokyo; it attracted some three hundred participants, 90 percent of whom were women.
- A nongovernmental organization called Kanagawa Onna no Space Mizura has been set up in Yokohama as a women's labor union to help settle sexual harassment cases out of court through direct talk with companies. The union consists of women who either work or live in Kanagawa Prefecture and already has assisted in settling some fifteen cases.
- The Japan Federation of Employers' Associations, Nikkeiren, agreed at its April 1993 meeting that each member company should develop guidelines to stop and prevent sexual harassment at work. While specific measures have not yet been developed, the federation's monthly magazine has featured the topic.
- A municipal assembly member, Kazuko Kitaguchi, said she was sexually harassed by a male Kumamoto Prefectural Assembly member, and demanded that the local government offer support services for sexually

harassed women by setting up a counseling service. The service is now offered at the Kumamoto Municipal Women's General Affairs Center.

- The Tokyo Metropolitan Government plans to set up a committee to address sexual harassment issues and, by 1995, to compile a manual for companies on how to stop and prevent sexual harassment. In early 1992 the government published two brochures titled "What is Sexual Harassment?" and "Sexual Harassment: A Labour Relations Issue." The brochures provide general information about sexual harassment and the results of a survey the government conducted in 1991. One brochure provides information for managers, supervisors, and employees on how to deal with harassment; the second brochure gives advice to individuals about what they can do and where to go for additional help and information. Both brochures contain facts from actual cases presented to the government.

- The Osaka Prefectural Government has sponsored three legal consultation sessions for sexual harassment victims since 1991 and has handled one hundred thirty-two cases.

- The government's Labor Minister began circulating a twenty-five minute video in 1993 to its male middle managers, urging the managers to reconsider their treatment of female office workers by showing how negative treatment, such as sexual harassment, can demoralize employees. The ministry decided to produce the video after a 1990 survey showed 35 percent of the respondents said that "insufficient understanding from managers and male colleagues" is the major obstacle to workplace equality.

However, Masaomi Kaneko, head of labor-related matters for the Tokyo Metropolitan Government, said many companies believe that providing in-house training and education on sexual harassment will hurt their corporate image. They believe people will interpret such a move as a sign that the company has problems with harassment.

United Kingdom

In 1991, a business-led initiative called Opportunity 2000 was launched in the United Kingdom to improve the position of women at work. As late as 1993, many people claimed that widespread cynicism exists about the program, primarily because it raised expectations which were hard to meet during the following years of recession.

However, a report issued by Opportunity 2000 at the end of the program's first year indicated that the initiative has had an impact on the daily working lives of women. The survey was conducted by Business in the Community, the umbrella organization responsible for Opportunity 2000, and Ashridge Management College. They conducted interviews with chief executives, board members and line managers from the original sixty or so companies that joined the effort. The survey collected data on the practical steps taken by companies to improve their attractiveness as employers to women. The steps included new policies and procedures on:

- Sexual harassment: the number of companies offering training on sexual harassment has more than doubled from 12 percent to 28 percent, although training is not necessarily offered to all staff;
- Specialized training: training programs are provided to encourage women to enter nontraditional jobs; single-sex training is provided to help women build confidence and develop their own style;
- Recruitment: female candidates are frequently included on the short lists for job interviews; managers are trained in competency-based interviewing to eliminate bias

against female candidates;

- Assessment and appraisal: gender-neutral techniques of rating job performance have been developed; sensitivity to needs of clients and the ability to build relationships with other employees are included in performance reviews;
- Working arrangements: organizations offer flexible working hours, including job sharing, working from home, part-time work, and temporary contracts; other benefits address family care and help with child care; and
- Pay and working conditions: organizations now provide identical terms and conditions of employment to their staff regardless of position; many review pay to see that equal pay for equal work is provided.

Most people believe that the commitment to Opportunity 2000 by chief executives and board members has driven many of the positive changes, but that to some extent the messages have failed to filter down to lower levels of management. Many women reported in a survey by the Institute of Management that they believe it is the "old boys' network" that is more of a barrier than anything, and that this prejudice must be eliminated before other changes can have a true and lasting impact.

United States

A recent editorial in *USA Today* reported that only 16 percent of rapes are reported and that only 62 percent of those reported lead to arrests. Half of the rapists convicted serve less than a year behind bars. These statistics, from a three-year study by the Senate Judiciary Commit-tee, resulted in the Senate unanimously passing the Violence Against Women Act.

The purpose of the anti-violence act is to change the practice of state and local justice officials of taking a less than aggressive stance against offenders in such gender-based crimes as rape and sexual assault or battery. The bill would encourage police, prosecutors, and judges who have primary responsibility for punishing violent crimes against women to treat these crimes more seriously. The study cited as an example of crimes not being taken seriously the fact that rape cases are 40 percent more likely to be dismissed than robbery cases.

Specifically, the act authorized $500 million to create a Commission on Violence Against Women, provide more rape crisis centers and battered women's shelters, and toughen federal penalties, particularly where abusers cross state lines. The most controversial section of the bill would allow some victims to sue their attackers in federal court because of a violation of the victims' civil rights. In these cases, the women would have to prove that the crime was motivated by gender bias, and would include only felonies, not divorce or state civil rights cases.

According to the *USA Today* editorial, "The [bill] is certainly not out of proportion to the problem.

"Every fifteen seconds a woman is beaten by her husband or boyfriend. Every six minutes a woman is raped. Yet some people—prosecutors included—insist on blaming the victims for the problems.

"The legislation is not a total answer. That can only come with a new attitude from police, prosecutors and judges.

"But the Violence Against Women Act declares an end to open season on woman. And that's a good start."

10

FINAL THOUGHTS:
IS THE END IN SIGHT?

... the [Thomas-Hill] hearings changed the level of awareness more than they changed the level of understanding. Those were political hearings. Those were the leaders of our country. It was not a pretty sight.

Susan L. Webb,
*CBS Evening News
with Dan Rather*

A recent story reported from Japan: "You might assume that when one partner decides to have a sex-change operation, the other would get the message: The marriage is over. But what if the other partner is similarly inclined? In Beijing a husband and wife recently exchanged sexual organs in a nineteen-hour operation. The advantages to the arrangement: The couple won't have to amend their marriage license, shop for gender-appropriate clothing or hunt for new names. Wang became Hou, and Hou became Wang."

Stories such as this cause concern and wonder as to whether things about and between men and women are getting better, worse, or simply more confused. Consider this second story:

In Utah, women at an appliance repair shop were surprised to see a male coworker using the women's rest-room. He had decided that since he'd been taking hormones for a sex change, it was time for him to use the ladies' room. The women employees demanded that he be banned; male workers did not want him using their restroom either. So, the male employee filed a sex/gender harassment charge with the Utah Anti-Discrimination Division. The result was that the division investigation suggested the employer use an "occupied" sign until he undergoes surgery to become a she.

Finally, should you think that such stories are few and far between, a third case, involving The Boeing Co., manufacturer of airplanes, as reported in the *Seattle Post Intelligencer* in March 1993 by the Associated Press: The Washington State Supreme Court ruled that The Boeing Co. did not discriminate when it fired a transsexual employee for wearing excessively feminine attire in violation of company directives. The plaintiff, listed as Jane Doe, filed a handicap discrimination action against Boeing after she was fired in 1985, saying the company did not accommodate her gender dysphoria, or discomfort with her anatomical sex.

Doe was hired as a Boeing engineer in 1978 when she was biologically a male. In 1984, Doe decided that she was a transsexual—a person who has a sense of discomfort and inappropriateness about his or her anatomical sex. In April of that year, she began hormone treatments and electrolysis for removal of body hair. She also changed her masculine name to a feminine name.

A year later Doe told Boeing supervisors and coworkers that she planned to have a sex change operation and that for one full year before the surgery she would have to adopt the social role of a woman.

Boeing informed Doe that while she was physically still a male, she could not use the women's restroom or dress in feminine attire. She was told she could wear male attire or unisex clothing, which the company said included blouses, sweaters, slacks, flat shoes, nylon stockings, earrings, lipstick, foundation, and clear nail polish. She was told not to wear excessively feminine attire such as dresses, skirts, or frilly blouses. She also was informed that after the sex change operation, she could then use the women's restroom.

After a short period of time, Doe began dressing in a way

Boeing described as excessively feminine, and other employees began filing complaints regarding Doe's attire and use of the women's restroom. Boeing then fired Doe.

The court said, "While gender dysphoria is an abnormal condition, we hold that ... Boeing did not discharge her because of that condition. We hold that Boeing's action met this standard [to accommodate an abnormal condition by those steps necessary to enable the employee to perform his or her job] and did not discriminate against Doe by reason of her abnormal condition."

Such stories show the confused nature of men and women about being men and women in today's environment. Though the stories may initially sound funny, amusing, or bizarre, closer inspection shows the problems they cause for the individuals involved, and in fact, for us all.

Understanding the problem of sexual harassment, as well as sexual victimization and violence against women, requires an understanding of the roles of men and women and the ways in which these roles and our societies are changing, particularly in light of today's changing world. Such a discussion requires travel on a slightly curving road—not in circles—but a route with some twists and turns—a scenic route. The beginning of the journey is an examination of our world as it exists today.

Thomas Kuhn is a twentieth-century philosopher well known for his discussion of what he termed "paradigm shifts"—a complex sounding term for a simple but very interesting occurrence. Kuhn said history, our progress, should be seen as a set of stair steps, not as a smooth sloping ramp. Every so often we experience a "transforming era"—a period in history when circumstances change so much that a major shift in our assumptions is required. In other words, things outside of us change so much, that the assumptions on which we have relied to guide our lives and our behavior are no longer accurate, and as a result, our internal beliefs must change as well—a very unsettling feeling for most of people.

Rosabeth Moss Kanter, author of the business best-sellers *Men and Women of the Corporation, Changemasters* and *When Elephants Learn to Dance*, said our present situation, including changes in labor forces, world trade, technology, and politics is not unusual taken in isolation. The fact that change is taking place in these areas is not unusual, but the fact that profound changes are occurring in all the areas at the same time is almost unheard of. Such periods as we are living in now occur only every hundred years or so, she said.

John Naisbitt, author of *Megatrends, Megatrends 2000,* and *Megatrends for Women,* said today is a very special time in history in which the two crucial elements for social change have come together—a serious change in people's values coupled with economic necessity. In other words, not only do people believe in and want to make some changes in the way they operate in the world—but they have to—economic necessity forces it.

Others have suggested an even simpler picture. We're all familiar with the little glass globes filled with water and fake snow—that kind we were so entranced with as kids, where the scene inside is a little house, or village, or Santa Claus or snowman, all calm and peaceful with the snow at the bottom of the globe. When someone picks up the ball and shakes it, the scene inside becomes chaotic—the snow swirls and the figures inside are temporarily lost. That's a picture of us and our world right now. We're living in a time of turmoil and difficulty and confusion for everyone—but that's the bad news.

The good news is that this is a very exciting, cutting- edge time, a seldom even once-in-a-lifetime experience, but one that requires special and new skills and attitudes for survival and success. The old ways of living and making a living won't work in this new time we're in and that we will be facing for a while. In fact we will all need to be unique and strong.

To look at the overall, broader picture of our world and our roles in it, particularly as men and women, we must take a look backwards, then look at now, and finally look closely at the future—a look ahead.

ROLES, RULES, AND CONTRACTS

As I travel the country, no matter the destination, I hear different versions of the same story from people: complaints, criticisms, gripes about bosses, work, kids, spouses, government, taxes, politicians—the list is endless. The point is, while they're not necessarily new gripes, and in many cases they're certainly valid complaints, the theme of the song is the same—that something's wrong, things are not working out the way they're supposed to or the way people had planned.

People talk of the good old days (now meaning the fifties and sixties in the United States) with longing and a half-hearted wish to go back. My grandmother always said that people get nostalgic and look backwards because they are so old that there's not much future to look to, or because they are so unhappy or insecure now, that spending time looking back simply feels better. Maybe this feeling that something's wrong accounts for the recent increased desire to look back, from songs to movies to clothing. In any event, let's do that, just look back thirty years or so.

For many people, looking back evokes a nice, calm picture. Most will admit that there were problems, but with hindsight, the problems seem smaller, neater, and much more manageable and more easily solved than today's problems. It is a pretty, rosy picture, but if you suspend the rosy glow for just a minute, and do some analyzing, here is what you'll see:

There were certain roles, rules, and relationships in effect thirty years ago that told us clearly and specifically how we were supposed to be, think, and act. Sometimes these rules were spoken, but mostly they were unspoken, but widely known and accepted in our society.

For example, in the work world of employers and employees, the rules were that the employer was pretty much in charge of things and used a fairly militaristic style of management—following the styles that served during wartime. As employees, you were expected to be hardworking, reliable, follow orders, and, just in case, the union could help you— but if both parties followed the rules, then the employer could expect loyal, productive workers, and the employees could expect pretty good working conditions, fair wages, and fair treatment, all the way to retirement. As a boss you knew how to act, and that was bossy—the manager or supervisor was in charge and responsible for making decisions, inspecting the work—and as a subordinate, your relationship to the boss was complementary—you followed orders, and let the boss carry the decision-making responsibility. No one was talking about participative management or quality circles or total quality management. Mostly the world of work was a man's world, and men knew how to behave at work—like men, being assertive, and decisive, and analytical. The employers, the managers, the supervisors, and most of the workers were men, and that's how men acted in general and at work in particular.

When the women worked, it was seldom in career endeavors, and they were limited to certain jobs, like teaching, secretarial work, and nursing ... they knew how to act at work too. In their jobs, women behaved like women were supposed to behave—nurturing, and smiling and secondary to the bosses/men, just like at home.

As for home, the roles and rules and relationships were clear, too: husband-wife, mother-father, parent-child, brother-sister, with clear boundaries and specified behaviors. The rules were simple—stay faithful to your spouse (at least publicly), work hard and save what you could, teach your kids good solid values, and the reward was a good and happy life.

The typical American worker was a white man, the breadwinner in his family who worked full time in an office or factory, belonged to or would join a union, was about 40 years of age and planned to retire at 65 with social security and company retirement benefits, and was motivated by job security and a steady pay plan in an industrial society.

The typical American woman was at home, or hoping to be at home, so if she worked it was just for a few extras. She had two or three kids, ran the Brownies or helped with little league, and depended on her husband for social, emotional, financial and decision-making support.

As for our boys and girls, it was the parents, combined with television and teachers, advertisers, and all the other socializing forces available, who taught our boys and girls to grow up in the image of the current men and women—to obey the rules and roles, to be good little boys and girls, and grow up to be good men and women.

People believed in the value of working hard, in faithfulness, in true honesty, that certain things separated the men from the boys, that men were men and women were women and never the twain shall meet. But the most important belief of all was in contracts and consequences. There was a promise made by society to all of us that a contract existed with certain positive consequences to follow, guaranteed to follow if we only followed the rules.

For example, if you followed the rules at work, employers could expect loyal workers, high productivity, reasonable profits, efficiency, and longevity of work relationships. As an employee, if you followed the rules, you could expect a loyal employer, job security, fair wages, and a good retirement to then go off and do what you'd really been wanting to do, play, not work—because work was work, not fun, and you had fun when work was finished. As a family member when you followed the rules, you would end up with a good life—a faithful, lifelong spouse, a nice home, good, hardworking kids, grand-kids, and a happy old age.

The contract also was made with the kids: that all this did work, if they just played by the rules, they could have not only what their parents had but even more, since every generation goes beyond the last ... it's in the contract ... right? This was a time when things were calm, and simple, and most of all stable—two plus two always equalled four and you didn't have to think or worry too much. The rules and rewards were known and certain and we could expect good things to come for us and our children and our childrens' children.

But then, we all remember when the first cracks in the United States began to appear in this happy time, in the dream, and in the rules and the contract: with Vietnam, and body counts and draft lotteries, with the Civil Rights Movement and the brutality witnessed nightly on the national news, with the first, then second Kennedy assassination, with the loss of Martin Luther King. All this speaks volumes about how visible the crack was, with everyone, it seemed, getting divorced or doing drugs or both. These were challenges to the older, stable ways that once worked. The cracks in our dream went unattended by us, and they grew and eventually spread worldwide.

The ultimate crack was the ultimate betrayal of the ultimate rule: that if you did what you were supposed to do, good things would come your way. But we were good and we did follow the rules and look what it got us—like the book titled *When Bad Things Happen to Good People*. And it worsened. The cracks grew from hippies and free love and grass to the real crack ... crack cocaine, and AIDS, and poverty and oil spills and abortion rights. And the refrain began to echo ... something's wrong, something's wrong, something's wrong.

What exactly went wrong was quite simply that the roles, rules, relationships, contracts and consequences were all wrong. They called for certain behaviors and values that fit a certain society, but it was the society of thirty years ago. When the society changed, and changed drastically as Kuhn, or Kanter, and Naisbitt attest, people didn't change, but held on to the same old ways of thinking and behaving that had worked in the past. When ways of thinking and acting do not fit the time and circumstances, then those ways of being are destructive to the organism, the people, the culture.

In individuals, a serious change in values took place as well. People actually began to think that work should be fun. John Naisbitt said, "In their hearts people know that work should be fun and that it should be related to the other parts of their lives ... ." When companies cannot or will not meet this demand and tell their employees to have fun on their own time, the employees do just that. Increasingly people are quitting company jobs and starting their own businesses in record numbers. All it takes is an idea, a kitchen table, a client, and twenty-five dollars to get your business cards printed at the copy shop.

In families, new types and styles of families—the single parent family headed by a mom, and now the single parent family headed by a dad—are replacing the old two-parent household. The American family of a mom, dad and two kids is in the minority these days. It's not more likely to be a family with his kids, her kids and their kids united under one roof.

As for values to be instilled: now we're supposed to deal not just with honesty, but ethics and ethical dilemmas (half of us can't define that, much less explore it with our children). AIDS and safe sex, condoms and drugs— those are not optional issues, but matters of life and death.

The point of this discussion is that people can no longer play the old roles of boss–subordinate, husband–wife, mother–father, parent–child, man–woman, boy–girl of the 1950s. Behaving in the old ways of the old days in a new day and age is "destructive to the organism." Having men be one way and women be the opposite, or bosses being leaders and subordinates only followers—these kinds of opposite (and supposedly equal) roles just don't work in today's complex world.

Some people call for what is labeled "androgyny"—an often misunderstood term that some believe means unisex behavior, cross-dressing or homosexuality. What androgyny really means is quite simply the integration of masculine and feminine characteristics within each person, encouraging the expression of male and female behaviors. Androgynous people have a greater capacity for flexibility and to be situationally appropriate rather than predictable and rigid. Because the complex world of today is requiring flexibility, androgynous people tend to adapt more easily and be more successful and happy in life and living.

Some have called it situational life—not being wishy-washy, but while knowing your core and basic values, also being flexible and acting appropriately to the situation and circumstances you find yourself in. What this means is that there are no more rules—the new rules are that there are no hard and fast rules, only principles and values to guide us. That means contrary to those times when we would sit back and relax and be calm, now more often we must take charge, think and then choose.

This same values shift, coupled with economic necessity, finally hit the work world itself in the early 1980s. No doubt you are are familiar with what I call the "Excellence Sweepstakes"—the self-improvement mode for business that really hit and started with Peters' and Waterman's book *In Search of Excellence*. Since 1982 that book has sold more that eight million copies in fifteen translations. Such sales of a business book were unheard of before.

This happened because exactly the same thing happed in business or organizational life that happed in people's personal lives—old ways of behaving just didn't work anymore. The excellence gurus labeled these "Workworld Assumptions Being Challenged." They said that whether you are in the private or public business sector, you can no longer operate on some time-proven assumptions, such as big is always better, analyze everything, the manager's job is to make all decisions, control everything at all times, get the incentives right and high productivity always follows, and it's all over if we stop growing. The traditional military or male values that we've used in business and government, that helped to get us to where we are today, rather abruptly became anti-productive.

The experts say that we must look to the opposite side of these traits and see that what appear to be traditionally female characteristics also can be valuable at work—small can be better, intuition counts a lot, decision-making should be shared and pushed down the organizational ladder, organizations (like people) should loosen up and be more flexible and spontaneous. Health and fun and other values can be more important than growth alone.

Examples of major cultural shifts, in the United States and around the world, that are affecting us all—businesses, organizations, and individuals—include:

- The *Wall Street Journal* reported that more and more workers are resisting business travel—or refusing to go on trips outright—because of family reasons. Employers say this pattern is similar to one approximately ten years ago, when employees began refusing to relocate, also citing family concerns. According to the *Journal*, when an American Express department scheduled a conference on Halloween, one-sixth of the employees refused to go, saying they wanted to spend that time with their children. American Express began scheduling future conferences later in November to avoid the problem. IBM encourages its managers to use teleconferencing and shorter trips. IDS Financial Services and Principal Financial Group help with overnight child or elder care when their employees must take trips.

- Between 1985 and 1989, the fastest-growing family group in the United States was single fathers, with a 33 percent increase. The census bureau says there are now about 1.4 million single-father families in the United States, compared with 8.7 million single-mother families. According to *Issues in HR*, this growth of single-father households reflects long-term social trends, especially in the areas of custody laws and decisions by never-married fathers to take care of their children. The magazine also said employers may now have to redefine their assumptions when it comes to family care—that while single fathers have the same needs as single mothers, they often face unequal leave policies and biased attitudes of supervisors—most of whom are male—who "think that men taking advantage of family friendly policies aren't serious about their careers."

• For women, the percentage of female officers in the Fortune 50 companies increased between 1990 and 1992 from 2.2 percent to 5.1 percent, growing from twenty-one to seventy-one. The *Wall Street Journal* reported that women are emerging from the twenty-five to thirty-year climb from MBA graduate to top corporate positions, and that analysts predict that 20 percent of top executives will be women by the year 2000. Journalist Cathy Trost said that despite concerns about the glass ceiling, "women's penetration to officer level is higher than previously reported." She also said that approximately half of large companies do not have a woman on their board yet, and that female directors have increased by only 3 percent in the last five years.

Bringing About the End of Harassment

Contemplating the changes and trends discussed above can hopefully provide insight and understanding into how and why we seem to be in such a mess in general, and in the sexual harassment mess in particular. But specifically what you can do, especially if you're a victim of harassment, is a continuing question.

I hesitate to tell victims of sexual harassment exactly what to do. First, each person is an adult and must make their own decisions and choices; it can be that inability or unwillingness to choose or act that exacerbates the sexual harassment problem itself. But also important is the fact that it is the victim of the harassment who will suffer (or enjoy) the consequences of their actions—not I. The person who is on the receiving end of the harassment knows the situation better than anyone, and as an advisor I can only present options.

There are many resources available for those who believe they are experiencing sexual harassment, all with their own lists of dos and don'ts, and all fairly similar. Some are more general, such as "empower yourself," "remember that you have choices," "take time to heal" (an especially good one), or "get control." Some are more specific. The steps below are from my booklet, *Twenty-five Things to Do If Sexual Harassment Happens to You*:

1) Admit that a problem exists; don't deny it to yourself. You may choose, as a strategy, to ignore it and see if it goes away, but choosing to ignore it is quite different than denying it exists. Denial will only compound an already confused situation.

2) Recognize sexual harassment for what it is—deliberate or repeated sexual behavior that's unwelcome. Ask yourself if the behavior is sexual or directed at you because of your sex or gender? Is it happening on purpose or is it accidental? Is it repeated over and over? Is it knowingly unwelcome? Have you said or indicated that you don't like it? Do you participate or initiate the behavior?

3) Keep in mind the most important point, whether the behavior is a truly major issue (usually the more obvious kinds like "put-out-or-get-out") or less severe but still inappropriate (occasional yet repeated jokes or innuendoes)—it's a problem that usually won't just go away.

4) Remember that whatever "kind" of behavior it is, it's still costing everybody. You're paying the price with a higher stress level, and your job efficiency and effectiveness is most likely affected too. It's damaging to

you, both personally and professionally; it needs to be stopped.

5) Keep in mind that your company or organization has an interest in stopping this kind of behavior at work too. Sexual harassment can be damaging to an organization in terms of absenteeism, loss of productivity, and lowered morale and motivation.

6) Accept responsibility for taking part in solving the problem; not blame but responsibility. Take control of the bad situation you're caught up in.

7) Speak up and tell the person that you don't like his or her behavior. Tell them calmly and in private. This is usually best, especially if it's the first time you've said something about it and if it's a less serious behavior. Some people feel more comfortable writing a letter to the harasser. If so, keep a copy for yourself.

8) Use an "I-Statement" saying, for example:
When: you call me honey/touch me/tell me jokes/etc., (describe the behavior you don't like),
I feel: very upset/embarrassed/angry/offended, (tell them what your feelings are), because: I want to be taken seriously/want to be treated as an equal/ want respect/etc. (tell them why it bothers you).

Sometimes it helps to write out your I-statement and rehearse it ahead of time.

9) Use the "broken record technique" by acknowledging the person's response and then repeating your I-statement. (If the offending employee responds by saying he/she didn't mean to hurt your feelings, or that you're too sensitive, etc., you can say, *"I understand that you didn't mean to hurt my feelings; however, when you ... I felt ... because ... "* You do not need to change your original I-statement.

10) Request what you do or don't want by saying, *"Please always call me by my name/don't touch me/don't tell me those jokes."* Be specific.

11) Try this mini-plan once or twice. If you don't get results from the offending employee, you'll have to move to another step.

12) Ask a coworker for support and even help in talking with the offender. Sometimes the offender can hear a message more clearly from a friend or buddy.

13) Go to a supervisor or manager to get additional help if the behavior does not stop.

14) Don't assume the behavior will stop if you ignore it; 75 percent of the time, sexual harassment problems get worse when ignored.

15) Don't try to deal with severe harassment alone (even the first time) in more serious cases—let someone in the company know about it immediately—get help.

16) If a mini-plan doesn't work, or if the problem is more complex or serious, a more thorough plan might be called for. In this case, it's important to find and maintain your balance and perspective by looking at all the elements of the problem.

17) Examine the situation itself first. What does the other person say or do? What do you say or do? When, where, and how often does it happen? Does it happen to others? On a scale of 1 to 10, how severe do you consider each event?

18) Write the answers to these questions down. Writing it out can help you clarify the issues and give yourself some objectivity. Write a description, as factually as possible, of each event.

19) Then take a look at the other person and write your thoughts. What's going on with this person? Why are they treating you the way they are? Is it possible that the other person is unaware of the negative effects the behavior has on you? Is the other person trying to be friendly or joking, or perhaps truly attracted to you? Is this person aware of the effects of the behavior but doesn't care—is the person insensitive to your

feelings or how you've asked to be treated? Or is this person treating you this way deliberately and maliciously after your repeated objections?

20) Take a look at yourself. Have you, or are you now, participating in the problem? Don't heap blame on yourself. That's a common trap. Just make sure you've looked at all sides and considered all aspects. How about your self-image at work. Does your image project how you want to be treated? Have you said "no" directly and specifically so there's no misunderstanding of your non-verbal messages?

21) Based on your analysis of the problem, now comes strategic planning. List all the ideas you can think of that would help stop the behavior and solve this problem. Then group or organize these ideas into three plans—Plan A, Plan B, and Plan C. Some of the ideas might be included in more than one plan.

22) Make your plans specific with regard to time, place, and actions. Think through all the consequences of each plan. Keep in mind that you have two simultaneous goals at this point: to get the behavior stopped and to maintain your effectiveness in your job.

23) Include other people in your plans. Don't try to be a hero and handle it all alone, especially with harassers who seem to be insensitive or malicious. Call on those friends, supervisors, or managers that you think can be of help.

24) Keep your plans flexible. The response of the harasser or of the manager or company representative may change your plans and/or your timetable. Solving this problem involves other people and their time and effort—not just your own. Be reasonable.

25) Implement plan A, B, or C as necessary. If you've gone through the ideas above, you should be able to put your plan into action more calmly and confidently to get the results you want.

These are some very specific steps to take if you think you're being sexually harassed, and it is just a suggested list, not a totally comprehensive one. No doubt, with thought, each person can come up with more ideas to help themselves and others.

More About the End of Harassment— For Us All

Sometimes when we're caught in a problem, especially one as emotionally charged as sexual harassment, it's easy to overlook the big picture and to forget how to stay thoughtful and focused on the truly important things in life. The ideas that follow can, I believe, benefit anyone willing to try to apply the principles to themselves and their lives. I think they are particularly good food for thought for those who experience sexual harassment or for those who want to think more philosophically about what we can do to eliminate the problem.

Charles Garfield, in his book *Peak Performers*, lists five major characteristics of individuals who will be highly successful, both personally and professionally, those who will make contributions and who will essentially be happy with life in a world such as the one we face. Garfield says that we must make every effort to develop these characteristics in all peoples of the world.

The five characteristics:

1) People for today's world and the world of the coming years will have a mission in life, and while that may sound lofty, all it means is that they have a goal or goals that inspire or motivate them to action, that their goals for their lives almost take upon the characteristics of a vision, not an hallucination, not imaginary, or unrealistic or negative, but an image of a desired state of affairs that motivates them as individuals. Garfield said this is

the call to action, the click that starts things moving.

2) These people also have the belief and attitude that they can get things to turn out right, not just once, but regularly. They have plans and objectives that are not necessarily precise or written in stone, but that guide them toward their goals, working with others and sometimes charting new paths and ways of doing things.

3) These people have a thorough familiarity with their strengths and weaknesses and work on those areas to continually grow and develop as people, as well as to gain needed work skills and abilities. In other words, these folks know and take care of themselves with positive self-esteem, respect and confidence.

4) These people work with others as team members—a small team like a group at work, church or school, or a large team, like society or our world as a whole—they encourage and foster the feeling of spirit among others they come in contact with—directly or indirectly, just by their presence—as role models that others look to.

5) These people understand and navigate a critical path, not a perfect path—they often get off course, as most of us are likely to do, but they correct that course, and get back on target, moving toward their goals.

These factors pertain to individuals and the part they play in the world in finding solutions to major and minor problems—problems of the world as well as their own individual problems. All these factors are about people empowering themselves and helping others to do the same. These are characteristics of people who will not allow sexual harassment to continue to happen to them or to others in their lives. These are not the characteristics of victims or harassers.

Joline Godfrey, author of *Our Wildest Dreams: Women Entrepreneurs Making Money, Having Fun, Doing Good*, tells of young women who have begun to develop in just the way Garfield describes. Godfrey said that while both our boys and girls are at risk in today's world, the girls are especially vulnerable: 40 percent of teenage women get pregnant at least once before age 20; the school drop-out rate for teenage women in urban areas is often as high as 60 percent; nearly 75 percent of teenage mothers under age 17 do not finish high school; as adults, 80 percent of all working women are still clustered in eighty of the four hundred ten job classifications listed by the U.S. Department of Labor; and, the average woman still earns only 72 cents for every dollar a man makes.

The exciting news Godfrey reports is about teenage women who are taking charge and exploring entrepreneurship. "A 17-year-old woman in New York City is the inventor of the No. 1 selling toy (a fabric covered balloon) in the country today. A young woman in Pennsylvania started her muffin business when she was 11, selling door to door; at 15, with the help of her family, she opened her first shop. And in a national business competition for teen women, one hundred calls a day come in from young women eager to put their business dreams on paper."

Godfrey said the young women of today certainly don't need job retraining. Young girls have learned to cooperate, be responsive and communicative, and they bring these usually unappreciated traits to a business world that now knows such traits are desperately needed. In short, what the excellence gurus said years ago is coming true ... both male- and female-type traits prove invaluable to business and society alike.

So, the good news about the world of today: we are making progress—in the work world, employers are choosing or being forced to push toward distinction in quality of products and quality of work life; in families, growing is taking place with men and women trying new roles; in their roles, men and women have the opportunity to try out new and less limiting behaviors; in relationships, we have the opportunity to enjoy each other more, regardless of gender; in our values, there is more diversity than ever before; and in our children, our boys and girls, there is the experience of expanded opportunities never before available as a result of our willing-ness to change and grow.

Of course, not all countries are experiencing the same pressures and changes at the same time. Those difficulties faced by industrial countries are quite different from the stark, often life-threatening changes in less industrialized or agrarian societies. But we are all moving, some fast, some slow, but overall, in the same general direction.

The bad news, though (and I say bad news tongue in cheek) is that despite people's hopes, some dreams will just not come true:

- Many people want to believe that things will "get better," but better meaning things will go back like they "used to be" in the good old days. Not so. Sorry, but we're mov-ing too fast to reverse gears. Things will get better, but not by going backwards.
- Many people want to believe that things will slow down. That's a maybe. But the slow down will be gradual and perhaps imperceptible, since things are moving so fast already.
- Some want to believe that we'll get new rules to replace the old rules about how to behave and live. Wrong. The most likely rule will be no rule … just lots of choices.
- And one of the saddest beliefs of all: some people believe that only a few of us can be highly successful, that most people just don't have what it takes to make it in today's world. Agreed, it's going to be a hard road to follow, not only in areas related to being male or female, but in all areas of life around the globe. But if you look closely at the five characteristics listed above, you too can certain-ly see, that they reside in us all, each and every one of us, man, woman, boy, girl, in every country and culture of the globe.

ABOUT THE AUTHOR

Susan L. Webb is a consultant and trainer specializing in the area of human relations. She has researched, designed, and presented workshops and seminars on leadership, supervisory skills, team building, sexual and racial harassment, stress management, and the changing roles of men and women in the work force.

Since 1981, more than three thousand companies and organizations have used her training programs, publications, or consulting services to stop and prevent harassment in the workplace. Ms. Webb has trained more than sixty thousand employees throughout the United States in the area of sexual harassment. She travels extensively, lecturing on other management issues as well.

Ms. Webb has written four books and numerous articles and has been featured in many national professional journals, newspapers, magazines, and broadcasts, including *Time, The New York Times, NBC Nightly News*, the *Christian Science Monitor, National Public Radio, Forbes, Working Woman, Management Review, Industry Week, Training Magazine, Personnel Administrator, USA Today, CNN, Larry King Live, CBS Evening News, The Oprah Winfrey Show* and *Eye to Eye with Connie Chung*. She is editor of *The Webb Report*, a national newsletter on sexual harassment. Ms. Webb frequently consults and provides expert witness testimony on the subject of sexual harassment and conducts investigations into allegations of harassment and other personal conflicts.

She received her bachelor's degree in economics and a master's degree in human relations from the University of Oklahoma. In 1981, she established the Pacific Resource Development Group to fill a need for high-quality training and consulting services.

Ms. Webb lives with her husband in Seattle.

Additional copies of *Shockwaves: The Global Impact of Sexual Harassment* may be ordered by sending a check for $11.95, paperbound, or $19.95, hardbound (please add the following for postage and handling: $2.00 for the first copy, $1.00 for each additional copy) to:

MasterMedia Limited
17 East 89th Street
New York, NY 10128
(212) 260-5600
(800) 334-8232
(212) 348-2020 (fax)

Susan L. Webb is available for keynotes and seminars. Please contact MasterMedia's Speakers' Bureau for availability and fee arrangements.
Call Tony Colao at (908) 359-1612.

RESOURCES

The following resources offer a global overview of sexual harassment, gender-related issues, and problems of women and men everywhere. Organized geographically and by specific topic, the list begins with the United States and expands to an international focus.

UNITED STATES ORGANIZATIONS, AGENCIES, AND SERVICES

In the Workplace

Ad Hoc Sexual Harassment Coalition is a broad-based coalition of women's and civil rights groups organized in response to the "now what do we do" question following the Thomas–Hill hearings.
C/O LAUREN WECHSLER, MS. FOUNDATION FOR WOMEN
141 FIFTH AVENUE, NEW YORK, NY 10010
212/353-8580

AFL–CIO union privilege provides nationwide legal services at no charge to most AFL-CIO members. Initial consultation and follow-up are free; other attorney's fees are discounted 30 percent. Many locals also have their own legal services plan.
1444 I STREET N.W, 8TH FLOOR, WASHINGTON, DC 20005
202/842-3500

American Arbitration Association, a non-profit organization, offers mediation and arbitration services through local

offices nationwide, and fact-finding teams for neutral investigations of workplace disputes, including sexual harassment.
140 W. 51ST STREET, NEW YORK, NY 10020
212/484-4000

American Bar Association (ABA) provides a booklet listing local lawyer referral services by state and county. Many associations give legal referrals.
750 NORTH LAKESHORE DRIVE, CHICAGO, IL 60611
312/988-5555

American Civil Liberties Union champions the rights set forth in the Declaration of Independence, opposes censorship, and supports civil rights for homosexuals. It publishes *First Principles*, a monthly newsletter, and *Civil Liberties,* a bimonthly newspaper.
132 WEST 43RD STREET, NEW YORK, NY 10036
212/944-9800

American Federation of State, County, and Municipal Employees provides a booklet for state and local union members on how to stop sexual harassment and offers training workshops for its members.
1625 L STREET NW, WASHINGTON, DC 20036
202/429-5090

American Psychological Association offers pamphlets on how to choose a therapist and gives referrals to state and local associations that provide names of specialists who deal with psychological problems associated with sexual harassment.
750 1ST STREET NE, WASHINGTON, DC 20002
202/336-5500

American Society for Training and Development, a national organization of professional workplace trainers, provides information and referrals on sexual harassment training.
1640 KING STREET, ALEXANDRIA, VA 22313
703/683-8100

Asian-American Legal Defense and Education Fund provides legal advice and attorney referrals for Asians and Asian Americans.
99 HUDSON STREET, 12TH FLOOR, NEW YORK, NY 10013
212/966-5932

Association for Union Democracy provides nationwide attorney referrals, legal advice, counseling and organizational assistance for women in unions, as well as training, workshops, and educational programs on sexual harassment.
WOMEN'S PROJECT, 500 STATE STREET, BROOKLYN, NY 11217
718/855-6650

Business and Professional Women/USA, a national membership organization of working women with more than three thousand local chapters, publishes position papers on sexual harassment.
2012 MASSACHUSETTS AVENUE NW, WASHINGTON, DC 20036
202/293-1100

Catalyst, a national research and advisory organization, helps corporations foster the careers and leadership capabilities of women. Catalyst publishes a wide variety of reference tools, manuals, and reports, including *Beyond the Transition: The Two-Gender Work Force and Corporate Policy* and *New Roles for Men and Women*. It also publishes *Career Series* for women who are searching for their first job, and *Perspective,* a monthly newsletter.
250 PARK AVENUE SOUTH, NEW YORK, NY 10002-1459
212/777-8900

Center for Working Life, a national nonprofit organization, provides workshops and sexual harassment training in the workplace, support groups for women who have been sexually harassed (including a group specifically for blue-collar women workers), and short-term counseling for women who have been sexually harassed.
600 GRAND AVENUE, SUITE 305, OAKLAND, CA 94610
510/893-7343

Child Care Action Campaign is dedicated to establishing a national system of quality, affordable child care. It provides advocacy, education, and information for corporations, childcare organizations, and the media. Its publications include a bimonthly members' newsletter, *Child Care Action News*, as well as various fact sheets, such as *Who's Caring for Your Kids?—What Every Parent Should Know About Child Care*, and *Child Care—The Bottom Line*.
99 HUDSON STREET, SUITE 1233, NEW YORK, NY 10013
212/334-9595

Clearinghouse on Women's Issues is a nonpartisan organization made up of members of other women's groups. It disseminates information on women's rights, particularly on issues of discrimination on the basis of sex or marital status, by holding luncheons featuring various speakers. It publishes a monthly newsletter.
P.O. BOX 70603, FRIENDSHIP HEIGHTS, MD 20813

Coalition of Free Men is an educational organization that believes men are victims of discrimination and works to fight discrimination, which it sees evidenced in the fact that only men are drafted and in that men typically are given the most dangerous jobs in society. It works to promote friendships between men. The coalition publishes a bimonthly newsletter, *Transitions*, and brochures such as *Men's Movement: A Perspective; Sex Discrimination in Language Against Men;*

and *How To Conduct Men's Studies.*
P.O. Box 129, Manhasset, NY 11030
516/482-6378

Coalition of Labor Union Women (CLUW), a national
organization with seventy local chapters, provides education
on sexual harassment, organizes conferences and workshops,
testifies and lobbies for legislation, supports strikes and boy-
cotts, and publishes a newsletter and other written materials
for union women. It also makes referrals to attorneys and legal
rights groups for union workers and can provide sample contract language, resolutions, and policies on sexual harassment.
15 Union Square, New York, NY 10003
212/242-0700

Commission on the Economic Status of Women is a legislative advisory commission established to study the economic status of women. It has found that divorce laws, employment discrimination, and child-care costs contribute to
women's poverty. It conducts research, holds public hearings,
and publishes reports, such as *Employment Rights* and
Parental Leave and the Legal Rights of Pregnant Employees.
State Office Building, Room 85
100 Constitution Avenue, St. Paul, MN 55155
612/296-8590

Communications Workers of America provides internal
training for union members and staff as well as written materials on sexual harassment.
501 3rd Street, Washington, DC 20001
202/434-1110

Department of Defense is responsible for presenting the
official positions of the military on current issues, including
sexual harassment. It maintains one officer responsible for
information on women in the military and publishes a

brochure that discusses sexual harassment in the military.
OFFICE OF THE ASSISTANT SECRETARY OF DEFENSE FOR PUBLIC AFFAIRS
PENTAGON, ROOM 2E777, WASHINGTON, DC 20301-1400
703/697-5737

Equal Rights Advocates provides legal advice and counseling, in both English and Spanish, and makes referrals to women's groups nationwide.
1663 MISSION STREET, SUITE 550 SAN FRANCISCO, CA 94103
415/621-0672 (GENERAL INFO)
415/621-0505 (COUNSELING HOTLINE)

Federally Employed Women (FEW) is a national non-profit membership organization of federally employed women with chapters throughout the United States. It provides assistance in dealing with sexual harassment in the federal sector, and written materials on how federal workers can stop sexual harassment, find and select an EEO attorney, and go to court.
400 EYE STREET NW, SUITE 425, WASHINGTON, DC 20005
202/898-0994

Federation of Organizations for Professional Women gives telephone advice and counseling on sexual harassment as well as written sexual harassment materials. It has support groups in Washinton, D.C., area. Limited legal assistance may be available through the Professional Women's Legal Fund.
2001 S STREET NW, SUITE 500, WASHINGTON, DC 20009
202/328-1415

Fund for the Feminist Majority researches methods that empower women. The hotline provides information, referrals, and strategies for dealing with sexual harassment. The fund also publishes a report that includes an overview and critical analysis of sexual harassment laws and an examination of women's experiences of sexual harassment.
1600 WILSON BOULEVARD, ARLINGTON, VA 22209

703/522-2214 (GENERAL INFO)
703/522-2501 (SEXUAL HARASSMENT HOTLINE)

HUD, the U.S. Department of Housing and Urban Development, has a housing discrimination hotline that can be reached by calling 800/669-9777. The automated system will transfer the call to the closest HUD Office of Fair Housing and Equal Opportunity. A HUD brochure with an insert on sexual harassment is available by calling 800/245-2691 and asking for the "National Media Campaign Brochure."

IMPACT International, Inc. makes referrals to local programs for teaching women self-defense skills in an atmosphere of strong personal support.
800/345-KICK OR 301/589-1349

Institute for Women and Work provides a bibliography of sexual harassment resource materials and training seminars on sexual harassment, primarily for union members.
SCHOOL OF INDUSTRIAL AND LABOR RELATIONS
CORNELL UNIVERSITY, 15 EAST 26TH STREET, 4TH FLOOR
NEW YORK, NY 10010
212/340-2812

Men International believes current divorce and custody laws discriminate against men. The group works to strengthen the traditional male image, particularly in the role of the father. Through its computerized network, the group also serves as a clearinghouse and resource center.
MEN INTERNATIONAL INFORMATION NETWORK
3409 HYDE PARK DRIVE, CLEARWATER, FL 33519
813/787-3875

National Conference of State Legislatures Women's Network provides information about media coverage, assessing laws and enforcement mechanisms in your city, county and state.
SUE MULLINS, 515/583-2156

National Council for Research on Women works to strengthen ties with other national and international organizations. The council also provides resources for feminist research, policy analysis, and educational programs for women and girls.
THE SARA DELANO ROOSEVELT MEMORIAL HOUSE
47-49 EAST 65TH STREET, NEW YORK, NY 10021
TEL: 212/570-50, FAX 212/570-5380

National Employment Lawyers Association offers a national directory listing of eleven hundred employment law attorneys, including brief descriptions of their practices. Send a self-adressed, stamped envelope for more information.
535 PACIFIC AVENUE, SAN FRANCISCO, CA 94133

National Federation of Business and Professional Women's Clubs is a research, education, and lobbying organization that works for equity and self-sufficiency for working women. It provides financial assistance to women seeking to improve their employment and education opportunities and maintains an extensive library of materials relating to women and work, such as *Jobs for the Future,* and publishes *National Businesswomen Magazine* six times a year.
2012 MASSACHUSETTS AVENUE NW, WASHINGTON, DC 20036
202/293-1200

National Lawyers Guild makes referrals to experienced attorneys who are members of the Guild, an association of progressive attorneys.
ANTI-SEXISM COMMITTEE

131 George Street, San Jose, CA 95110
408/287-1916

National Organization for Changing Men is an organization of men and women devoted to supporting positive changes in men. They are pro-feminist, support gay rights, and encourage men to have nonsexist relationships with women, to develop a more sensitive and involved role as fathers, and to relate better to other men. NOCM has many task groups that deal with such issues as male/female relationships, fathering, and publish their newsletter, *Brother.*
794 Penn Avenue, Pittsburgh, PA 15221
412/371-8007

National Resource Center for Consumers of Legal Services provides nationwide legal referrals to attorneys experienced in sexual harassment cases and publishes materials on how to choose a lawyer.
P.O. Box 340, Gloucester, VA 23061
804/693-9330

National Women's Law Center is a national nonprofit organization focusing on policy areas important to women and provides research and testimony on sexual harassment.
1616 P Street NW, Suite 100, Washington, DC 20036
202/328-5160

National Women's Political Caucus provides a model sexual harassment policy for congressional members, and an honor roll of members of Congress who have adopted sexual harassment policies.
1275 K Street NW, Suite 750, Washington, DC 20005
202/898-1100

9 to 5, National Association of Working Women is a nonprofit membership organization of U.S. office workers, with local chapters throughout the country. The toll-free confidential telephone hotline, staffed by trained job counselors, provides information and referrals on how to deal with sexual harassment and other problems on the job. Members get books and reports at a discount, and legal referrals to attorneys. A newsletter is published five times a year. Some chapters offer support groups and referrals to training resources.

614 SUPERIOR AVENUE NW, CLEVELAND, OH 44113
216/566-9308 (GENERAL INFORMATION)
800/522-0925 (HOTLINE)

NOW Legal Defense and Education Fund provides research and referrals on a broad range of issues affecting women and the law and offers a comprehensive list of publications on sexual harassment. NOW LDEF also offers a Legal Resource Kit for victims and consults with corporations and other organizations on issues involving sexual harassment guidelines and procedures.

99 HUDSON STREET, 12TH FLOOR, NEW YORK, NY 10013
212/925-6635

Pacific Resource Development Group is a consulting firm specializing in sexual harassment. Since 1980, services have included consulting, training, investigation, and expert witness testimony. (See also, Premiere Publishing.)

145 NW 85TH STREET, SUITE 104, SEATTLE, WA 98117
800/767-3062

Premiere Publishing, Ltd. is the sister corporation of Pacific Resource, and is responsible for publishing and distributing of a wide variety of sexual harassment products, including video and audiotapes, a monthly newsletter, *The Webb Report*; an investigator's manual, training manuals, and employee handbooks.

145 NW 85TH STREET, SUITE 103, SEATTLE, WA 98117
800/767-3062 OR 206/782-8310

Select Committee on Children, Youth, and Families was created in 1983 to conduct an ongoing assessment of the condition of American children and families, and to make recommendations to Congress and the public on how to improve public and private policies. It publishes reports and transcripts of hearings on family issues.
U.S. HOUSE OF REPRESENTATIVES
385 HOUSE OFFICE BUILDING, ANNEX 2
WASHINGTON, DC 20515

Society for Human Resource Management is a membership organization that provides human resource managers with information and advice on developing sexual harassment policies, procedures, and programs.
606 N. WASHINGTON STREET, ALEXANDRIA, VA 22314
703/548-3440

Tele-Lawyer provides legal advice over the phone at a reasonable per-minute charge. Staff lawyers also will review documents such as employment contracts and do legal research.
19671 BEACH BOULEVARD, SUITE 207
HUNTINGTON BEACH, CA 92648
800/835-3529

Tradeswomen, Inc. offers peer support, networking, and advocacy for women in nontraditional, blue-collar jobs. It publishes the quarterly *Tradeswoman Magazine* and the monthly *Trade Trax* newsletter.
P.O. BOX 40664, SAN FRANCISCO, CA 94140
415/821-7334

United Auto Workers Union (UAW) provides written and video training materials and workshops for UAW and other union members.
800 EAST JEFFERSON, DETROIT, MI 48214
313/926-5212

U.S. Department of Labor Women's Bureau provides a detailed list of sexual harassment resources, including organizations, training materials, court cases, and articles.
200 Constitution Avenue NW, Room S3311
Washington, DC 20210
202/523-6665

Wider Opportunities for Women (WOW), a national nonprofit organization, focuses primarily on women in nontraditional employment. It provides reports and materials on sexual harassment, and consulting and training for employers.
1325 G Street NW, Washington, DC 20005
202/638-3143

Women Employed Institute is a membership group providing telephone counseling on sexual harassment in the Chicago area, local attorney referrals, fact sheets, and prevention training for area employers.
22 West Monroe, Suite 1400, Chicago, IL 60603
312/782-3902

Women for Racial and Economic Equality is a political activist organization working to end racism and economic inequality through the enactment of a Women's Bill of Rights. It publishes a bimonthly journal, *WREE-View of Women.*
198 Broadway, Room 606, New York, NY 10038
212/385-1103

Women's Alliance for Job Equity (WAJE) provides information and public education seminars in the Philadelphia area, regular job-problem meetings, peer support program, legal referrals for WAJE members, and onsite training programs for local employers.
1422 Chestnut Street, Suite 1100, Philadelphia, PA 19102
215/561-1873

Women's Law Project gives information and legal referrals in the Philadelphia area.
125 SOUTH 9TH STREET, SUITE 401, PHILADELPHIA, PA 19107
215/928-9801

Women's Legal Defense Fund, a national nonprofit membership organization, provides public education, written information, advocacy, and targeted litigation on sexual harassment.
1875 CONNECTICUT AVENUE NW, SUITE 710
WASHINGTON, DC 20009
202/986-2600

Women's Rights Litigation Clinic provides legal advice and counseling, written materials on sexual harassment, and technical legal support in some cases.
RUTGERS UNIVERSITY LAW SCHOOL
15 WASHINGTON STREET, NEWARK, NJ 07102
201/648-5637

Work and Family Center of the Conference Board is a national clearinghouse designed to meet the needs of the business community, government agencies, and other organizations concerned with changes in work and family relationships. It supports research on child care, parental leave, relocation policies, and other related issues, and publishes *Family Supportive Policies: The Corporate Decision* and the *Bibliography on Work and Family Issues*.
845 THIRD AVENUE, NEW YORK, NY 10022
212/339-0356

Workers' Rights Clinic rotates among several locations. It provides a legal clinic for low-income workers in the San Francisco Bay Area who have employment problems, including sexual harassment. Services include telephone and in-person legal advice and counseling. PHONE 415/864-8208

W.R.A.T.H. (Women Refusing to Accept Tenant Harassment) provides advice to women sexually harassed by landlords or others related to housing.
607 ELMIRA ROAD, SUITE 299, VACAVILLE, CA 95687

In the Schools

American Association of University Women Legal Advocacy Fund funds sexual harassment cases brought by university women students, faculty, and staff against institutions of higher education.
1111 16TH STREET N.W., WASHINGTON, DC 20036
202/785-7744

American Federation of Teachers (AFT) provides a booklet on sexual harassment, for AFT union members.
HUMAN RIGHTS DEPARTMENT
555 NEW JERSEY AVENUE NW, WASHINGTON, DC 20001
202/879-4400

Center for Afro-American Studies provides information on activities of African-American women in response to the sexist and racist treatment of Anita Hill.
C/O ELSA BARKELY BROWN, UNIVERSITY OF MICHIGAN
ANN ARBOR, MI 48109
313/747-4887

Center for Research on Women conducts, disseminates, and promotes research in the field of women's studies, focusing on southern women and women of color in the United States. It operates a computerized information retrieval service called the Research Clearinghouse that contains more than two thousand entries for books, journal articles, unpublished manuscripts, and multimedia materials. The center publishes a newsletter, as well as *Southern Women* and

Research Clearinghouse Publications twice yearly, and *Research Papers* three times a year.
CLEMENT HALL, MEMPHIS STATE UNIVERSITY
MEMPHIS, TN 38152
901/678-2770

Center for Research on Women is directed by Nan Stein with the purpose of examining and remedying sexual harassment in the school systems.
SEXUAL HARASSMENT IN SCHOOLS PROJECT, WELLESLEY COLLEGE
WELLESLEY, MA 02181
616/283-2500

Center for Women in Government provides sexual harassment training for New York state employees and serves workers nationwide through training videos, digests of important sexual harassment cases and laws, and pamphlets on sexual harassment.
UNIVERSITY OF ALBANY, DRAPER HALL, 310
135 WESTERN AVENUE, ALBANY, NY 12222
518/442-3900

Center for Women Policy Studies focuses on policy issues affecting the social, legal, and economic status of women, and offers publications on sexual harassment, peer harassment, and campus rape, including a guide for women students who encounter harassment. It publishes more than 100 papers originally issued by the Association of American Colleges, including the first nationally distributed papers on sexual harassment in academia.
2000 P STREET NW, SUITE 508, WASHINGTON, DC 20036
202/872-1770

College and University Personnel Association provides a book on sexual harassment in business, industry, and education, and a video on sexual harassment in higher education.
1233 20TH STREET NW, WASHINGTON, DC 20036
202/429-0311, EXT. 23

Kidpower provides referrals to local programs to help children become safer and more confident through effective self-defense skills. It also provides workshops for parents, teachers, and others on how to teach children these skills.
P.O. BOX 1212, SANTA CRUZ, CA 95061
408/426-4407

National Association for Women in Education provides materials on sexual harassment on college campuses.
1325 18TH STREET NW, SUITE 210, WASHINGTON, DC 20036
202/659-9330

National Education Association (NEA) provides training, videos, and brochures on sexual harassment to union members. Contact local or state NEA offices for more information.
HUMAN AND CIVIL RIGHTS DEPARTMENT
1201 16TH STREET NW, WASHINGTON, DC 20036
202/833-4000

Project Esteem: The Hawaii Department of Education provides *Sexual Harassment: It's Uncool,* a dramatic poster to spark discussion. The poster includes a definition of sexual harassment and reporting information.
1390 MILLER STREET, SUITE 416, HONOLULU, HI 96813

Project of the Center for the Study of Communication provides information on gender issues.
UNIV. OF MASSACHUSETTS FOUNDATION FOR MEDIA EDUCATION
P.O. BOX 2008, AMHERST, MA 01004-2002
413/545-2341

Fair Employment Practice Agencies

The following agencies handle discrimination complaints under state or municipal laws. State agencies are listed first, followed by local offices. All state agencies are included, regardless of complaint procedures or enforcement powers.

Alaska

State Commission for Human Rights
431 West 7th Avenue, Suite 101
Anchorage, AK 99501
907/276-7474

Anchorage Equal Rights Commission
620 East 10th Avenue, Suite 204
Anchorage, AK 99501

Human Rights Commission Southcentral Region
P.O. Box AH, 314 Goldstein Boulevard
Juneau, AK 99811
907/465-3560

Arizona

Civil Rights Division, Attorney General's Office
1275 West Washington Street
Phoenix, AZ 85007
602/255-5263

Southern Arizona Office
402 West Congress Street, Suite 315; 100 North Stone Street
Tucson, AZ 85701

Governor's Office of Affirmative Action
1700 West Washington Street, State Capitol Room 804
Phoenix, AZ 85007

California

Department of Fair Employment and Housing
1201 I Street, Suite 211
Sacramento, CA 95814
916/445-9918

California District and Field Offices,
Department of Fair Employment and Housing

1529 "F" Street
Bakersfield, CA 93301
805/395-2728

1900 Mariposa Mall
Suite130
Fresno, CA 93721
209/445-5373

322 West First Street
Room 2126
Los Angeles, CA 90012
213/620-2610

1111 Jackson Street
Oakland, CA 94607
415/464-4095

375 West Hospitality Lane
Room 280
San Bernardino, CA 92408
714/383-4711

110 West C Street
Suite 1702
San Diego, CA 92101
619/237-7405

30 Van Ness Avenue
San Francisco, CA 94102
415/557-2005

888 North First Street
Room 316
San Jose, CA 95112
408/227-1264

28 Civic Center Plaza
Room 330
Santa Ana, CA 92701
714/558-4159

5730 Ralston Street
Room 302
Ventura, CA 93003
805/654-4513

Colorado

Civil Rights Commission, Room 600C
State Services Building
1525 Sherman Street
Denver, CO 80203
303/866-2621

Colorado Branch Offices, Civil Rights Commission

2860 South Circle Drive
North Building
Suite 2103
Colorado Springs, CO 80906

800 8th Avenue
Suite 223
Greeley, CO 80631
303/356-9221

222 South 6th Street
Room 417
Grand Junction, CO 81501
303/248-7329

720 North Main
Suite 222
Pueblo, CO 81003
303/545-3520

Connecticut

Commission on Human Rights and Opportunities
Central Office
90 Washington Street
Hartford, CT 06115
203/566-3350

Connecticut Regional Offices, Commission on Human Rights and Opportunities

Capital Region
1229 Albany Avenue
Hartford, CT 06112

Eastern Region
302 Captain's Walk
New London, CT 06320

West Central Region
232 North Elm Street
Waterbury, CT 06702

Southwest Region
1862 East Main Street
Bridgeport, CT 06610

Delaware

Department of Labor, Anti-Discrimination Section
Wilmington State Office Building
820 North French Street, 6th Floor
Wilmington, DE 19801
302/571-2900

State Human Relations Commission
William Service Center
805 River Road
Dover, DE 19910
302/736-4567

Georgtown Service Center
Route 113-Bradford Street Extension
Georgetown, DE 19947

District of Columbia

D.C. Office of Human Rights
2000 14th Street NorthWest, 3rd Floor,
Washington, DC 20009
202/939-8740

Florida

Commission of Human Relations
325 John Knox Road
Suite 240, Building F
Tallahassee, FL 32399
904/488-7082 or 800/342-8170

Lee County Department of Equal Opportunity
P.O. Box 398
Fort Meyers, FL 33902-0398
813/334-2166

Georgia

Georgia Office of Fair Employment Practices
156 Trinity Avenue SouthWest, Suite 208
Atlanta, GA 30303

Governor's Council on Human Relations
State Capitol, Room 249
Atlanta, GA 30334
404/656-6757

Augusta/Richmond County
Human Relations Commission
Suite 400, 500 Building
Augusta, GA 30902

Hawaii

Department of Labor & Industrial Relations
Enforcement Division
888 Mililani Street, Room 401
Honolulu, HI 96813
808/548-3976

Idaho

Commission on Human Rights
450 West State Street
Boise, ID 83720
208/334-2873

Illinois

Department of Human Rights
One Illinois Center
100 West Randolph Street, Suite 10-100
Chicago, IL 60601
312/917-6200

Springfield Regional Office
Stratton Office Building, Room 623
Springfield, IL 62706
217/785-5100

Indiana

Civil Rights Commission
32 East Washington Street, Suite 900
Indianapolis, IN 46204
317/232-2600

Iowa

Civil Rights Commission
211 East Maple Street
2nd Floor, State Office Building
Des Moines, IA 50319
515/281-4121 or 800/457-4416

Kansas

Commission on Civil Rights, Landon State Office Building
900 SouthWest Jackson, 8th Floor, Suite 851S
Topeka, KS 66612
913/296-3206

Kansas Branch Offices, Commission on Civil Rights

212 South Market
Wichita, KS 67202
913/265-7466

Wichita Civil Rights and Equal Employment
Opportunity Commission
455 North Main Street, 10th Floor
Wichita, KS 67202

Kentucky

Commission on Human Rights
701 West Muhammad Ali Boulevard
P.O. Box 69
Louisville, KY 40201
502/588-4024

832 Capital Plaza Tower
Frankfort, KY 40601
502/564-3550

Maine

Human Rights Commission
State House, Station No. 51
Augusta, ME 04333
207/289-2326

Maryland

Commission on Human Relations
20 East Franklin Street
Baltimore, MD 21202
301/333-1700

514 Race Street
Cambridge, MD 21613
301/228-0112

Professional Arts Building
Room 305, 5 Public Square
Hagerstown, MD 21740

Massachusetts

Commission Against Discrimination
McCormack State Office Building
1 Ashburton Place
Boston, MA 02108
617/727-3990

*Massachusetts District Offices,
Commission Against Discrimination*

145 State Street
Springfield, MA 01103

22 Front Street
P.O. Box 8008
Worcester, MA 01614

222 Union Street
New Bedford, MA 02740

Michigan

Department of Civil Rights
303 West Kalamazoo
Lansing, MI 48913
517/334-6079

Department of Civil Rights
Michigan Plaza Building
Detroit, MI 48226
313/256-2663

Michigan District Offices, Department of Civil Rights

221 East Roosevelt
Battle Creek, MI 49017

State Office Building
125 East Union Street
Flint, MI 48502

Grand Rapids State
Office Building
350 Ottawa Street, NW
Grand Rapids, MI 49502

State Office Building
301 East Louis B. Glick Highway
Jackson, MI 49201

309 N. Washington Square
Leonard Plaza Building
Room 103
Lansing, MI 48913

State Office Building
411 East Genesee
Saginaw, MI 48605

242 Pipestone
Benton Harbor, MI 49022

2542 Peck
Muskegon Heights, MI 49444

Pontiac State Bank Building
28 North Saginaw
10th Floor
Pontiac, MI 48058

L'Anse-Baraga
Upper Peninsula, U.S. 41
Arnheim, Pelkie, MI 49958

Minnesota

Department of Human Rights
500 Bremer Building
7th and Robert Streets
St. Paul, MN 55101
612/296-5663

Missouri

Commission on Human Rights
315 Ellis Boulevard
P.O. Box 1129
Jefferson City, MO 65102
314/751-3325

Missouri Regional Offices, Commission on Human Rights

625 North Euclid
Suite 605
St Louis, MO 63108
314/444-7590

1601 East 18th Street
Suites 320 and 340
Kansas City, MO 64108
816/472-2491

526 D South Main
Sikeston, MO 63801
314/471-7185

Montana

Human Rights Commission
Room C -317, Cogswell Building
Capital Station, Box 1728
Helena, MT 59624
406/444-2884

Nebraska

Nebraska Equal Opportunity Commission
P.O. Box 94934
301 Centennial Mall South
Lincoln, NE 68509
402/471-2024

Nebraska Branch Offices, Equal Opportunity Commission

5620 Ames Avenue
Suite 110
Omaha, NE 68104

4500 Avenue I
Box 1500
Scottsbluff, NE 69361

Lincoln Commission
on Human Rights
129 North 10th Street, Room 318
Lincoln, NE 68508

Omaha Human Relations Dept.
1819 Farnam Street, Suite 502
Omaha, NE 68102

Nevada

Equal Rights Commission
515 East Tropicana
Suite 590
Las Vegas, NV 89158
702/386-5304

668 Galletti Way
Sparks, NV 89431
702/789-0288

New Hampshire

Commission for Human Rights
61 South Spring Street
Concord, NH 03301
603/271-2767

New Jersey

Division on Civil Rights, Department of Law & Public Safety
Headquarters Office
1100 Raymond Boulevard
Newark, NJ 07102
201/648-2700

New Jersey Branch Offices, Division on Civil Rights, Department of Law & Public Safety

436 East State Street
Trenton, NJ 08608
609/292-4605

370 Broadway
Paterson, NJ 07501
201/345-1465

130 Broadway
Camden, NJ 08102
609/757-2850

New Mexico

Human Rights Commission
930 Baca Street
Santa Fe, NM 87501
505/827-6420

New York

State Division of Human Rights
55 West 125th Street
New York, NY 10027
212/870-8400

New York Branch Offices, State Division of Human Rights

Alfred East Smith
State Office Building
25th Floor
Albany, NY 12225
518/474-2705

364 Hawley Street
Binghamton, NY 13901
607/773-7713

349 East 149th Street
Bronx, NY 10451

1360 Fulton Street
4th Floor
Brooklyn, NY 11216
718/622-4600

69 Delaware Avenue
Buffalo, NY 14202
716/847-3713

State Office Building
Veterans Highway
Hauppage, NY 11787
516/360-6434

100 Main Street
2nd Floor
Hempstead, NY 11550
516/538-1360

270 Broadway
9th Floor
New York, NY 10007
212/587-5041

NYS Harlem Office Building
163 West 125th Street
2nd Floor
New York, NY 10027

120-55 Queens Boulevard
Kew Gardens, NY 11424
718/520-3373

259 Monroe Avenue
Rochester, NY 14607
716/238-8250

351 South Warren Street
Syracuse, NY 13202
315/428-4633

30 Glenn Street
3rd Floor
White Plains, NY 10603
914/949-4394

North Carolina

Human Relations Council
121 West Jones Street
Raleigh, NC 27603
919/733-7996

Office of Administrative Hearing
424 North Blount
Raleigh, NC 27601
919/733-2691

North Dakota

Department of Labor
State Capital, 5th Floor
Bismark, ND 58505
701/224-2660

Ohio

Civil Rights Commission
220 Parsons Avenue
Columbus, OH 43215
614/466-2785

Ohio Branch Offices, Civil Rights Commission

615 West Superior Avenue NW
Cleveland, OH 44113
215/622-3150

Southeast Regional Office
220 Parsons Avenue
Columbus, OH 43215
614/466-5928

North-Southwest
Regional Office
800 Miami Tower
40 West Fourth Street
Dayton, OH 45402
513/228-3612

Northwest Regional Office
510 Gardner Building
506 Madison and Superior
Toledo, OH 43604
419/241-9164

Southwest Regional Office
Masonry Office Building
2nd Floor
707 Race Street
Cincinnati, OH 45202
513/852-3344

South–Northeast
Regional Office
302 Peoples Federal
Building
39 East Market Street
Akron, OH 44308
216/253-3167

Oklahoma

Human Rights Commission, Room 480
2101 North Lincoln Boulevard
Oklahoma City, OK 73105
405/521-2360

Oregon

Bureau of Labor and Industries
Civil Rights Division, State Office Building
1400 SouthWest Fifth Avenue
Portland, OR 97201
503/229-5900 or 800/452-7813

Oregon Branch Offices, Bureau of Labor and Industries

165 East 7th Street
Room 220
Eugene, OR 97401

700 East Main
Medford, OR 97504

3865 Wolverine Street NE
Building E-1
Salem, OR 97310

Pennsylvania

Human Relations Commission
101 South Second Street, Suite 300
Harrisburg, PA 17105-3145
717/787-4410

Pennsylvania Branch Offices, Human Relations Commission

State Office Building
11th Floor
300 Liberty Avenue
Pittsburgh, PA 15222

3405 North 6th Street
Harrisburg, PA 17110
717/787-9780

711 State Office Building
Broad & Spring Garden
Philadelphia, PA 19130
215/238-6940

Puerto Rico

Department of Labor and Human Resources
Anti-Discrimination Unit
505 Munoz Rivera Avenue
Hato Rey, PR 00918
809/754-5353

Rhode Island

Commission for Human Rights
10 Abbott Park Place
Providence, RI 02903
401/277-2661

South Carolina

Human Affairs Commission
2611 Forest Drive
Columbia, SC 29204
803/737-6570

South Dakota

Division on Human Rights
State Capitol Building
222 East Capitol, Suite 11
Pierre, SD 57501
605/773-3177

Tennessee

Human Development Commission
Capitol Boulevard Building, Suite 602
226 Capitol Boulevard
Nashville, TN 37219
615/741-2424

Tennesse Field Offices, Human Development Commission

170 North Main Street	540 McCallie Avenue
Room 1113	6th Floor West, Room 605
Memphis, TN 38103	Chattanooga, TN 37402

Texas

Commission on Human Rights
P.O. Box 13493
Capitol Station
Austin, TX 78711
512/475-1178

Austin Human Relations Commission
P.O. Box 1088
Austin, TX 78767

Corpus Christi Human Relations Commission
101 North Shoreline
Corpus Christi, TX 78408

Fort Worth Human Relations Commission
1000 Trockmorton Street
Fort Worth, TX 76102

Utah

Industrial Commission
Anti-Discrimination Division
160 East 3rd Street South
Salt Lake City, UT 84151
801/530-6801

Vermont

Attorney General of Vermont
Civil Rights Division, Pavilion Office Building
109 State Street
Montpelier, VT 05602
802/828-3171

Virginia

Department of Labor and Industry
P.O. Box 12064
Richmond, VA 23241
804/786-2376

Alexandria Human Rights Office
405 Cameron Street
Alexandria, VA 22313

Fairfax County Human Rights Commission
Circle Towers Office Building
Suite 206
9401 Lee Highway
Fairfax, VA 22030

Virgin Islands

Department of Labor
P.O. Box 3159 53A, 54A & B
Kronprindfens Code
Charlotte Amalie
St. Thomas, VI 00801
809/776-3700

Washington

Washington State Human Rights Commission
402 Evergreen Plaza Building
711 South Capitol Way
Mail Stop FJ-41
Olympia, WA 98504
206/753-6770

Washington Branch Offices, State Human Rights Commission

Columbia Building
1516 2nd Avenue
Suite 400
Seattle, WA 98101
206/464-6500

32 North 3rd Street,
Suite 441
Yakima, WA 98901
509/545-2379

West 905 Riverside Avenue
Suite 416
Spokane, WA 99201
509/ 456-4473

West Virginia

Human Rights Commission
1036 Quarrier Street
215 Professional Building
Charleston, WV 25301
304/348-2616

Wisconsin

Department of Industry, Labor, and Human Relations
Equal Rights Division
201 East Washington Avenue
Madison, WI 53702
608/266-6860

Wisconsin Branch Offices, Department of Industry, Labor, and Human Relations, Equal Rights Division

819 North 6th Street
Room 255
Milwaukee, WI 53203
414/224-4384

718 West Clairemont Avenue
Eau Claire, WI 54701
715/836-5135

424 South Monroe Street
Green Bay, WI 54301
414/497-4170

1328 Schofield Avenue
Schofield, WI 54476
715/359-0471

Wyoming

Fair Employment Commission
Hathaway Building
Cheyenne, WY 82002
307/777-7261

135 North Ash Street
Room 180
Casper, WY 82601
307/234-8650

Commission of Labor & Statistics
Herschler Building
Cheyenne, WY 82002

U.S. Equal Employment Opportunity Commission

The **Equal Employment Opportunity Commission (EEOC)** aims to eliminate discrimination in the workplace. To achieve this purpose, the commission investigates cases of alleged discrimination, including cases of sexual harassment; helps victims prosecute cases; and offers educational programs for employers and community organizations. The EEOC publishes a packet of information about sexual harassment.

1801 L STREET NW
WASHINGTON, DC 20507
202/663-4900
800/USA-EEOC
800/872-3362 (SPANISH ALSO)

Equal Employment Opportunity Commission Administrative Offices
2401 E STREET, NW
WASHINGTON, DC 20507
202/634-6922 OR 800/USA-EEOC

EEOC District, Area, and Local Offices

Following is an alphabetical directory of EEOC's twenty-three "full-service" district offices, and the area and local offices serving those districts.

Albuquerque Area Office (Phoenix District)
Western Bank Building, Suite 1105
505 Marquette NW
Albuquerque, NM 87101
505/766-2061

Atlanta District Office
Citizens Trust Building, Suite 1100
75 Piedmont Avenue NE
Atlanta, GA 30335
404/331-6091

Baltimore District Office
109 Market Place, Suite 4000
Baltimore, MD 21202
301/962-3932

Birmingham District Office
212 Eighth Avenue North, Suite 824
Birmingham, AL 35203
205/254-0082

Boston Area Office (New York District)
JFK Building, Room 409-B
Boston, MA 02203
617/223-4535

Buffalo Local Office (New York District)
Guaranty Building, 28 Church Street
Buffalo, NY 14202
716/846-4441

Charlotte District Office
5500 Central Avenue
Charlotte, NC 28212
704/567-7100

Chicago District Office
Federal Building, Room 930-A
536 South Clark Street
Chicago, IL 60605
312/353-2713

Cincinnati Area Office (Cleveland District)
Federal Building, Room 7015
550 Main Street
Cincinnati, OH 45202
513/684-2851

Cleveland District Office
1375 Euclid Avenue, Room 600
Cleveland, OH 44115
216/522-7425

Dallas District Office
8303 Embrock Drive
Dallas, TX 75247
214/767-7015

Dayton Area Office (Cleveland District)
Federal Building, Room 60
200 West 2nd Street
Dayton, OH 45402
513/225-2753

Denver District Office
1845 Sherman Street, 2nd Floor
Denver, CO 80203
303/837-2771

Detroit District Office
Patrick V. MacNamara Federal Building, Room 1540
477 Michigan Avenue
Detroit, MI 48226
313/226-7636

El Paso Local Office (Dallas District)
First National Building, Suite 1112
109 North Oregon Street
El Paso, TX 79901
915/541-7596

Fresno Area Office (San Francisco District)
1313 P. Street, Suite 103
Fresno, CA 93721
209/487-5793

Greensboro Local Office (Charlotte District)
324 West Market Street, Room B-27
Post Office Box 3363
Greensboro, NC 27402
910/333-5174

Greenville Local Office (Atlanta District)
Century Plaza, Suite 109-B
211 Century Drive
Greenville, SC 29607
803/233-1791

Houston District Office
405 Main Street, Sixth Floor
Houston, TX 77002
713/226-2601

Indianapolis District Office
Federal Building, U.S. Courthouse
46 East Ohio Street, Room 456
Indianapolis, IN 46204
317/269-7212

Jackson Area Office (Birmingham District)
McCoy Federal Office Building
100 West Capitol Street, Suite 721
Jackson, MS 39269
601/965-4537

Kansas City Area Office (St. Louis District)
911 Walnut, 10th Floor
Kansas City, MO 94106
816/374-5773

Little Rock Area Office (New Orleans District)
Savers Building, Suite 621
320 West Capitol Avenue
Little Rock, AR 72201
501/378-5060

Los Angeles District Office
3660 Wilshire Boulevard, 5th Floor
Los Angeles, CA 90010
213/251-7278

Louisville Area Office (Memphis District)
601 West Broadway, Room 104
Louisville, KY 40202
502/582-6082

Memphis District Office
1407 Union Avenue, Suite 502
Memphis, TN 38104
902/521-2617

Miami District Office; Metro Mall
1 Northeast First Street, 6th Floor
Miami, FL 33132
305/536-4491

Milwaukee District Office
310 West Wisconsin Avenue, Suite 800
Milwaukee, WI 53203
414/291-1111

Minneapolis Local Office (Milwaukee District)
110 South Fourth Street, Room 178
Minneapolis, MN 55401
612/349-3495

Nashville Area Office (Memphis District)
Parkway Towers, Suite 1100
Nashville, TN 37219
615/251-5820

Newark Area Office (New York District)
60 Park Place, Room 301
Newark, NY 07102
201/645-6383

New Orleans District Office
F. Edward Hebert Federal Building
600 South Maestri Place, Room 528
New Orleans, LA 70130
504/589-2329

New York District Office
90 Church Street, Room 1505
New York, NY 10007
212/264-7161

Norfolk Area Office (Baltimore District)
Federal Building, Room 412
200 Granby Mall
Norfolk, VA 23510
804/441-3470

Oakland Local Office (San Francisco District)
Wells Fargo Bank Building
1333 Broadway, Room 430
Oakland, CA 94612
415/273-7588

Oklahoma Area Office (Dallas District)
Alfred P. Marrah Federal Building
200 NW Fifth Street, Room 703
Oklahoma City, OK 73102
405/231-4911

Philadelphia District Office
127 North 4th Street, Suite 300
Philadelphia, PA 19106
215/597-7784

Phoenix District Office
135 North Second Avenue, Fifth Floor
Phoenix, AZ 85003
602/261-3882

Pittsburgh Area Office (Philadelphia District)
Federal Building, Room 2038A
1000 Liberty Avenue
Pittsburgh, PA 15222
412/644-3444

Raleigh Area Office (Charlotte District)
178 West Hargett Street, Suite 500
Raleigh, NC 27601
919/856-4064

Richmond Area Office (Baltimore District)
400 North 8th Street, Room 6206
Richmond, VA 23240
804/771-2692

San Antonio Area Office (Houston District)
727 East Durango, Suite 601-B
San Antonio, TX 78206
512/229-6051

San Diego Local Office (Los Angeles District)
San Diego Federal Building
880 Front Street
San Diego, CA 92188
619/293-6288

San Francisco District Office
10 United Nations Plaza, Fourth Floor
San Francisco, CA 94102
415/556-0260

San Jose Local Office (San Francisco District)
U.S. Courthouse and Federal Building
280 South First Street, Room 4150
San Jose, CA 95113
408/291-7352

Seattle District Office
Arcade Plaza Building
1321 Second Avenue, 7th Floor
Seattle, WA 98101
206/442-0968

St. Louis District Office
625 North Euclid Street
St. Louis, MO 63108
314/425-6585

Tampa Area Office (Miami District)
700 Twiggs Street, Room 302
Tampa, FL 33602
813/228-2310

Washington Area Office (Baltimore District)
1717 H Street N.W., Suite 400
Washington, DC 20006
202/653-6197

INTERNATIONAL ORGANIZATIONS, SERVICES, POLICIES, AND PRACTICES

The Global Campaign for Women's Human Rights
1333 H STREET NW, SUITE 700
WASHINGTON, DC 20005
TEL.: 202/682-1270; FAX 202/682-2154

The International Programme for the Improvement of Working Conditions and Environment (PIACT) was established by the International Labour Organisation in 1976 at the request of the International Labour Conference and after extensive consultations with member states. The purpose of PIACT is to promote or support action by member states in setting and reaching definite objectives aimed at "making work more human." The Programme is concerned with improving the quality of working life in all aspects. To achieve these aims, PIACT uses and coordinates the traditional means of ILO action, including: the preparation and revision of international labour standards; operational activities, such as the dispatch of multidisciplinary teams to assist member states on request; tripartite meetings between representatives of governments, employers, and workers, including industrial committees to study the problems facing major industries, regional meetings, and meetings of experts; action-oriented studies and research; and clearinghouse activities, especially through the International Occupa-tional Safety and Health Information Centre (CIS) and the Clearinghouse for the Dissemination of Information on Conditions of Work.

Australia

Federal Level: The Sex Discrimination Commissioner, on behalf of the Human Rights and Equal Opportunity Commission (a nonjudicial administrative body established by the federal government), is required by the Sex Discrimination Act of 1984, to investigate alleged violations of the Act, including those involving sexual harassment. The Commission must promote an understanding and acceptance of the legislation, and prepare and publish guidelines to prevent sex discrimination, and intervene in any proceedings on issues of discrimination, including sexual harassment.

Queensland: The Anti-Discrimination Commission, established by the Anti-Discrimination Act of 1991, consists of the Anti-Discrimination Commissioner and staff. The Commission investigates complaints of sexual harassment and attempts to resolve complaints through conciliation. The Commission also reviews existing and proposed legislation to insure consistency with the Act and conducts research and educational programs to promote the purposes of the Act. On request of the Minister, the Commission must research and develop additional grounds of discrimination for possible inclusion in the

Act. The Commission is also to promote the public's understanding and acceptance of human rights in Queensland.

Austria

The Equality of Treatment Committee, established within the Federal Ministry of Labour and Social Affairs, investigates alleged infringements of the principle of equality of treatment, which could include complaints about sexual harassment. For complaints of sexual harassment, a female lawyer for equality of treatment issues and a female deputy were appointed to provide advisory services and to give support to employees; they present cases to the Equality of Treatment Committee based on one or more violations of the equality of treatment rule. The Committee and the responsible lawyer can assist the complainant when harassment is interpreted to be discrimination on the basis of sex.

Belgium

Two governmental institutions have initiated the Belgian Government's actions regarding sexual harassment—the Commission of Women's Employment and the Secretary of State for Social Emancipation, both of which are under the authority of the Ministry of Employment and Labour. Although the Commission of Women's Employment has legal authority to examine problems relating to sexual harassment in the public sector, usually such questions are referred to the Consultative Commission for the Settlement of Differences regarding Equal Treatment of Men and Women in the Public Service.

Canada

The federal Canadian Human Rights Commission receives complaints of sexual harassment by federal government

employees or people employed in a federal undertaking.
The Ontario Human Rights Commission receives complaints
of sexual harassment by employees of the private sector and
state public sector in the Province of Ontario.
The Status of Women Canada conducts research, and provides
information on Canadian women.
151 SPARKS STREET, 10TH FLOOR
OTTAWA, ONTARIO; K1A 1C3.

*The Canada-U.S. Free Trade Agreement & Women: An As-
sessment* is a manual provided by the Minister of Supply and
Services Canada.
COMMUNICATIONS BRANCH, STATUS OF WOMEN CANADA
151 SPARKS STREET, 10TH FLOOR
OTTAWA, ONTARIO; K1A 1C3; PHONE 613/995-3901

Czechoslovakia

Czechoslovakia has no specialized institutional authority to
deal with sexual harassment in the workplace, although the
Ministry of Labour would normally handle complaints of violation of the Labour Code, which could be applicable to sexual harassment.

Denmark

The Equal Opportunities Council, under authority of the
Equal Opportunities Act, may by request or on its own initiative, examine any issue under the Act, which would include a
complaint of sexual harassment.

Finland

The Equality Ombudsman and Equality Board supervise the
implementation of the Equal Opportunities Act and the state
labour inspectors, under the Labour Protection Act, and have

the principle responsibility for enforcement of the Act.

France

The office of the Secretary of State for Women's Rights, which is under the authority of the Ministry of Labour, Employment and Vocational Training, has proposed initiatives for new legislation specifically addressing sexual harassment, with respect to changes in the Penal Code and changes in the Labour Code.

Germany

At the federal level, no particular institution is responsible for sexual harassment cases in the workplace. However, public institutions continue to appoint female equal opportunities officers with a view to achieving equality of treatment. It is the duty of these officers to determine whether or not established rules and policies on equal treatment during recruitment and hiring activities, promotion, transfer, training, and any other benefits or services, are followed. The issue of sexual harassment is also within the duties of these officers.

Under the Anti-Discrimination Act of the State of Berlin, an equal opportunities women's officer is responsible for pursuing any allegations of sexual harassment in the workplace.

Also in Germany, the works council has rights and duties to protect against discrimination on the basis of sex, and to control standards for the worker's safety and the free development of the worker's personality. The works council may challenge termination decisions in court and also influence personnel decisions, such as promotions or transfer, or guidelines for selection during recruitment. The Works Constitution Act allows an employee to make a complaint to the appropriate individuals in an organization if the person feels discriminated against by the employer or by other employees, or feels unfairly treated in any other respect. These provisions could apply to complainants of sexual harassment by supervisors or other employees.

Greece

As a result of the enactment of Act No. 141 on equality in 1984, a section entitled the Sex Equality Section was established within the Ministry of Labour. In addition, sex equality offices are a part of employment inspections and have a responsibility for supervising provisions of the Act, as well as for finding any existing discrimination. The issue of sexual harassment could fall within the scope of the labour offices.

Ireland

The Employment Equality Act of 1977 created the Employment Equality Agency. The agency works toward the elimination of discrimination in employment, including sex discrimination and sexual harassment. It conducts research and provides information, reviews legislation, and conducts investigations. The Agency can act on behalf of complainants alleging sexual harassment when a case is referred before the Labour Court or an equality officer.

Japan

Under the Equal Employment Opportunity Act, an Equal Opportunity Mediation Commission exists at each Prefectural Women and Young Worker's Office. The Commission is composed of three people who deal with complaints of sexual harassment.

The Labor Standards Act is enforced by the Labor Standards Bureau, a Prefectural Labor Standards Office and the Labor Standards Inspection Office. The Ministry of Labor controls and supervises these offices, and complaints of sexual harassment relating to wage discrimination would come within the scope of these labor offices.

Luxembourg

The Labor and Mines Inspector and the Employment Administration supervise the implementation of the Equal Opportunities Act. Complaints of sexual harassment to the labor inspector are kept absolutely confidential. Labor inspectors may enter business premises without notification to ensure enforcement of lawful working conditions, and are not to indicate to the employer if the inspection is the result of a complaint. However, according to information provided to the International Labour Organi-zation, as of January 1992, the labor inspector was not actively following up on complaints of sexual harassment, stating that sexual harassment is not a work condition issue, but a criminal matter.

Netherlands

Under the Men and Women (Equal Treatment) Act, the Commission for Equal Treatment for Men and Women in Employment was established. The Commission may investigate on its own initiative or because of complaints of unequal treatment at work; it has the responsibility to investigate complaints of sexual harassment and decide if a complaint is valid. However, the Commission's decisions are not legally binding and to date, no complaint about sexual harassment has been submitted to it. The Commission may make its decisions public and is required to submit an annual report on its activities to the Ministry of Social Affairs and Employment.

New Zealand

The Human Rights Commission was established by the Human Rights Commission Act in 1977. The Commission's goals are to work towards the elimination of discrimination, to encourage or assist research, to promote equality between people, to conduct formal investigations, to act as a mediator, and to make recommendations on its formal investigations. An Equal Opportunities Tribunal (EOT) rules on proceedings brought under the Act. The issue of sexual harassment falls within the responsibilities of the Commission.

The Employment Tribunal was established under the Employment Contracts Act. Its goal is to provide fair and just resolution of differences between parties in employment contracts by mediation or adjudication.

Norway

An Equal Status Ombud and an Equal Status Appeals Board supervise implementation of the Equal Status Act. In cases where sexual harassment could potentially constitute sex discrimination, the issue would be the responsibility of the Equal Status Ombud.

Portugal

A Commission on Equality in Work and Employment was established within the Ministry for Employment and Social Security, with a view to promoting the application of the decree, by Legislative Decree No. 392 on equal opportunity in the private sector. The Commission's duty is to promote studies and inquires to eliminate discrimination against women in matters of work and employment. Legislative Decree No. 426 expanded the Commission's scope to the public employment sector. Sexual harassment falls within the Commission's responsibilities.

Spain

The Women's Institute is responsible for women's issues in Spain. It is an autonomous governmental body under the authority of the Ministry of Social Affairs.

Sweden

The Equal Opportunities Ombudsman and the Equal
Opportunities Board supervise compliance of the Equal
Opportunities Act, including those related to sexual harassment at work. Both the Ombudsman and the Board are
appointed by the government. The Ombudsman works for
employer compliance with the Act on a voluntary basis and
to promote equality at work in other ways.

Switzerland

The Office for the Equality of Rights between Man and
Woman is under the authority of the Department of Justice
and Police. The issue of sexual harassment is within the duties
of this office.

United Kingdom

The Equal Opportunities Commission (EOC) was established
as a result of the Sex Discrimination Act 1975. The
Commission's goals are to work toward the elimination of discrimination, to promote equality between men and women,
to undertake or assist research, to review discriminatory provisions in health and safety legislation, to conduct formal
investigations, and to make recommendations and reports on
its formal investigations. There are separate Commissions for
Great Britain and for Northern Ireland. The British EOC
included a short reference to sexual harassment in a Code of
Practice issued in 1985, and which addressed eliminating discrimination on the basis of sex and the promotion of equality
of opportunity in employment. The Northern Ireland EOC has
produced a booklet, *Sexual Harassment Is No Laughing
Matter,* describing the alternatives available to women, trade

unions, and employers for dealing with the problem.

United States

Federal: The Equal Employment Opportunity Commis-sion (EEOC) is an independent agency established by federal statute, the 1964 Civil Rights Act, to deal with claims violating the federal laws protecting equal opportunity in employment. Sexual harassment claims are brought before the EEOC, which must investigate, make findings, attempt to resolve the conflict between the parties by informal conciliation, and if conciliation fails, to either bring an enforcement action in federal district court or issue a right to sue letter to the complainant to bring a private legal action.

California: The Fair Employment and Housing Commission (FEHC) is an independent state agency, established by state statute to deal with claims violating state laws protecting equal opportunity in employment and housing. Sexual harassment claims are brought before the FEHC, which must investigate and adjudicate claims of sexual harassment brought under the state law forbidding sexual harassment.

Other States and Municipalities: Most states and many municipal governments have local agencies, usually called Human Rights Commissions, responsible for insuring compliance with state and local laws and ordinances related to discrimination in employment and other areas, such as housing. The power, authority, and scope of each agency varies.

The U.S. Merit Systems Protection Board's. *Sexual Harassment In The Federal Government: An Update.* Issued by the U.S. Government Printing Office in 1988, is a comprehensive study of sexual harassment in the federal sector. It nearly duplicated in methodology and findings the results of the Merit Systems' 1980 study on sexual harassment.

NOTE: Most information on agencies in other countries that are responsible for handling sexual harassment came from the Internatioal Labour Organisation's publication, *Combating Sexual Harassment at Work.*

Experts on Women's Issues Worldwide

Human Rights Abuse in the Family

Charolette Bunch, Director
CENTER FOR WOMEN'S GLOBAL LEADERSHIP
RUTGERS UNIVERSITY, DOUGLAS COLLEGE CAMPUS
27 CLIFTON AVENUE, NEW BRUNSWICK, NJ 08903
TEL.: 908/932-8782 OR 7118; FAX: 908/932-1180
Feminist author, organizer, teacher, and activist, Ms. Bunch
has been a leading figure in the international women's movement for more than two decades. The Global Center has organized more than 800 women's organizations worldwide to
support the Global Campaign for Women's Human Rights. Ms.
Bunch has been a leader in the NGO preparatory meetings for
the UN World Conference on Human Rights.

Roxanna Carrillo
UNIFEM (UNITED NATIONS DEVELOPMENT FUND FOR WOMEN)
304 EAST 45TH STREET, NEW YORK, NY 10017
TEL.: 212/906-6454; FAX: 212/906-6705
A Peruvian, Ms. Carrillo will represent UNIFEM at the World
Human Rights Conference. She is well known throughout
Latin America for her work on violence against women as a
development issue.

Rhonda Copelon, Associate Professor of Law and Co-Director
INTERNATIONAL WOMEN'S HUMAN RIGHTS CLINIC (IWHR)
CUNY LAW SCHOOL
65-21 MAIN STREET, FLUSHING, NY 11367
TEL.: 718/575-4329; FAX: 718/575-4478
Ms. Copelon is a leading legal authority on reproductive
health issues and women's human rights who's currently
involved in the legal issues concerning gender justice and war
crimes in connection with the UN proposal for a war crimes

tribunal on the former Yugoslavia. She has written on domestic violence and rape as torture, and served as a member of the expert committee that drafted the proposed Inter-American Convention to Prevent, Punish, and Eradicate Violence Against Women.

Marsha Freeman, Deputy Director
INTERNATIONAL WOMEN'S RIGHTS ACTION WATCH (IWRAW)
HUBERT H. HUMPHREY INSTITUTE OF PUBLIC AFFAIRS
UNIVERSITY OF MINNESOTA, 301-19TH AVENUE SOUTH
MINNEAPOLIS, MN 55455
TEL.: 612/625-5093; FAX: 612/625-6351
Author of numerous articles and papers, Ms. Freeman specializes in women's human rights, gender bias and the implementation of the Women's Human Rights' Treaty in the developing world.

Dr. Shauna Swiss, Director of the Women's Program
PHYSICIANS FOR HUMAN RIGHTS
100 BOYLSTON STREET, SUITE 702, BOSTON, MA 02116
TEL.: 617/695-0041; FAX: 617/695-0307
A physician, Dr. Swiss is an expert on the physical, psychological and social consequences of violence, torture, and rape in war. She has written and spoken internationally on her recent trips to Liberia and the former Yugoslavia, and collaborates with women's health organizations to build local capacity to develop community-based programs for women who have been victims of rape and other war-related trauma.

War Crimes Against Women in Conflict Situations

Jessica Neuwirth, Director
EQUALITY NOW
226 WEST 58TH STREET, NO. 4, NEW YORK, NY 10019
212/586-0906
Formerly with Amnesty International, Ms. Neuwirth is an

attorney who founded Equality Now to mobilize actions (letter writing, fax campaigns, video witnessing, and media events) on behalf of individual women whose rights are violated and to promote women's rights at local, national, and international levels. The Women's Action Network distributes "Women's Actions," bulletins in English, French, and Spanish that provide information about specific abuses and recommend concrete actions to be taken.

Nelia Sancho Liao, Director
ASIAN WOMEN-HUMAN RIGHTS COUNCIL
P.O. Box 190, 10991 MANILA, PHILIPPINES
632/921-5571
A former political prisoner under the Marcos regime and an ex-beauty queen, Ms. Liao founded the Asian Women's Human Rights Council. It has conducted a series of tribunals throughout Asia on military sexual slavery from World War II to current conflicts in Asia.

Dorothy Q. Thomas, Director
WOMEN'S RIGHTS PROJECT, HUMAN RIGHTS WATCH
1522 K STREET NW, SUITE 910, WASHINGTON, DC 20005
TEL.: 202/371-6592; FAX: 202/371-0124
Ms. Thomas specializes in monitoring and documenting human rights abuses against women, with an emphasis on violence throughout the world. Special reports have been issued on Peru, Brazil, Pakistan and Kuwait. A report on Burmese prostitutes in Thailand will be issued shortly.

Violations Against Women's Bodies: Health, Sexuality, Reproduction

Rebecca Cook, Professor
Faculty of Law, University of Toronto
78 Queen's Park, Toronto, Ontario, Canada M5S 2C5
Tel.: 416/978-4666; Fax: 416/978-7899
An internationally known attorney who frequently writes and speaks on international law, reproductive rights, health issues, and women's human rights, Ms. Cook directs the **International Human Rights Law Programme** and teaches International Human Rights Law, Reproductive Health Law, and Ethical and Legal Issues in Health Care. She also serves as a legal advisor to the Ford Foundation, the World Health Organization in Geneva and the Commonwealth Secretariat in London.

Seble Dawit, Visiting Associate
The Center for Women's Global Leadership
Douglass College
27 Clifton Avenue, New Brunswick, New Jersey 08903
Tel.: 908/932-8782; Fax: 908/932-1180
An Ethiopian attorney, Ms. Dawit specializes in women's health issues and human rights. Formerly on the staff of the International Women's Health Coalition, she is in the forefront of new legal strategies to take effective action against genital mutilation.

Lynn Freedman, Associate Director
Development, Law & Policy Program
60 Haven Avenue, #B3, New York, NY 10032
Tel.: 212/305-6971; Fax: 212/305-7024
An attorney, Ms. Freedman is known for her expertise in the public health aspects of reproductive rights and law.

Anika Rahman, Staff Attorney
THE CENTER FOR REPRODUCTIVE LAW AND POLICY,
INTERNATIONAL PROGRAM
120 WALL STREET, NEW YORK, NY 10005
TEL.: 212/514-5534; FAX: 212/514-5538
Ms. Rahman's work focuses on reproductive health issues in developing nations. She also has worked on redress for victims of sexual harassment and legal issues involving the rights of immigrants, specifically battered immigrant women in the United States. Ms. Rahman has conducted extensive research on issues relating to dowry laws in India and Muslim personal law in the South Asian region.

Nahid Toubia, Associate
THE EBERT PROGRAM IN REPRODUCTIVE HEALTH
AT THE POPULATION COUNCIL
ONE DAG HAMMARSKJOLD PLAZA, NEW YORK, NY 10017
TEL.: 212/339-0632; FAX: 212/755-6052
The first woman surgeon in Sudan, Ms. Toubia is internationally known for her expertise on abortion-related injury and death and genital mutilation. She is also a member of several scientific and technical advisory committees of the World Health Organization and sits on the advisory committee of the Women's Rights Watch Project of Human Rights Watch.

Socio-Economic Human Rights of Women

Leni Marin, Senior Program Specialist
FAMILY VIOLENCE PREVENTION FUND
BUILDING ONE, SUITE 200, 1001 POTRERO AVENUE
SAN FRANCISCO, CA 94110
TEL.: 415/821-4553 (EXT. 556); FAX: 415/824-3873
As coordinator of the Fund's Battered Immigrant and Refugee Women's Rights Project, Ms. Marin played a leadership role in organizing the Coalition for Immigrant and Refugee Rights and Services/Immigrant Women's Task Force's historic hear-

ing: "Documenting Human Rights Abuses Against Immigrant and Refugee Women in the United States." An immigrant from the Phillippines, Ms. Marin has devoted her time to work on behalf of critical services for immigrant and refugee women and battered women and their children.

Celina Romany, Associate Professor of Law and Co-Director
INTERNATIONAL WOMEN'S HUMAN RIGHTS CLINIC (IWHR)
CUNY LAW SCHOOL, 65-21 MAIN STREET, FLUSHING, NY 11367
TEL.: 718/575-4329; FAX: 718/575-4478
Recognized in feminist legal theory and the reconceptualization of women's rights as human rights, Ms. Romany studies the links between violence against women and issues of race, gender, and class, and civil, political, social, and economic rights.

Sima Wali, Executive Director
REFUGEE WOMEN IN DEVELOPMENT (RefWID), INC.
810 FIRST STREET NE, SUITE 300, WASHINGTON, DC 20002
TEL.: 202/289-1104; FAX: 202/289-8173
A refugee from Afghanistan, Ms. Wali has represented refugee women in national and international conferences and she is an expert on the special concerns of refugees and women's human rights.

Political Participation

Florence Butegwa, Regional Coordinator
WILDAF (WOMEN IN LAW AND DEVELOPMENT IN AFRICA)
P.O. BOX 4622, HARARE, ZIMBABWE
TEL.: 2634-729-151 OR 2634-467-11; FAX: 2634-731-901(902)
An attorney with extensive international experience, Ms. Butegwe is widely regarded as an expert on international law and women's human rights. She has been instrumental in developing a network of women's organizations in fifteen

African countries to facilitate communications among women's human rights advocates.

Arvonne Fraser, Director
INTERNATIONAL WOMEN'S RIGHTS ACTION WATCH (IWRAW)
HUBERT H. HUMPHREY INSTITUTE OF PUBLIC AFFAIRS
UNIVERSITY OF MINNESOTA
301 19TH AVENUE SOUTH, MINNEAPOLIS, MN 55455
TEL.: 612/625-2505; FAX: 612/625-6351
Following decades of leadership in the U.S. and international women's rights communities, Ms. Fraser is an expert on the proposed Convention to Eliminate Discrimination Against Women (CEDAW), which has been ratified by one hundred twenty-one nations, but has yet to be ratified by the United States. She recently headed the U.S. delegation to the UN Commission on the Status of Women and is considered an expert on the history of the Women's Human Rights Treaty.

Marge Schuler, Director
INSTITUTE FOR WOMEN, LAW & DEVELOPMENT (IWLD)
733 15TH STREET NW, SUITE 700, WASHINGTON, DC 20005
TEL.: 202/393-3663; FAX: 202/393-3664
An expert on legal literacy and informal education, Ms. Schuler has been instrumental in supporting the creation of women's rights organizations and networks that link advocates in Asia, Africa, and Latin America. This work is an outgrowth of her organization of the Third World Forum on Women, Law and Development in 1985. Ms. Schuler has written extensively on women's rights strategies from a cross-cultural perspective and has edited several books that draw on women's experiences from around the world.

Maria Suarez
FEMINIST INTERNATIONAL RADIO ENDEAVOR (FIRE)
APARTADO 88, SANTA ANA, COSTA RICA
TEL.: 506-421-821; FAX: 506-491-929
Founder and Coordinator of Feminist International Radio Endeavor (FIRE), headquartered in Costa Rica, Ms. Suarez is known throughout Central America as an expert on women's human rights.

NOTE: The names of leaders and their descriptions are from the Global Campaign for Women's Human Rights.

REFERENCES

Books

Adams, Caren, et al. *No Is Not Enough: Helping Teen-agers Avoid Sexual Assault.* San Luis Obispo, CA: Impact Publishers, 1984.

Backhouse, Connie. *Fighting Sexual Harassment: An Advocacy Handbook.* Cambridge: Alliance Against Sexual Coercion, 1981.

Backhouse, Constance and Leah Cohen. *Sexual Harassment On The Job: How To Avoid The Working Woman's Nightmare.* Englewood Cliffs, N.J.: Prentice-Hall, Inc., 1981.

Bell, Ruth. *Changing Bodies Changing Lives.* New York: Random House, 1980.

Benson, Donna and Gregg Thomson. *Sex, Gender And Power: Sexual Harassment On A University Campus.* Berkeley: University of California, 1979.

Bravo, Ellen and Ellen Cassedy. *The 9 to 5 Guide To Combating Sexual Harassment.* New York: Wiley, 1992.

Burton, Clare. *The Promise & The Price: The Struggle For Equal Opportunity In Women's Employment.* Sydney, Australia: Allen & Unwin, 1991.

Clarke, Elissa. *Stopping Sexual Harassment.* Detroit: Labor Education and Research Project, 1980.

Coeli Meyer, Mary and Jeanne Oestriech, Frederick J. Collins, and Inge Berchtold. *Sexual Harassment.* New York: Petrocelli Books, Inc., 1981.

Cooper, Kenneth C. *Stop It Now: How Targets & Managers Can End Sexual Harassment.* St. Louis: Total Communications Press, 1985.

Croninger, Bob and Barbra Morris, and Eleanor Lin, and Jacquie Terpstra. *Tune In To Your Rights ... A Guide for Teenagers About Turning Off Sexual Harassment.* Michigan: Regents of the University of Michigan, 1985.

Dzeich-Wright, Billie and Linda Weiner. *The Lecherous Professor: Sexual Harassment on Campus.* Champaign: University of Illinois Press, 1992.

Farley, Lin. *Sexual Shakedown.* New York: Warner Communications Company, 1978.

Griffin, Thomas M. "Sexual Harrassment and Title IX." West's Education Law Reporter 18 (1984): 513-520.

Gutek, Barbara A. *Sex And The Workplace.* San Francisco: Jossey-Bass Inc. Publishers, 1985.

Harragan, B.L. *Games Mother Never Taught You: Corporate Gamesmanship for Woman.* New York: Warner Communications Company, 1979.

Horn, Patrice D. and Jack C. Horn. *Sex In The Office: Power and Passion In The Workplace.* Reading, MA: Addison-Wesley Publishing Company, 1982.

Ivory Power: Sexual Harassment on Campus. Albany: State University of New York Press, 1990.

MacKinnon, Catharine A. *Sexual Harassment of Working Women: A Case of Sex Discrimination.* New Haven: Yale University Press, 1979.

Male/Female Roles: Opposing Viewpoints. San Diego: Greenhaven Press, Inc., 1989.

Mezey-Gluck, Susan. *In Pursuit of Equality.* New York: Yale St. Martin's Press, 1991.

Nieva, V.F. and Barbara A. Gutek. *Women and Work: A Phsyiological Perspective.* New York: Praeger, 1981.

Paludi, Michele A. and Richard B. Barickman. *Academic and Workplace Sexual Harassment : Resource Manual.* Ithaca: State University of New York Press, 1992.

Paludi, Michele. *Working 9 to 5: Women, Men, Sex, and Power.* Albany: State University of New York Press, 1991.

Petrocelli, William and Barbara Kate Repa. *Sexual Harassment On The Job.* Berkeley: Nolo Press, 1992.

Phelps, Timothy M. and Helen Winternitz. *Capitol Games: Clarence Thomas, Anita Hill, and the Story of a Supreme Court Nomination.* Westport, CT: Hyperion, 1992.

Powell, Elizabeth. *Talking Back to Sexual Pressure.* Minneapolis: CompCare Publishers, 1991.

Sargent, Alice. *Beyond Sex Roles.* New York: West Publishing, 1977.

Schwartz, Felice North. *Breaking With Tradition: Women and Work, The New Facts of Life.* New York: Warner Books, Inc. 1992.

Sex Equity Handbook for Schools. New York: Longman, 1982.

Sexual Harassment and Teens; Minneapolis: (1992). $17.95. Free Spirit Publishing Inc., 1992.

Sexual Harassment in Employment and Education; Seattle: (1992). NW Women's Law Center, 1992.

Sexual Harassment: Current Controversies. San Diego: Greenhaven Press, Inc., 1992.

Sexual Values: Opposing Viewpoints. San Diego: Greenhaven Press, Inc., 1989.

Siegel, Deborah L. *Sexual Harassment: Research and Resources.* New York: The National Council for Research on Women, 1991.

Strauss, Susan with Pamela Espeland. *Sexual Harassment and Teens.* Minneapolis: Free Spirit Publishing, Inc., 1992.

Strauss, Susan. *Sexual Harassment To Teenagers: It's Not Fun, It's Illegal.* St. Paul: Minnesota Department of Education, Equal Educational Opportunities Section, 1987.

Sumrall, Amber Coverdale and Dena Taylor, Andrea Dworkin, and Margaret Randall. *Sexual Harassment: Women Speak Out.* Freedom, CA: The Crossing Press, 1992.

Till, F.J. *Sexual Harassment: A Report On the Sexual Harassment of Students.* Washington, DC: National Advisory Council on Women's Educational Programs, 1980.

Wagner, Ellen J. *Sexual Harassment In The Workplace: How to Prevent, Investigate, and Resolve Problems in Your Organization.* New York: AMACOM, 1992.

Webb, Susan L. *Step Forward: Sexual Harassment in the Workplace.* New York: MasterMedia, 1991.

Periodicals and Special Reports

Center for Sex Equity in Schools. "Sexual Harassment Is No Laughing Matter." Title IX Line: Special Issue (Fall 1983). Ann Arbor: University of Michigan School of Education.

Copeland, Lois and Leslie R. Wolfe. "Violence Against Women as Bias Motivated Hate Crime: Defining the Issues." Washington, DC: Center for Women Policy Studies, 1991.

de Nys, Mary, and Leslie R. Wolfe. "Learning Her Place: Sex Bias in the Elementary School Classroom." *Peer Report 5* (Autumn 1985).

Field, Anne. "Harassment on Campus: Sex in a Tenured Position?" *MS.* (September 1989): 68-73, 100-102.

Fitzgerald, Louise F. *Sexual Harassment in Higher Education: Concepts & Issues.* National Education Association, 1992.

Flerchinger, Billie Jo and Jennifer J. Fay. *Top Secret.* Santa Cruz: Network Publication, King County Rape Relief.

Gilligan, Carol. *In A Different Voice.* Cambridge: Harvard University Press, 1982.

Griffin, Thomas M. "Sexual Harassment and Title IX." West's Education Law Reporter 18 (1984): 513-520.

Hall, Roberta, and Bernice Sandler. "The Classroom Climate: A Chilly One for Women?" Paper written for the project on the Status and Education of Women, Association of American Colleges, 1982.

Kaser, Joyce and Marlene Ross. "Preventing Sexual Harassment of School Employees." *Educational Leadership* (November 1983): 53-57.

Mead, Margaret. "A Proposal: We Need Taboos on Sex at Work." *Redbook* (April 1978): 31, 33,38.

National Advisory Council on Women's Educational Programs. *A Report on the Sexual Harrassment of Students.* Washington, DC: NACWEP, U.S. Department of Education, 1980.

Project on the Status and Education of Women. *Sexual Harassment: A Hidden Issue.* Washington, DC: Association of American Colleges, 1978.

Riley, Susan. *A Fair Shot/An Equal Chance.* Quincy: Project SCOPE, Massachusetts Department of Education, 1980.

Rossein, Merrick. "Sex Discrimination and the Sexually Charged Work Environment." The New York University Review of Law and Social Change 9 (Fall 1981): 271-305.

Rowe, Mary P. "Ideas for Action: Dealing with Sexual Harassment." *Harvard Business Review* 59:3 (May-June 1981): 42-46.

Sadker, Myra and David Sadker. " Sexism in the Classroom." *Vocational Education Journal* (October 1985): 30-32.

Safran, Claire. "What Men Do to Women on the Job: A Shocking Look at Sexual Harassment." *Redbook* (November 1976): 149, 217-223.

Sexual Violence Facts and Statistics. The Illinois Coalition Against Sexual Assault, 123 South Seventh Street, Suite 500, Springfield, IL 62701. 1993.

Stein, Nan D. "It Happens Here Too: Sexual Harassment in the Schools." *Education Week* (November 17, 1991): 32,25.

Stringer, Gayle M. and Deanna Rants-Rodriguez. *So What's It To Me?* Sexual Assault Information for Boys. Renton, WA: King County Rape Relief, 1987.

Top Secret: A Discussion Guide. Santa Cruz: Network Publication, King County Rape Relief, 1985.

Toufexis, Anastasia. "Our Violent Kids." *Time* (June 12, 1989): 52-58.

Vandell, Kathy and Lauren Fishbein. "Equitable Treatment of Girls and Boys in the Classroom," a brief prepared for the American Association of University Women, 1989.

Who's Hurt and Who's Liable: Sexual Harassment in Massachusetts Schools: A Curriculum and Guide for School Personnel. (1986). Free. Massachusetts Department of Education, ATTN: Bureau of Equity and Language Services, 1385 Hancock Street, Quincy, MA 02169-5138. 617/770-7545.

Videos

Dreamworld: Desire/Sex/Power in Rock Video is a powerful one-hour video depicting images from a variety of music videos. The accompanying narration describes the patterns in the images and how they contribute to attitudes about women as easy prey for sexual assault.

428 • <small>SHOCKWAVES</small>

No Laughing Matter: High School Students and Sexual Harassment. (1982) is a twenty-five minute videotape that presents the stories of three high school teens who are involved in incidents of sexual harassment at school and work. Comments by teachers and administrators regarding the prevention of sexual harassment are interspersed with the stories. $25. Massachusetts Department of Education, ATTN: Bureau of Educational Technologies, 1385 Hancock Street, Quincy, MA 02169-5183. 617/770-7508.

Touch (video for grades K-6) and *No Easy Answer* (curriculum and video for grades 6-12) deal with sexual abuse prevention. The thirty-minute videos can be used alone or to supplement existing abuse prevention programs in schools, churches, and community groups.

ADDITIONAL RESOURCES FROM THE AUTHOR

The following resources are available from:
PREMIERE PUBLISHING, LTD.
145 NW 85TH STREET, SUITE 103
SEATTLE, WA 98117
TEL.: 800/767-3062

Videos

Sexual Harassment... Shades of Gray Video Training Package is a five-tape video package for training all employees—executives, managers, supervisors, and general employees. It is a program for organizations who want to change behavior, not just introduce the subject with a quick overview. The videos present the information in a nonthreatening setting with a sincere, direct, thought-provoking approach and an indepth look at the sexual harassment problem. The video package includes five tapes, the Resource Manual, the Training Manual, a Leader's Guide, and twenty-five participant handbooks. (The series also is available on audiocassette.) ISBN 1-878269-15-1.

Sexual Harassment... Shades of Gray Resource Manual is the result of fourteen years of research and training involving more than fifteen hundred companies and organizations. It eliminates the need for costly and time-consuming research by presenting the current, historical, and legal aspects of the issue. It is designed to offer practical and useful information, for immediate implementation in the workplace. ISBN 1-878269-02-X.

Sexual Harassment... Shades of Gray Training Manuals enable trainers to set up sexual harassment training programs for all employees in a number of days rather than the months usually required. It is a "how to" manual, with specific and detailed instructions for implementing the entire training effort from beginning to end. The Resource Manual is included as part of the Training Manuals set. ISBN 1-87826-01-1.

Sexual Harassment: Investigator's Manual explains how to conduct comprehensive investigations into complaints of harassment by thorough fact-finding and indepth analysis of allegations. It provides one of the best methods for organizations to limit their liability—by providing prompt, appropriate, remedial action to all complaints. ISBN 1-878269-25-9.

Sexual Harassment: Guidelines for Managers, Supervisors, and Employees is a handbook to help employees at all levels stop inappropriate, illegal, and costly behavior that is taking place on the job. It is also effective as a handout in training programs; more than one hundred thousand have been used to date by all types and sizes of companies and organizations. ISBN 1-878269-00-3.

Sexual Harassment... Shades of Gray Trainee Kits provide employees at all levels with important printed information to take back to the job after training. Each kit includes a handbook (described above), a sexual harassment identification chart, an employee booklet (one of three chosen from the list below), a special selection of articles about harassment, and three recent issues of *The Webb Report*.

Six Simple Steps to Stop Sexual Harassment is a booklet that details the steps that companies, organizations, and their managers and supervisors can take to stop and prevent sexual harassment in the workplace. It applies to organizations of any size. Also available on audiocassette. ISBN 1-878269-05-4.

How to Handle Sexual Harassment Complaints offers step-by-step guidelines to follow when dealing with a complaint or incident of sexual harassment so it is effectively resolved in-house. Also available on audiocassette. ISBN 1-878269-06-2.

25 Things to Do If Sexual Harassment Happens to You is a booklet that provides clear, reasonable advice for employees to handle sexual harassment when it happens to them so that the problem is resolved within the company or organization. Also available on audiocassette. ISBN 1-878269-07-0.

Step Forward: Sexual Harassment in the Workplace is a book that every employee should have. It is a practical, no-nonsense guide to what sexual harassment is and what every manager, supervisor, and employee should do about it. ISBN 1-94361-51-2.

Shades of Gray Training Transparencies consists of a set of seven color transparencies for use in sexual harassment training, covering these major topics: the history of sexual harassment; what is sexual harassment; what does the law say; what are the costs of harassment; about victims; about harassers; closing comments.

The Webb Report is a monthly newsletter published since January 1985 to keep individuals up to date on the problem of sexual harassment. It provides current information on what's happening across the United States in Federal and State courts with regard to Title VII and Title IX actions, state anti-discrimination laws, and tort actions. It also includes current information about sexual harassment in other countries. ISBN 1-053-0932.

Certified Shades of Gray Consultants

Pacific Resource's *Shades of Gray* Consultants are trained and certified to conduct workshops, seminars, and speaking engagements, and to provide clients with all *Shades of Gray* materials—videos, manuals, handbooks, and subscriptions to *The Webb Report.* The certified consultants and their geographical areas are:

Nationwide

Susan L. Webb
Pacific Resource Development Group, Inc.
145 NW 85th, Suite 104
Seattle, WA 98117
206/782-7015, or 800/767-3062

California

Dona Bertain
Bertain and Associates Consulting
702 Mangrove
Chico, CA 95926
916/898-9023

Colorado

Carolyn Allen Zeiger, Ph.D.
The Athena Group
1780 South Bellaire, Suite 506
Denver, CO 80222
303/782-5060

Massachusetts

Craig D. Morrill & Janet S. Robbins
Medical Training Associates
19 Stockholm Avenue
Rockport, MA 01966
800/822-0550

North Dakota

Michelle Lozuaway-McComsey
Progress Consulting
808 Eighth Street South
Fargo, North Dakota 58103
800/383-6985 FAX 707/235-828

North Carolina

Byron C. Pruitt
The Employers Association
8848 - H Red Oak Boulevard
Charlotte, NC 28217
704/522-8011

Ohio

Linda Treasure
Treasure Associates
P.O. Box 14301
Dayton, OH 45413
513/339-9965

Washington

Marion Weldon
Weldon & Associates
P. O. Box 30148
Seattle, WA 98103
206/462-6212

Washington, DC

Grace A. Whitman
2025 Pennsylvania Avenue NW, Suite 1008
Washington, DC 20006
202/785-0530

Texas

Norman Werback
WerbackRose
13615 Welch Road, Suite 104
Dallas, TX 75244
214/492-8450

To learn more about the *Shades of Gray* Consultants program or how you might become certified, please call 800/767-3062 and ask for a copy of the prospectus.

If you know of additional resources that should be added to the list of resources in future editions of *Shockwaves,* please mail them to the author. 145 N.W. 85th, Suite 103, Seattle, WA 98117, USA.

OTHER MASTERMEDIA BOOKS

At bookstores, or call (800) 334-8232
to place your credit card order.

AGING PARENTS AND YOU: A Complete Handbook to Help You Help Your Elders Maintain a Healthy, Productive, Independent Life, by Eugenia Anderson-Ellis, is a complete guide to providing care to aging relatives. It gives practical advice and resources to the adults who are helping their elders lead productive lives. Revised and updated. ($9.95 paperbound)

BALANCING ACTS!: Juggling Love, Work, Family, and Recreation, by Susan Schiffer Stautberg and Marcia L. Worthing, provides strategies to achieve a balanced life by reordering priorities and setting realistic goals. ($12.95 paperbound)

BEATING THE AGE GAME: Redefining Retirement, by Jack and Phoebe Ballard, debunks the myth that retirement means sitting out the rest of the game. The years between 55 and 80 can be your best, say the authors, who provide ample examples of people successfully using retirement to reinvent their lives. ($12.95 paperbound)

BEYOND SUCCESS: How Volunteer Service Can Help You Begin Making a Life Instead of Just a Living, by John J. Raynolds III and Eleanor Raynolds, C.B.E., is a unique how-to book targeted at business and professional people considering volunteer work, senior citizens who wish to fill leisure time meaningfully, and students trying out career options. The book is filled with interviews with celebrities, CEOs, and average citizens who talk about the benefits of service work. ($9.95 paperbound, $19.95 hardbound)

Other MasterMedia Books

THE BIG APPLE BUSINESS AND PLEASURE GUIDE: 501 Ways To Work Smarter, Play Harder, and Live Better in New York City, by Muriel Siebert and Susan Kleinman, offers visitors and New Yorkers alike advice on how to do business in the city as well as how to enjoy its attractions. ($9.95 paperbound)

BREATHING SPACE: Living and Working at a Comfortable Pace in a Sped-Up Society, by Jeff Davidson, helps readers to handle information and activity overload, and to gain greater control over their lives. ($10.95 paperbound)

CITIES OF OPPORTUNITY: Finding the Best Way to Work, Live, and Prosper in the 1990s and Beyond, by Dr. John Tepper Martin, explores the job and living options for the next decade and into the next century. This consumer guide and handbook, written by one of the world's experts on cities, selects and features forty-six American cities and metropolitan areas. ($13.95 paperbound, $24.95 hardbound)

THE CONFIDENCE FACTOR: How Self-Esteem Can Change Your Life, by Dr. Judith Briles, is based on a nationwide survey of six thousand men and women. Briles explores why women so often feel a lack of self-confidence and have a poor opinion of themselves. She offers step-by-step advice on becoming the person you want to be. ($12.95 paperbound, $18.95 hardbound)

DARE TO CONFRONT! How To Intervene When Someone You Care About Has a Drug or Alcohol Problem, by Bob Wright and Deborah George Wright, shows the reader how to use the step-by-step methods of professional interventionists to motivate drug-dependent people to accept help they need. ($17.95 hardbound)

THE DOLLARS AND SENSE OF DIVORCE: The Financial Guide for Women, by Dr. Judith Briles, is the first book to combine the legal hurdles by planning finances before, during, and after divorce. ($10.95 paperbound)

THE ENVIRONMENTAL GARDENER: The Solution to Pollution for Lawns and Gardens, by Laurence Sombke, focuses on what each of us can do to protect our endangered plant life. A practical source book and shopping guide. ($8.95 paperbound)

FINANCIAL SAVVY FOR WOMEN: A Money Book for Women of All Ages, by Dr. Judith Briles, divides a women's monetary lifespan into six phases, discusses the specific areas to be addressed at each stage, and demonstrates how to create a sound lifelong money game plan. ($15.00 paperbound)

FLIGHT PLAN FOR LIVING: The Art of Self-Encouragement, by Patrick O'Dooley, is a life guide organized like a pilot's flight checklist, that ensures you'll be flying "clear on top" throughout your life. ($17.95 hardbound)

GLORIOUS ROOTS: Recipes for Healthy, Tasty Vegetables, by Laurence Sombke, celebrates the taste, texture, and versatility of root vegetables. Contains recipes for appetizers, soups, stews, and baked, broiled, and stir-fried dishes—even desserts. ($12.95 paperbound)

HOT HEALTH-CARE CAREERS by Margaret T. McNally, R.N., and Phyllis Schneider, provides readers everything they need to know about training for and getting jobs in a rewarding field where professionals are always in demand. ($10.95 paperbound)

HOW TO GET WHAT YOU WANT FROM ALMOST ANYBODY, by T. Scott Gross, shows how to get great service, negotiate better prices, and always get what you pay for. ($9.95 paperbound)

KIDS WHO MAKE A DIFFERENCE, by Joyce M. Roché and Marie Rodriguez, is a surprising and inspiring document of some of today's toughest challenges being met—by teenagers and kids! Their courage and creativity allowed them to find practical solutions. ($8.95 paperbound, with photos)

THE LIVING HEART BRAND NAME SHOPPER'S GUIDE, by Michael E. DeBakey, M.D., Antonio M. Gotto, Jr., M.D., Lynne W. Scott, M.A., R.D./L.D., and John P. Foreyt, Ph.D., lists brand-name supermarket products that are low in fat, saturated fatty acids, and cholesterol. Revised edition. ($14.95 paperbound)

THE LIVING HEART GUIDE TO EATING OUT, by Michael E. DeBakey, Antonio M. Gotto, Jr., and Lynne W. Scott, is an essential handbook for people who want to maintain a health-conscious diet when dining in all types of restaurants. ($9.95 paperbound)

THE LOYALTY FACTOR: Building Trust in Today's Workplace, by Carol Kinsey Goman, Ph.D., offers techniques for restoring commitment and loyalty in the workplace. ($9.95 paperbound)

MAKING YOUR DREAMS COME TRUE: A Plan For Easily Discovering and Achieving the Life You Want, by Marcia Wieder, introduces an easy, unique, and practical technique for defining, pursuing, and realizing your career and life interests. Filled with stories of real people and helpful exercises, plus a personal workbook, this clever volume will teach you how to make your dreams come true—any time you choose. ($9.95 paperbound)

MANAGING IT ALL: Time-Saving Ideas for Career, Family, Relationships, and Self, by Beverly Benz Treuille and Susan Schiffer Stautberg, is written for women who are juggling careers and families. More than two hundred career women (ranging from a TV anchorwoman to an investment banker) were interviewed. The book contains many humorous anecdotes on saving time and improving the quality of life for self and family. ($9.95 paperbound)

Other MasterMedia Books

MANAGING YOUR CHILD'S DIABETES, by Robert Wood Johnson IV, Sale Johnson, Casey Johnson, and Susan Kleinman, brings help to families trying to understand diabetes and control its effects. ($10.95 paperbound)

MANAGING YOUR PSORIASIS: A Resource Guide, by Nicholas J. Lowe, M.D., is an innovative manual that couples scientific research and encouraging support with a focus on the impact of stress on psoriasis, and how patients can take charge of their health. ($10.95 paperbound, $17.95 hardbound)

MANN FOR ALL SEASONS: Wit and Wisdom from The Washington Post's *Judy Mann,* shows the columnist at her best as she writes about women, families, and the impact and politics of the women's revolution. ($9.95 paperbound, $19.95 hardbound)

MIND YOUR OWN BUSINESS: And Keep It in the Family, by Marcy Syms, CEO of Syms Corporation, is an effective guide for any organization, small or large, facing what is documented to be the toughest step in managing a family business—making the transition to the new generation. ($12.95 paperbound, $18.95 hardbound)

MISS AMERICA: The Pursuit of the Crown, by Ann-Marie Bivans, is an authorized guidebook to the Pageant, containing eyewitness accounts, complete historical data, and a realistic look at the trials and triumphs of the potential Miss Americas. ($27.50 hardbound)

OFFICE BIOLOGY: Why Tuesday Is the Most Productive Day and Other Relevant Facts for Survival in the Workplace, by Edith Weiner and Arnold Brown, teaches how in the '90s and beyond we will be expected to work smarter, take better control of our health, adapt to advancing technology, and improve our lives in ways that are not too costly or resource-intensive.

Other MasterMedia Books

($12.95 paperbound, $21.95 hardbound)

ON TARGET: Enhance Your Life and Advance Your Career, by Jeri Sedlar and Rick Miners, is a neatly woven tapestry of insights on career and life issues gathered from audiences across the country. This feedback has been crystallized into a highly readable guidebook for exploring who you are and how to go about getting what you want from your career and your life. ($11.95 paperbound)

OUT THE ORGANIZATION: New Career Opportunities for the 1990s, by Robert and Madeleine Swain, is written for the millions of Americans whose jobs are no longer safe, whose companies are not loyal, and who face futures of uncertainty. It gives advice on finding a new job or starting your own business. (Revised $12.95 paperbound, $17.95 hardbound)

THE OUTDOOR WOMAN: A Handbook To Adventure, by Patricia Hubbard and Stan Wass, details the lives of adventurous women and offers their ideas on how you can incorporate exciting outdoor experiences into your life. ($14.95 paperbound)

PAIN RELIEF: How to Say No to Acute, Chronic, and Cancer Pain, by Dr. Jane Cowles, offers a step-by-step plan for assessing pain and communicating it to your doctor, and explains the importance of having a pain plan before undergoing any medical or surgical treatment. This landmark book includes "The Pain Patient's Bill of Rights," and a reusable pain assessment chart designed to help patients and their families make informed decisions. ($22.95 paperbound)

POSITIVELY OUTRAGEOUS SERVICE: New and Easy Ways To Win Customers for Life, by T. Scott Gross, identifies what the consumers of the '90s really want and how business can develop effective marketing strategies to answer those needs. ($14.95 paperbound)

POSITIVELY OUTRAGEOUS SERVICE AND SHOWMANSHIP, by T. Scott Gross, reveals the secrets of adding personality to any product or service and offers a wealth of nontraditional marketing techniques employed by top showmen, from car dealers to restaurateurs, amusement park operators to evangelists. ($12.95 paperbound)

THE PREGNANCY AND MOTHERHOOD DIARY: Planning the First Year of Your Second Career, by Susan Schiffer Stautberg, is the first and only undated appointment diary that shows how to manage pregnancy and career. ($12.95 spiralbound)

REAL BEAUTY ... REAL WOMEN: A Handbook for Making the Best of Your Own Good Looks, by Kathleen Walas, International Beauty and Fashion Director of Avon Products Inc., offers expert advice on beauty and fashion to women of all ages and ethnic backgrounds. ($19.95 paperbound)

REAL LIFE 101: The Graduate's Guide To Survival, by Susan Kleinman, supplies welcome advice to those facing "real life" for the first time, focusing on work, money, health, and how to deal with freedom and responsibility. Revised. ($9.95 paperbound)

ROSEY GRIER'S ALL-AMERICAN HEROES: Multicultural Success Stories, by Roosevelt "Rosey" Grier, is a wonderful collection of personal histories, told in their own words by prominent African Americans, Latins, Asians, and Native Americans; each tells of the people in their lives and choices made to achieve public acclaim and personal success. ($9.95 paperbound, with photos)

SELLING YOURSELF: How To Be the Competent, Confident Person You Really Are! by Kathy Thebo and Joyce Newman, is an inspirational primer for anyone seeking to project a competent, confident image. Drawing on experience, their own and others,' these entrepreneurs offer lessons in simple techniques that can add up to big successes. ($11.95 paperbound)

SHOCKWAVES: The Global Impact of Sexual Harassment, by Susan L. Webb, examines the problem of sexual harassment today in every kind of workplace around the world. Practical and well-researched, this manual provides the most recent information, including legal changes in progress. ($11.95 paperbound, $19.95 hardbound cover)

SIDE-BY-SIDE STRATEGIES: How Two-Career Couples Can Thrive in the '90s, by Jane Hershey Cuozzo and S. Diane Graham, describes how two-career couples learn the difference between competing with a spouse and become a supportive power partner. Published in hardbound as *Power Partners.* ($10.95 paperbound, $19.95 hardbound)

THE SOLUTION TO POLLUTION: 101 Things You Can Do To Clean Up Your Environment, by Laurence Sombke, offers step-by-step techniques on how to conserve more energy, start a recycling center, choose a biodegradable product, and even proceed with individual clean-up projects. ($7.95 paperbound)

THE SOLUTION TO POLLUTION IN THE WORKPLACE, by Laurence Sombke, Terry M. Robertson, and Elliot M. Kaplan, supplies employees with everything they need to know about cleaning up their workplace, including recycling, using energy efficiently, conserving water, and buying recycled products and nontoxic supplies. ($9.95 paperbound)

SOMEONE ELSE'S SON, by Alan A. Winter, explores the parent-child bond in a contemporary story of lost identities, family secrets, and relationships gone awry. Eighteen years after bringing their first son home from the hospital, Trish and Brad Hunter discover they are not his natural parents. Torn between their love for their son, Phillip, and the question of whether they should help him search for his biological parents, the couple must also struggle with the issue of their own biological son. Who is he—and do his parents know their baby was switched at birth? ($18.95 hardbound)

STEP FORWARD: Sexual Harassment in the Workplace, by Susan L. Webb, presents the facts for dealing with sexual harassment on the job. ($9.95 paperbound)

THE STEPPARENT CHALLENGE: A Primer For Making It Work, by Stephen J. Williams, Ph.D., shares firsthand experience and insights into the many aspects of dealing with step relationships—from financial issues to lifestyle changes to differences in race or religion that affect the whole family. Peppered with personal accounts and useful tips, this volume is must reading for anyone who is a stepparent, about to become one, or planning to bring children to a second or subsequent marriage. ($13.95 paperbound)

STRAIGHT TALK ON WOMEN'S HEALTH: How to Get the Health Care You Deserve, by Janice Teal, Ph.D., and Phyllis Schneider, is destined to become a health-care "bible" for women concerned about their bodies and their future health. Well-researched, but devoid of confusing medical jargon, this handbook offers access to a wealth of resources, with a bibliography of health-related books and contact lists of organizations, healthlines, and women's medical centers. ($14.95 paperbound)

TAKING CONTROL OF YOUR LIFE: The Secrets of Successful Enterprising Women, by Gail Blanke and Kathleen Walas, is based on the authors' professional experience with Avon Products' Women of Enterprise Awards, given each year to outstanding women entrepreneurs. The authors offer a specific plan to help you gain control over your life, and include business tips and quizzes as well as beauty and lifestyle information. ($17.95 hardbound)

Other MasterMedia Books

TEAMBUILT: Making Teamwork Work, by Mark Sanborn, teaches businesses how to increase productivity, without increasing resources or expenses, by building teamwork among employees. ($12.95 paperbound, $19.95 hardbound)

A TEEN'S GUIDE TO BUSINESS: The Secrets To a Successful Enterprise, by Linda Menzies, Oren S. Jenkins, and Rickell R. Fisher, provides solid information about starting your own business or working for one. ($7.95 paperbound)

TWENTYSOMETHING: Managing and Motivating Today's New Work Force, by Lawrence J. Bradford, Ph.D., and Claire Raines, M.A., examines the work orientation of the younger generation, offering managers in businesses of all kinds a practical guide to better understand and supervise their young employees. ($12.95 paperbound, $22.95 hardbound)

WHAT KIDS LIKE TO DO, by Edward Stautberg, Gail Wubbenhorst, Atiya Easterling, and Phyllis Schneider, is a handy guidebook for parents, grandparents, and babysitters who are searching for activities that kids *really* like. Written by kids for kids, this is an easy-to-read, generously illustrated primer for teaching families how to make every day more fun. ($7.95 paperbound)

WORK WITH ME! How To Make the Most of Office Support Staff, by Betsy Lazary, shows you how to find, train, and nurture the "perfect" assistant and how to best use your support-staff professionals. ($9.95 paperbound)

YOUR HEALTHY BODY, YOUR HEALTHY LIFE: How To Take Control of Your Medical Destiny, by Donald B. Louria, M.D., provides precise advice and strategies that will help you live a long and healthy life. Learn also about nutrition, exercise, vitamins, and medication, as well as how to control risk factors for major diseases. Revised and updated. ($12.95 paperbound)